DRAWN
TO THE
DARK

DRAWN TO THE DARK

Explorations in Scare Tourism
Around the World

CHRIS KULLSTROEM

PELICAN PUBLISHING COMPANY
GRETNA 2017

Library of Congress Cataloging-in-Publication Data

Names: Kullstroem, Chris, 1979- author.
Title: Drawn to the dark : explorations in scare tourism around the world / Chris
  Kullstroem.
Description: Gretna [Louisiana] : Pelican Publishing Company, 2017. |
  Includes bibliographical references and index.
Identifiers: LCCN 2016045967| ISBN 9781455622948 (pbk. : alk. paper) | ISBN
  9781455622955 (e-book)
Subjects: LCSH: Dark tourism.
Classification: LCC G156.5.D37 K85 2017 | DDC 133—dc23 LC record available at
https://lccn.loc.gov/2016045967

Printed in the United States of America

Published by Pelican Publishing Company, Inc.
1000 Burmaster Street, Gretna, Louisiana 70053

To the monster fans around the world.

Rock on.

Contents

Acknowledgments

This book is the result of dozens of Monster Heroes. Some bravehearted souls opened their doors to a wandering haunter. Others risked their own sanity by joining me on the adventures. Many others showed their support from the home front, ranging from travel suggestions to ensuring that my cat wouldn't end up becoming a hobo. To you all, I give my undying gratitude for making the journey possible and for sharing it with me every step of the way.

Thank you:

Dud Adam
Stephen Bailly
Lesley Bannatyne
Victor Bariteau
Robert Benedek
Michael Bolton
Glenn Budzeck
Richard Budzeck
Lori Castor
Child & Family Agency of
    Southeastern Connecticut
Keri Chiveralls
Nicola, Franca, and Paolo Cicoli
Mollie Clarke
Tony Clifford
Nevin Cody
Michael and Jon Covault
Markus Csar
István Csertő

Brent Curry
David Daniels
Eileen De Souter
Edward Douglas
The Dunedin Writers' Group
Dan and Nancy Durkee
Adam Fitch
Stan Franzeen
Steve Gibson
Mark Gillan
Jan Girke
Paul Godwin
Gavin Goszka
Patricia Grant
Thomas Gullotta
Josh Hailey
Christoph Haubner
Taka Hayashi
Joey Heyneke

Johan Hiemstra
Nobert Hundsberger
Susan Irving
Greg Jones
Manny and Theoni Katehis
Kevin Keegan
Shawna Kionka
Alexandra, Zsuzsana, and László Kiss
Cheryl LaBeau
Christian Langkamp
Brian Lighthouse
David Lindblom
Shoon Lio
Eileen Lopaze
Alex Mac
Duane Mackey
Carl Magedera
Warren Maxwell
Jon Michael Miller
Tibi Molnar
Taylor Morris
Mark, Beth, and Callie Muncy
Bertram Neuner
Bernie Noonan
Patrick Nottingham
Andreas Oberhuemer
Steve O'Connor
Thomas O'Duffy
Julian C. Palmer
Andras Petsch

Randy Ping
Julianna Rathonyi
Joe Raymond
Sandra Yepes Rios
David Sampson
Ashley Saunders
Kevin Schwartz
Sabrina Selfridge
George Sharrow
Adam Shaughnessy
Alan Shobert
Sidney Smith
Clemens Spectler
Nigel Speirs
Dom Spens
Lori Stanis
Paul Steiner
Kelly Stevens
Ray Stevens
Fern Strong
Hikaru Suzuki
Dick Terhune
Dávid Tófalvi
Pam Tole
Ross Troiano
Ruben Vasque
James Walsh
Edward S. Whinnery
Desiree Williams
Joe Wisinski

Introduction

Monsters seem strange to some, or gruesome, or terrifying. But not to everyone—to some, their company is preferred.

Such has been my case for as long as I can remember. Since my days of falling asleep to the Cryptkeeper's maniacal laugh from *Tales from the Crypt* and Pennywise the Clown peeping out of storm drains in Stephen King's *It!*, monsters have been my passion. There's something engrossing about creatures that are only partially human or have come back from the dead to terrorize the living with almost godlike power. Years later, I would discover that there are many others—millions, in fact—equally drawn to skeletons and killer clowns, demons and devils. Some even create entire shows around them. There's a name for these wonderfully twisted, likeminded enthusiasts: haunters. Haunters use their love for the dark not for money or fame but for the simple pleasure of running unique performances for others who enjoy them.

This book is a story of haunter explorations. It's a journey in which I dedicated a year to looking at dark-themed characters and shows in eleven countries. We can think of such shows as a theatrical representation of what is commonly perceived to be scary, with all the characters, scenes, and interactions that entails. For those brave enough to inspect the draw, performance, and experience of scare tourism around the world, the depths of the human imagination await.

Up until now, I had focused my writing on American Halloween. As a New Englander, I grew up in a region that embraces the holiday. From cabins in the woods to the museums of Salem, Massachusetts, witches, vampires, and virtually every type of creature crawl out of the grave in October to celebrate. But after finishing graduate school in 2013 with a degree in social science, I wanted to broaden my knowledge of scare tourism. I wanted my next book to be about how other countries envisioned and portrayed their own dark characters, how their monsters and demons interacted with patrons, and how those patrons responded. Unlike those in the United States, most international shows, I knew, weren't associated with Halloween. Looking at them in a different context might reveal more about our own cultural fascination with that enchanting time of year, as well as the draw to dark characters overall. Not only would the travels be an exciting journey into the unknown, but they could lead to viewing scare tourism in a completely new light.

I already knew about some things that were going on. There were Krampus *laufs* (processions) based on a Christmas demon in Austria and Walpurgisnacht shows about witches and devils in Germany. There were vampire-based tourism in Transylvania and zombie camps in England. Allowing for additional shows to be determined en route, I planned for a full year of travels. It would mean leaving my job and apartment behind: something I had always wanted to do as a true monster explorer.

As I wrapped up my final months at work—a Connecticut nonprofit where my coworkers were as excited for me as they were terrified—some friends and I made a Kickstarter video. I set a goal of $10,000 for the book project and launched the video on Friday the thirteenth in September of 2013. When the project closed six weeks later on Halloween night, it had barely reached a third of the goal. It financially failed. That may have deterred some people, but let's face it: they don't call us "enthusiasts" for nothing. I had no problem using my own savings for the trip, even if it meant spending my last dollar. After all, people have been willing to die for their passions since the dawn of man, so what's going broke compared to that? And although I expected to doubt myself at any moment and run off screaming into the night like a camper from a chainsaw massacre, it never happened. I was as sure about doing the project as anything I had ever done.

I also had one source of support. Since 2009, the Couchsurfing organization had allowed me to conduct other monster-based travels across the United States, Europe, and Australia. Many of the hosts had been excited about the nature of my travels and eager to share the adventure with me. With their help, I knew that I could explore the universal draw of the dark.

On October 25, my life changed. I left the United States, with my Kickstarter campaign still under way, in the height of the Halloween season. I became officially homeless and unemployed. I knew that I might not be able to find free places to stay through Couchsurfing. I knew that I might run out of money and have to look for food in a dumpster. And I knew that when the travels were over and the book was finished, I might not even find a publisher who wanted it. But I also knew that those risks were nothing compared to the possibility that the completed work *would* reach people, would *teach* people, and just might change the way that I saw the monster culture I'd always known.

And with that, I flew off to discover whatever awaited me out there in the dark.

Bring it on.

Chapter 1

Oaxaca's Day of the Dead

"Life is short—let's party!"

The Boardinghouse

I woke up in the boardinghouse at the ungodly hour of 7:00 A.M. Barely distinguishable voices came from downstairs. Looking at the glowing alarm clock by my bedside, I let out a groan. Who could get up this early?

As my mind defogged, I remembered my arrival in Mexico the previous night. I had flown in with everything that I would need for a year of travels, in a single backpack and duffel bag: a pair of shorts; two pairs of long pants; long-sleeve, short-sleeve, and sleeveless shirts (two each); bathroom supplies; camera; notebook; and laptop. Unable to find an English-speaking Couchsurfing host in town, back in Connecticut I had contacted the organizer of Oaxaca's English-speaking library for recommendations on a place to stay. Michelle, an American who'd been living in Oaxaca for twenty years, had replied to my e-mail and referred me to a boardinghouse run by a friend. Michelle even picked me up at the airport, then drove me through crammed and chaotic traffic filled with more old VW Beetles than I'd seen since elementary school. We arrived at a large, yellow boardinghouse at 10:00 P.M., where the owner, Yolanda, welcomed me with a polite smile. Her ignorance of English perfectly matched my own of Spanish. She showed me to my upstairs bedroom, where a full-sized bed and private bath awaited. Both were neat and clean and a welcome relief after the rundown storefronts I'd seen along the drive. After a long shower, I passed out as soon as my head hit the pillow, excited about seeing both the living and the dead the next day.

I had heard stories about the Day of the Dead holiday, *Dia de los Muertos,* since I was a kid. Celebrated long before the sixteenth-century Spanish conquest of Mexico, the Day of the Dead is a time when the spirits of those who have died are believed to return. Families visit gravesites and make altars out of food and flowers to welcome them. The spirits of adults are said to return on November 1 and those of children on the following night. People dance in the streets as skeletons and bake breads into the shapes of corpses. The holiday's icon is Catrina. An elegantly dressed female skeleton, she represents joy in the face of death and mocks mankind's mortality. Her grinning skull demonstrates that death comes to us all, whatever our station in life. But unlike what I'd grown up with in the United States, neither Catrina nor any other deathly image around at this time is intended to be gruesome or scary. Rather, the traditions are based on remembering and honoring the dead, who are still acknowledged as being a part of the family. I had long dreamed of experiencing the holiday firsthand; the idea of celebrating death seemed nothing short of remarkable.

I had also read that Oaxaca was the place to go for the biggest Day of the Dead celebrations in Mexico. Parades, open-air theater, and sand-art competitions ran all week throughout the town. And what's more, Oaxaca would have something that made me feel particularly safe anywhere in Mexico: *tourists.*

After dragging myself out of bed, I staggered downstairs towards what sounded like a dozen women excitedly talking over each other. I came to a small dining area and saw four Caucasian women sitting at a large breakfast table. All from the United States, they spoke and gestured as energetically as teenagers, though they were clearly past retirement age. They turned to me with immediate interest.

"Good morning!" they said enthusiastically.

"Good morning," I mumbled with a sleepy smile.

"Come sit with us!" one said, waving towards them.

"Sit here, next to me!" cried another, patting an empty chair beside her.

They introduced themselves as Martha, Julie, Robin, and Gale. Through their eager overlapping, I learned that the four were friends from California, all in their seventies and spending a month in Oaxaca to study Spanish. While Yolanda quietly served fruit, toast, and eggs around us, the energetic crew asked about my own reasons for traveling. I told them about incorporating Day of the Dead traditions in a book about dark- and death-themed characters, expecting them to look at me as though I was completely nuts.

Instead, they seemed fascinated.

"Oh, that's wonderful!" Julie beamed beside me. "The Day of the Dead is a beautiful tradition. You'll love it...."

"More people should know about things they do here at this time," Robin said before Julie could continue.

"And you came here alone? How exciting!"

"*We* came here alone! Well, separately."

"But she's *all* alone—good for you!"

"How old did you say you were? Thirty-four? So young!"

"And you don't speak *any* Spanish? That's funny!"

"We've been here almost a week," Gale said from the head of the table. "Our Spanish classes run eight hours every day, then we have to do a few hours of homework each night."

"Oh my God," I said with a mouth full of toast. "You're all so ambitious."

"Of course!" Julie gave an enthusiastic shrug. "Why not? We did the same thing last year. We've never let our age stop us!"

Robin nodded. "We've never let *anything* stop us. Life's too short for that!"

I watched the four clear their plates with healthy appetites. They took turns practicing their Spanish with Yolanda, pronouncing each word with thick, American accents. Our host was patient with her elderly students and no doubt saw me as a complete slacker for not even attempting a word. I soon waved goodbye to my new friends as they rushed off to catch a shuttle for school. I secretly dubbed them the Fabulous Four and felt any preconceived notion I'd had of life slowing down after retirement fly out the window.

Death Portrayed in Beauty and Wonder

In town, the dead were everywhere. Plastic skeletons danced in shop windows. They waved from black-iron balconies, their flowered dresses and sombreros matching the yellow, green, or orange apartment buildings behind them. Life-sized paper-mâché skeletons stood in tuxedos or black dresses and flowing veils outside the shop entrances. Rouge-painted cheekbones emphasized dignified smiles. Death, it seemed, was nothing to mourn—whether you were dead or alive.

On the pedestrian street Alcalá, flocks of tourists gazed at the dead. They practiced their Spanish in American, British, and German accents while buying painted porcelain skulls set out on blankets lining the sidewalks. I followed the example of the crowd and kept to the shady side of the street. It must have been about eighty degrees in the shade and at least ten degrees hotter in the sun; I got the feeling that my shorts and tank top would be my daily outfit throughout my stay.

Inside the shops, altars produced beautiful explosions of yellow, orange, and red. Strands of marigolds arched over tables filled with breads, nuts, and fruits. Candles flickered beside framed portraits. Flower petals encircled pictures of the Virgin Mary. I knew that each display symbolized stages of life: birth, death, and the passage into heaven. Candy and bottles of mescal—the traditional drink of Oaxaca—had been laid out for spirits of the deceased to enjoy upon their return. In shop after shop I admired each display. I saw creativity in elaborate pieces of personal remembrance. I could only imagine what it would be like to grow up in a culture where the dead were honored in such a way. Almost half of my own family had died years earlier, including my mother, an uncle, and grandparents on both sides. As an atheist, I held no beliefs about spirits or an afterlife, but keeping a family's memories alive through beautiful works of art struck me as a wonderful tradition.

Beyond Alcalá, the dead also celebrated in the sand. Skeletons played guitar and danced beside their coffins in sand art surrounding the Basilica de la Soledad and Iglesia de Santo Domingo. They smiled in frames of vibrant marigolds and blooming corn: life surrounding death. From behind a rope barrier, I watched an artist work on a sand painting roughly thirty feet wide. Black sand rained from what resembled a small flour sifter as he colored hair falling across a skeletal woman's massive rib cage. I stared, completely engrossed, at the corpse's jet-black eyes and peaceful smile. Her deathly grace was no less beautiful than anything I'd seen among the living. I had never seen death portrayed in such a way—in beauty and wonder and almost admiration. This wasn't the image of corpses that I had grown up with. These weren't monsters maniacally laughing on late-night TV or crawling out of graves in horror films.

There was deeper meaning here.

"Life Is Short—Let's Party!"

On October 31, the Fabulous Four and I joined a bus tour to San Antonino Castillo Cemetery. As we sat in one of three coaches heading to the grounds before sundown, the women talked as energetically as ever. I chuckled while listening, eating a small loaf of bread shaped like a shrouded body. The *pan de muertos* tasted so good that I immediately wished I had bought at least a dozen more at the market.

"I can't believe how beautiful everything is in town," I said to Robin and Gale beside me. "The way the dead are portrayed is so moving."

"Isn't it incredible?" Gale agreed, nodding. "What a wonderful custom."

"They certainly don't do anything like that where we're from," Robin said. "Death isn't even discussed...."

Gale nodded before Robin could finish. "And here we are with a big bus of tourists going to a cemetery at night. Can you imagine something like that back home?"

"People would think it was morbid."

"Or depressing."

"But look around." Robin waved an arm, gesturing to the back of the bus. Every seat was filled. I also couldn't help but notice that I was the only one there younger than fifty. "You don't see anyone depressed. They're *enjoying* themselves. This is what life should be about!"

"That's why we come here," Gale said, her eyes wide with emotion. "That's probably why *everyone* comes here!"

As the coach pulled away from the curb, a man hopped onboard and steadied himself beside the driver. I stared at him as if star struck; he looked almost exactly like Christopher Walken. The only differences were his slightly shorter stature and darker skin and hair.

"Welcome, everyone, to our trip to San Antonino Castillo," he said into a handheld microphone. His thick, Mexican accent reverberated throughout the bus. He kept a firm grip on the safety rail while scanning the crowd, his tour-guide badge swaying from his neck with each bounce along the road. "Many of you have probably never been to a cemetery for *Dia de los Muertos*. There are some things you should know before we arrive."

Beside me, Robin and Gale grew quiet, turning their attention to our new guide. Martha and Julie did the same behind us, and the bus fell into a hush.

"The cemetery will quickly become very dark." Our nameless guide held up a finger as if in warning. "So you must be very careful when walking around the stones." He stared blankly for a moment, his finger frozen in front of him.

I tried to determine if he was serious or drunk.

I had a feeling it was both.

"You should take lots of pictures." As the bus took a sharp turn, the man stumbled and fell onto a woman in the front row. He quickly stood up and put a hand on her shoulder. "The families will not mind," he continued, looking back at his audience without missing a beat.

I turned and smiled between the seats at Martha and Julie. They responded with wry, questioning looks. The guide was nothing if not entertaining.

"They will be eating and drinking and celebrating," I heard him continue over the speakers, "because in Oaxaca, *Dia de los Muertos* is not a sad time. It is a good time."

I turned around and saw him leaning against the driver, ignoring the startled look that he got in response.

"In Oaxaca," he went on, "we have a saying." The guide threw up a hand with a wistful smile: "'Life is short—let's party!' And if we're broke, we do not get sad. We say: 'I'm broke... but let's party!'"

I covered my mouth to hide my quiet, hysterical laughter. Beside me, Gale and Robin did the same. I glanced back to see several others look at the guide with only confusion.

We arrived at our destination as the sun was beginning to set. Over a hundred tourists clasped their cameras while walking towards the massive graveyard. My eyes grew wide as I joined them; what stretched before us looked more like an extensive floral garden than any cemetery

I'd ever seen. Red, orange, and pink marigolds adorned almost every grave. White-marble crosses; long, flat table stones; and those resembling stone coffins were topped with additional pots of roses, carnations, and daisies. Some arrangements were so large that they obscured the stones completely. Orange candlelight flickered from small, glass jars, giving the appearance of lightning bugs hovering over the grounds. I admired it all in quiet fascination while the Fabulous Four and I separated down different walkways. I had been to cemeteries all over the United States and Europe but had never seen anything like this. An otherwise barren city of stone had been made into something as beautiful and lively as a nature preserve. Everything smelled invigorating yet soothing. I had flashbacks of giving bouquets of flowers to family and friends at birthday parties and anniversaries. I could barely believe that I was in a place of death at all.

Several families sat in lawn chairs encircling the graves. They clasped their hands peacefully on blankets over their laps. Children sat beside elderly grandparents; young couples held hands over their armrests. From a distance, I saw Martha and Julie speak to an older couple seated before a statue of Jesus. His outstretched arms were surrounded by white tulips.

"Puedo tomar una foto?" they asked. "May I take a photo?" It was what Señor Walken had suggested we ask, between his swaying and stumbling on the bus. The couple responded with a small smile and nod, then watched the tourists take a picture of the grave.

I continued walking the paths, watching others request permission to take photos. But despite everything I'd seen and learned, I just couldn't speak to someone visiting a family member at their graveside. I couldn't get over the feeling that it would be viewed as a sign of disrespect. It was as if the idea that had been engrained in me since childhood locked me into some kind of forced silence. Whenever I came upon anyone sitting beside a stone, I only greeted them, then bashfully walked on.

But despite the awkwardness, I looked at each family in admiration. It was a wonderful tradition they shared. Any differences in our beliefs didn't matter; I saw families coming together and celebrating their loved ones through beautiful acts of remembrance.

In Oaxaca's town square, the Zocalo, vendors abounded. Carts were heaped with balloons and toys, candy skulls and other sweets. Small children dressed as skeletons and devils held out pumpkin pails, begging for pesos. People sat outside restaurants lining the square, drinking, laughing, and watching the masses before them.

As I wandered amongst the crowd, my attention veered to a cart selling chili-flavored lollypops. A fan of anything involving sugar, I couldn't help but look at them in disgust. Why would anyone do such a hideous thing to candy?

I immediately bought one.

After one lick, my grimace of revulsion caught the attention of someone nearby.

"You don't like it?" I heard a male voice say.

I turned to find a tall, dark man beside me, appearing to be in his late thirties. He smiled and stood casually with his hands in his corduroy-pants pockets. His English contained only a trace of a Mexican accent.

"Ugh." I tossed the candy into an overflowing trashcan. "It's disgusting!"

"They're very popular here. But I've never liked them, either. I'm Ruben," he said, extending a hand.

"I'm Chris," I replied. "Nice to meet you."

"You, too. Are you here for the *comparsa?*"

"The *comparsa?*" I blankly repeated the word. "What's that?"

"It's kind of like a parade in America. But with lots of music and dancing."

"Oh!" My face lit up. "That sounds awesome."

Ruben, I learned, was originally from a small village in northern Mexico. After living in Arizona for several years, he had recently moved to Oaxaca. We exchanged stories and I told him about my cemetery excursion with the Fabulous Four.

"Lots of cemeteries around here are beautiful at this time," Ruben said. "And they're not all quiet like the one you went to. Some of them have music and parties."

"Really?" I tried picturing it. The idea of a loud spectacle didn't quite fit the peaceful remembrance that I'd seen. "That sounds different."

"Yes." Ruben nodded. "Oaxaca is very different from the United States. *Very.*"

As the sun began to set, an eruption of trumpets and drumming came from off in the distance. All around us, people gravitated towards the music. I smiled at the masses. It looked as though an unseen force had turned random wanderers into a single unit drawn to its power. Within moments, a half-dozen Mariachi players appeared. Dressed in red and black suits, they played trumpets and horns, drums and guitar with bonelike smiles painted to match their black, hollow eyes. The crowd quickly gathered around them, smiling at the upbeat sound and the dead who created it. Additional living corpses appeared from behind them. A skeletal bride danced beside an equally dead pope. Catrinas in colorful dresses swung their arms to the rhythm. Some appeared to be only partially dead, with half of their faces painted bone white and the other left as healthy, brown skin. Male skeletons danced in black suits and colorful shirts. I marveled at the entire troop moving to the loud beat of the Mariachi players. Death had arrived in Oaxaca with vibrant music and dance.

"Wow," I said to Ruben, "this is great!"

"Come on, we can dance, too." He wasted not a moment and took my hand to lead me into the celebration. "People don't just watch *comparsas;* they *join* them. That's what they're all about."

I followed his lead, laughing and boogying down. Above us, skeleton puppets cast deadly grins above a living Grim Reaper figure dancing in his long, black cloak. A vampire smiled sharp fangs and held out a hand to a woman watching from the crowd. In her shy eyes I saw the same trepidation that I had felt in the cemetery. She wanted to join the fun but didn't dare step out of her comfort zone. But after a moment she took the offered, bony-gloved hand. She immersed herself and let loose like the rest of us, laughing away in the dance of death.

"This is the *best,*" I said to Ruben over the music. "Now *this* is a party!"

On November 2, Ruben and I met up in the Zocalo once again. If I liked parties and cemeteries, he told me, he knew just the place to go for the official Day of the Dead.

"I haven't been to Oaxaca Cemetery before," he said. "It's called *Panteon General*. But I know it's very popular."

I didn't have to ask why. A thick cluster of people lined the road 5 de Febrero after sundown. Barely visible through the crowds, vendor tables on either side of the street sold *pan de muertos* and grilled meats, colorful candy and toys. Ruben and I walked shoulder to shoulder through the masses, and I pointed to a Ferris wheel off in the distance.

"Oh my God," I said in disbelief.

He looked towards the ride and smiled. "Oh, yeah. This is *Dia de los Muertos*. Of course there are rides and games."

"Beside a *cemetery?*"

He laughed. "Of course!"

Farther down the road, kids screamed in excitement as they ran to bumper cars and motorized plane rides. I could barely believe it when a tall, stone wall finally appeared beside the chaos. Beyond the entrance, rows of gravestones lay in peaceful darkness compared to the explosion of noise, color, and lights on the other side.

"I've never seen anything like this around a cemetery," I said. The two of us slowly followed the crowd into the burial grounds. "This definitely wouldn't fly back home."

Ruben chuckled, keeping his arms pressed tightly in front of him to avoid being crushed. "That's for sure."

"It'd be pretty cool, though," I said with a smile.

Beyond the stone wall, soft, orange lights glowed throughout the darkness. Candlelight danced in small glass jars and paper bags, extending for what seemed like miles beside large gravestones. The sounds of commotion slowly died away as we walked a wide, paved path. Moving silhouettes of people wrapped in blankets looked like floating specters on the graves. Just like at San Antonino Castillo, I saw that no one seemed to mind tourists taking pictures. Still, I lowered my camera at the sight of anyone beside a stone, while Ruben stood back and watched. After a while, a Mariachi band caught my eye. A family of six sat beside them, enjoying the guitar, trumpet, and violin played to a tall, cross monument adorned with flowers. After a few moments I felt a hand on my back and Ruben gently push me towards the players.

"It's okay to take pictures," he said. "They really won't mind."

"Are you sure?" I whispered. "I don't want to be rude." I glanced nervously at the family. But rather than the glares of bafflement or shock that I expected, they only continued to watch the band.

"They don't consider it rude."

I held up my camera for a few moments, keeping my attention on the seated listeners. Eventually an elderly woman glanced at me with mild interest. I took a picture of the band then quickly backed away. After we'd continued farther down the path, Ruben admitted that it was actually his first time being in a cemetery on November 2.

"What?!" I turned to him in the darkness. "But you grew up in Mexico. Wasn't it a tradition in your village?"

"For some people. But my mother never wanted to go to the cemeteries," he said with a shrug, "so I never went. But I knew you'd like it."

"So this is your first time in a cemetery for Day of the Dead?"

He smiled and nodded.

"Wow, then it's a new experience for both of us. I'm so glad we met!"

"Me, too," he said. "I probably never would have done this otherwise."

In an enclosed area of wall vaults, paper skulls hung above tables of breads, apples, pears, and nuts. Miniature Catrina dolls grinned beside sombrero-topped skeletons and plastic coffins. I stopped in surprise at the sight of someone wearing a Grim Reaper robe on a stone bench. I looked at him—or her—for several moments, immediately drawn to their quiet, foreboding presence. I remembered wearing a similar costume at Halloween parties, approaching people without saying a word just to creep them out. It had worked every time. But this person obviously had no such motive in mind. Instead, their sole intention seemed to be simply sitting in silence. The effect was tangible; just standing beside them I felt an encompassing sense of peace.

"You know, being here has given me a completely new perspective on death," I said once we were back out among the graves.

Ruben nodded. "Oaxacans base death traditions on celebration, not sadness or fear. That makes a big difference."

I smiled at the sentiment. Suddenly, something caught my eye in the distance. High above the grounds' shadowy outlines, two ghostly faces appeared. Dark, hollow eyes seemed to glow against pure-white skulls. Small sockets took the place of where noses should have been. Long, thin lines formed only traces of mouths. A black top hat slowly came into view above one of them, then a red bowtie and black tuxedo. I stared, awestruck, at a figure standing about ten feet tall. Stilts were certainly hidden beneath his pants legs, though they didn't hinder his movements as he glided down the walkway in long strides. Beside him, a red, broad-brimmed hat topped a female image of death. Black lace fell to her brow and her dress shimmered a captivating, deep red. A second pair of identical characters followed them, then a third. I gazed at each in wonder. The couples walked through the dark grounds, looking massive and beautiful. They turned their attention towards me as they passed, and I smiled up at intense vitality burning in their eyes through otherwise lifeless expressions. These weren't the smiling skeletons from the *comparsa,* dancing and mocking the fate of man. These were larger-than-life manifestations of death itself, and they had returned to where the living now awaited them.

Screamville Haunted House

The next evening, Ruben and I met up to walk around town. Down 20 de Noviembre, I held my breath through the smell of dead insects being sold for consumption at the open-air markets. Once free to breathe normally again, I told my friend about some children's plays I'd seen in a local park. I was particularly interested in the vampire and Hollywood-monster costumes that some of the kids had worn. I couldn't help but express joy at the combination of Halloween with Day of the Dead. As much as I loved the meaning behind the Mexican holiday, I was sure that Halloween could bring an equal amount of happiness to anyone who celebrated it.

"Halloween and Day of the Dead are slowly starting to blend," Ruben said. "That's okay with some people, but they don't want to lose their traditions. So the schools make sure to teach kids about the differences in the holidays."

I smiled at the thought. "That's good that they let kids celebrate both."

Since Ruben had spent several years in the States, he knew the history of Halloween as well as I did. It all goes back to the Celts of ancient Ireland. The Celts believed that in late October, a veil separating the world of the living from that of the dead becomes thin. Spirits were believed to be able to enter through it and, should they choose, cause harm to the living. To protect themselves, the Celts dressed in disguises to resemble walking spirits. They led parades out of town to drive the spirits away and left offerings outside their doors in hopes of being left in peace. The rituals took place on a night known as Samhain (pronounced *Sow*-in), meaning "summer's end," on October 31.

But the rise of Christianity changed those traditions. In the year 835, Pope Gregory IV moved the Catholic holiday All Saints' Day from May to the first of November. Pagan Samhain traditions were suddenly accepted as those meant for celebrating All Saints' Eve—or All *Hallows'* Eve. The poor began going from door to door and offered to say prayers for the homeowners in exchange for food, using lanterns made out of carved turnips to light their way. When the rituals came to America, they evolved into Halloween parades and trick or treating, with large, carved pumpkins replacing the smaller turnips of Europe.

And even now, centuries later, the customs continue to be handed down.

"I remember when I was a kid," I said, reflecting on the traditions, "the whole neighborhood came alive for Halloween. Everyone decorated their yards with jack-o-lanterns and put ghosts in the windows. And when I went trick or treating with my parents, people came to their doors dressed as witches and monsters. It was actually one of the rare times that we even *saw* our neighbors." I chuckled with a nostalgic smile.

Before I could continue, I stopped in my tracks. A large billboard in front of us made my eyes grow wide. A huge, hockey-masked figure was portrayed emerging from a dark, foggy wood. A bleeding red font beside him read: *Ven a sentir MIEDO, Screamville.*

"Look!" I said, frozen at the image. "What does that say?"

"That says, 'Come to get SCARED,'" Ruben translated, looking up at it.

I gasped loud enough to wake the dead.

"Oh my God—it's a haunted attraction!" I turned to him in astonishment. "We gotta go!"

Ruben smiled, studying the billboard as if trying to determine what made it so remarkable. "Okay. It gives the address; I know the area. It's actually not far from here."

We found Screamville on Gabino Garcia about fifteen minutes by foot from Oaxaca's city center. It was all I could do not to skip the entire way. It was one of those rare moments that I lived for: discovering a scare show in the least likely location. Ruben and I approached a large, black banner stretching across a wall of concrete, then stared through its opening in surprise.

"Is this what I think it is?" I asked. Before us, towering storage units overflowed with rusting car parts. Doors and fenders lined the ground. Tires, wires, and random pieces of metal created a dilapidated chaos around an expansive, dark lot.

"Yep," Ruben said. "It's a junkyard."

We purchased tickets for thirty pesos, just over two American dollars, at a cafeteria table decorated with flags and electric lights. Sparks shot out from cut, metal barrels while we wound through a roped queue line. Before reaching the entrance, I learned why Ruben hadn't been sure just what to expect based on Screamville's billboard: he had never been to a haunted attraction before.

"Really?" I asked him in amazement. "The whole time you were in the States, you never went to one?"

"Nope." He gave a sheepish smile, eyeing the dark surroundings that reeked of oil. Random pieces of car stretched in every direction; it looked as though an automobile mass murderer had gone on a rampage, then stacked his mutilations into separate piles.

"You'll love it," I said. "They're totally different from the Day of the Dead shows." I opened my eyes wide. "They're *scary!*"

"I know... ," he said, playfully flinching. "That's pretty much why I never went to one. I don't even like scary movies."

We handed our tickets to a worker dressed in a reflector vest, then entered a massive, steel storage unit.

"Yeah, I know what you mean," I said. "I couldn't even watch previews for them when I was a kid. I thought that my older brother was the bravest guy in the world for being able to watch them all night. Then one day I realized that he liked them because they were *cool,* not scary. And I've loved them ever since."

Before us, old tires formed a crude path along a cement wall. Orange flames flickered in glass jars, providing the only source of light and casting tall shelves of metal into shadow. Low, eerie music permeated the grounds. I felt as though Ruben and I had become the stars of a new horror film, one in which deranged killers chase an American tourist and her local friend into a Oaxaca junkyard. The ending, of course, would be bloodshed.

"This place is awesome," I said, scanning it all. "And what a great spot for a haunt!"

"It's definitely spooky...," Ruben whispered. He nervously peered down the narrow paths separating the towering shelves. After turning his attention forward once again, he paused before taking another step. I followed his gaze. Ahead, a girl slowly emerged from the darkness. She looked ghastly pale with dirty, matted hair falling over a white bathrobe. A dull scraping sound came from her slippers as she dragged her feet towards us. Ruben and I stared at her, moving not a muscle and holding her undivided attention.

"She's creepy," Ruben finally uttered.

"She *is*." I looked at her in fascination. As she continued inching our way, I envisioned a young woman who had once been preparing a peaceful, Sunday-morning bath. Within moments, everything had gone horribly wrong; she had obviously fallen prey to some widespread virus mutation. She had collapsed on the bathroom floor, only to revive hours later as a decayed, animated corpse craving human flesh. I pictured it all while admiring her vacant eyes and eerie stagger. In them I saw the perfect portrayal of the undead. *This* was the type of character that I had grown up with. This was a star from late-night horror films and Halloween haunt shows. This was no smiling image of death, dancing in a *comparsa*.

This was a *monster*.

I turned to Ruben and was taken aback by his frozen stare at the creature.

"She's great, huh?" I asked, nudging him.

As if suddenly remembering to blink, Ruben regained himself. He began to crack a smile. I led him past the decaying virus victim, who continued to stare at us after we had shuffled away.

"She was freaky looking!" Ruben finally said with a shudder.

"Yeah." I nodded with approval. "Very well done."

Farther along the corridor, long, transparent bags glimmered in the sparse light. They hung from the rafters with red smearing the inside of the plastic. I peered in one and saw thick rope binding together the cuffs of blue jeans and upside-down, black boots. Dark hoods were pressed against the bottom of each bag, concealing the identity of their wearers.

"They're body bags," I said ominously. "Murder victims suspended in the vaults of the junkyard."

Ruben traced the outline of the fake blood with his finger. "Ewww..."

I stepped back, smiling at the display. "Very nice."

We continued through the dark cell until strange spots dotted the cement. Blood-soiled sheets appeared along the ground, concealing large, man-shaped forms beneath. Ahead, a figure slowly materialized. I watched a distorted, male face come into view. A deep cut ran along his forehead, nose, and chin. Rotting, discolored flesh covered one eye, while the other glared at us in disgust. Additional scars along his mangled face matched stains on his faded jumpsuit. I could only presume that the vile creature had worked on as many people as he did cars—the hanging bodies and sheeted victims being among them.

Ruben gripped my arm, recoiling from the mechanic as we stepped his way. "Whoa... "

"Cool, huh?" I asked, stifling a chuckle.

"Yeah," Ruben said as if in a trance. He released his grip, then smiled at the vision of horror. "He *is* cool."

The path brought us through additional, disorientingly dark compounds. Gutted and crushed cars were complemented with whining organ music and smells of paint and oil. Creatures stepped out of the darkness, blood-stained and mangled, some wielding butcher knives threateningly by their side. They leered and crept towards us, then eerily stalked as we passed. I loved it all. It was the haunt experience that I had grown up with: one built around living, syndicated nightmares. It was a far cry from Celtic Samhain rituals based on protection from spirits. Rather, I knew that these types of haunts had developed from the popularity of horror films and small, charity-run haunted houses in the 1970s. During this time, small haunt shows were run as fundraisers for Halloween. People walked through spook houses bearing the same level of scares as dark carnival rides or Disneyland's Haunted Mansion. But when the hit movie *Halloween* connected the American holiday to serial killers on the rampage, haunt owners saw an opportunity. They could make moviegoers enjoy the same excitement as the characters in the slasher films, running for their lives from psychopaths ready to hack them to pieces. The walkthrough shows changed from playful skeletons and ghosts to murderers with axes and chainsaws. It was quite the transition—and one I'd always felt grateful to be able to enjoy.

As the trail wound outside, Ruben backed away from a set of deep, red eyes emerging from behind a tree. Yellow, razor-sharp teeth curled into a twisted smile and a plush, red nose looked almost comical in comparison with a shiny costume glistening in the night.

Ruben instinctively jumped back as the demented clown came fully into view. It smiled in delight at his reaction.

"That's messed up," Ruben said, clasping his hands to his chest.

I couldn't help but giggle, then gestured to the star of our dark theater. "But he's cool, right?"

The clown's smile widened as if to confirm the sentiment. Ruben's hands relaxed as he took a step towards me once again, then nodded.

"Oh yeah," he said. "He's cool."

Chapter 2

The Krampus in Salzburg

"This isn't Christmas!"

Bertram in Salzburg

I kept falling asleep on the bus.

On Thanksgiving Day, I arrived in Salzburg after forty-eight hours of travel from Oaxaca. I felt my head fall like a rock yet again, and I lifted it with a jerk while forcing my eyes wide open. My limited attention remained on simply remaining upright, keeping one hand on my duffel bag beside me. It felt strange to be wearing a winter coat, hat, and gloves after a month in central Mexico. Always one to prefer the cold over stifling heat, I normally would have reveled in the layers. Instead, my clothes felt like pillows, drawing my eyelids slowly down and making me oblivious to those nearby, who no doubt assumed I was drunk.

My Couchsurfing host, Bertram, had given me directions on where to go from the airport. I could find his office inside a large church in Salzburg's city center. After dragging myself down a darkened street, I knocked on a large, oak door at 8:00 P.M. I clamped my arms across my chest in the cold, estimating it to be about twenty degrees Fahrenheit. After a few moments, a man came to the door. I recognized the short, red hair, thick glasses, and reddish complexion from Bertram's Couchsurfing profile. Wearing jeans and a button-down shirt, he stared at me while others behind him sat engrossed in a meeting.

"Kann ich Ihnen helfen?" he asked blankly.

I could only imagine the sight I presented: a puffy-eyed, frozen stranger with a backpack and duffel bag, knocking at his church door after sundown.

"Are you Bertram?" I asked with effort.

He continued staring, then finally flinched in recognition. "Oh! Chris! I'm sorry, I forgot!"

"That's okay," I mumbled. I felt my tired skin stretch into a smile. So long as I had a place to go, I didn't care if he *had* forgotten. Bertram, apologizing that his meeting was running late, gave me directions and a spare key to his flat. I staggered off towards another bus, half-conscious but fully relieved to be going anywhere with a place to sleep.

My host and I officially met the next day. After finding his apartment on the fourth floor of an elevator-less building, I had collapsed onto his foldout couch in the living room and woken up fourteen hours later. My energy finally returned while he told me stories about others he'd hosted over the years. I was far from the only one, he assured me, who had arrived almost comatose after crossing time zones. I was, however, the only one who had specifically come for Krampus.

"Originally, Krampus was believed to be a creature that kept evil spirits away in winter," Bertram said while stirring a pot of pasta on the stove. His English was fluent with a thick Irish accent he'd picked up during a semester at Trinity. I sat across from him at his small kitchen table, the foldout couch mere feet away in the living room. Eating together has always been a big component of Couchsurfing. People prepare their favorite foods for the age-old, intimate custom of sharing a meal. Fortunately no one had ever seemed to mind when I made sandwiches for the people I'd hosted back in Connecticut; to me, there truly was no better food.

"But once Christianity spread," Bertram continued, "Krampus became the evil companion of St. Nicholas. On December fifth, St. Nicholas goes door to door and gives treats to children who have been good that year. Krampus goes with him, but *his* job is to *take* the children who have been bad."

I chuckled at the story. Krampus was certainly a stark contrast to the Santa and his elves that I had grown up with. I had learned about the monstrous, Alpine beast said to terrorize children during a haunted-attraction conference a year earlier. I could barely believe the stories. A monster that comes around before Christmas, the time of year when so many American haunters go through a bought of depression with the Halloween season having come to its end? It seemed like a total contradiction—but of the best kind.

"So Krampus came to *your* door when you were a kid?" I asked.

Bertram shrugged, stirring a pan of meat sauce. "Of course."

"Were you scared?"

He shot me a serious look. "*Any* kid would be scared at something like that in their house."

"But the person in costume never did anything to hurt you, right?"

"Oh no, Krampus would just kinda stand there while St. Nicholas gave me candy and things. There's no Santa Claus in Austria; you know that, right?"

"Ohhh," I said. I hadn't known that. "I thought Santa was all over Europe."

"No. We have the Christkind—that means 'Christ child'—who brings presents on Christmas Eve. People still dress as Krampus and St. Nicholas and go door to door in the villages on December fifth. In major towns, like Salzburg, though, we have *laufs*. Do you know what they are?"

"Yes, I've seen some online. They're like parades." I couldn't help but smile at the word; the last time I had attended something "like a parade," I had danced with vampires and skeletons in the streets. *Laufs,* I knew, were pretty different.

"Mmmm, kind of... Krampuses walk in the street like in American parades." Bertram studied a long string of spaghetti, then bit off a small piece to determine if it was cooked. He ate the remaining piece with a decisive nod, then shot me a look of warning. "But you have to watch out because each Krampus has a weapon. It's always a cow's tail, a horse's tail, or a bundle of branches. And when they walk by, they hit people pretty hard. It's not uncommon to find bruises from it the next day."

"Oh my God," I said, "I didn't know it got that rough."

"Oh, yeah." Bertram smiled as he set plates on the table. "And there are all kinds of styles in the costumes. It varies by region, but the culture is starting to change. Some masks are made from latex now and have LED eyes, but the traditional style is just wood and paint with sheep or goat horns. Lately there's been a big influence from horror films and Halloween in America."

I looked at him, surprised. It was the same thing that Ruben had said was happening with Day of the Dead traditions.

"You'll see," he continued. "The *lauf* running in town tonight is the biggest in Austria. There will be thirty groups in it, I read."

"Wow!" I tried to envision it while my stomach quietly growled. After two days of airport food, the pasta and sauce looked and smelled exquisite.

"It will also last about three hours, so you'll want to dress warm." Bertram smiled, taking a seat across from me. "Hopefully you won't get beat up too bad."

"What?" I chuckled. "You don't want to go with me?"

He shook his head. "I work at a *church*. This is our busiest time of year. We have concerts and all kinds of events going on almost every night. So it looks like you'll be enduring the Krampus demon on your own."

I couldn't help but smile at the thought. While steam wafted over the table, fogging up the small window by our side, I envisioned standing out on the streets, bundled up in the cold and cowering as massive Austrian monsters stampeded by me.

"No problem," I said happily. "I can totally do that."

The Krampus *Lauf*

A few hours later, I headed towards town. Hohensalzburg Fortress and Salzburg Cathedral loomed above the River Salzach. Multistoried, baroque buildings along the water shone in the sun, each appearing to be untouched by time. In the city center, holly and lights adorned every road. Small, wooden huts sold handmade Christmas ornaments and wreaths, hot wine and desserts. I followed the flood of tourists around Cathedral Square and saw dozens of Krampus-shaped cookies and candies, decorations and plush toys. I excitedly bought a red, foil-wrapped demon made from hollowed chocolate, only to frown when the taste reminded me of Easter. Beside me, a Chinese tourist pointed to a red Krampus mask hanging by a string.

"This isn't Christmas!" he joked, shaking his head in astonishment.

I laughed and nodded. "I know—it's awesome!"

At the corner of Linzer-Bundesstraße and Schillinghofstraße, I stood where Bertram had recommended I watch the *lauf*. Wooden barriers were set up next to the sidewalks. Small tents sold beer, hot chocolate, and bread with meat spread. Drawn to their sandwich-like quality, I bought two of the intriguing breads and found them simple, yet divine. As the sun began to set, I realized that going anywhere in Austria after dark would require more layers than even I was used to. I pulled down my hat to cover as much of my forehead and ears as possible. Amazingly, the few hundred people gathering around me didn't seem to shiver one bit. *How are they not* freezing? I thought. I made a mental note to buy thermal underwear the next day.

Fortunately, a distant sound of loud, dull bells distracted me from the cold. The crowd grew quiet as hatted heads looked down the empty, barricaded street. The sound grew closer: dozens of bells growing louder as if a stampede of cows was heading our way.

And then they appeared.

Black, shaggy beasts, each over six feet tall, ran in long strides down the street. Pointed horns reached more than two feet over their heads. As they got closer I made out sharp fangs set in horrifying snarls. They had long, crooked noses with nostrils angrily flared, yellow eyes, and pointed ears. Large bells clanked loudly from thick belts around their waists and grew almost deafening as the creatures approached. I stared at them in wonder, each captivating and beautiful, with fur slightly shining in the streetlights. After a year of waiting, I had found Krampus at last.

Once spying their weapons, however, I saw little else. The long, thick tails of black animal hair looked deadly as the creatures whipped them through the air. One Krampus ran to the barrier on the opposite side of the road and struck it with such force that the crowd immediately jumped back in unison. I flinched as an identical creature rushed right towards me. He threw back his weapon as if to strike, then stopped as I cringed with the people beside me. The beast's yellow eyes glared down at us. Deep-set lines along his pasty-fleshed face made him look like a demon from the underworld, though the long, black wool reflected the cold climate that I knew he was actually from. Throughout the street, similar creatures threateningly ran up to the crowds. They thrashed their weapons on the ground and slammed them against the barriers, making

DRAWN TO THE DARK

loud *whacks!* I couldn't help but feel grateful that none of them actually hit anyone.

After the monstrous group moved down the road, I turned to see another one approach. Ten different wooly beasts came running our way. I remembered what Bertram had said about costume styles varying by region. Long, sharp horns shot up above shiny, black manes, contrasting the rest of their white physique. Running faster than his predecessors, one creature charged the barrier in front of me. I instantly jumped back, staring at deep, red veins protruding from sunken, corpselike skin. The slits in his deep green eyes looked like those of a cat. In a flash he leaned over the barrier and harshly struck a man's legs beside me. The three-foot, black horse's tail whipped through the air, making the man cry out in anguish. He hopped in pain after multiple strikes. I looked at him in shock as his attacker walked away, then from the corner of my eye saw a similar devil run up to me and raise his own weapon. I immediately jerked back and felt only the tip of the long, dark hair strike my sneakers. A moment later, another approached so fast that I didn't have time to move. With a sharp *whack!* I felt a rush of pain below the back of my knee. I yelled out and instinctively grabbed my leg after the Krampus ran off. It throbbed like I couldn't believe. I felt as though I'd just been hit with a steel rod. *My God,* I thought, looking at the people around me in confusion, *you all came out here for* this?! I turned my attention back to the black-and-white beasts running around the street. They each took turns attacking men and women, who clutched each other at their approach. These were nothing like the monsters that I knew—the gruesome characters in haunted attractions that stalked and preyed while only *pretending* to pose a threat. There was no pretense of danger here; Krampus was the real deal. If it was pain we wanted, we would get it.

Within seconds, I felt the throbbing in my leg vanish. The man beside me who had endured much worse seemed completely fine. He watched the Krampus group before us move on, then turned and looked for the next one to approach. I followed his lead, laughing to myself. Our excitement at the prospect of getting attacked again seemed hilarious.

More creatures arrived by the dozen: white and gray, brown and black, some scrawny, others resembling the Abominable Snowman. I saw long, graying beards; long tongues hanging out between jagged teeth; and pointed, curled, or stubby horns. The only feature they shared was the reaction that it got from the crowd. It was always a combination of awe and fear as we cowered before fierce beasts that looked ready to tear us to pieces. They walked, ran, and even rolled on the pavement. I took pictures, recoiled, was hit, took more pictures, and froze, surrounded by dozens of others doing the same thing (except, it seemed, freezing). Although young children had been Krampus's original target, I saw them get off easy now. The creatures only waved and patted them on the head before moving on to a teenager upon whom they whaled mercilessly. The more brutal attacks were the rarest, I found, and if one Krampus used force, odds were that everyone in its group would do the same. But despite how hard they hit, no one seemed to mind. People of all ages jumped and hopped after being attacked, then laughed while rubbing their aching legs. Part of the fun, I realized, was in not knowing just what each Krampus would do.

That night, my head hit the pillow on Bertram's foldout couch yet again. I was as exhausted as I'd been after two days of airports and flights. I had survived three hours and thirty groups of brutal, Austrian beasts. The next morning, I stared in disbelief at a large black-and-blue mark behind my knee. My first reaction was to take a picture and e-mail it to my friends back home. It was my battle scar, and, somehow, I was proud of it.

Bertram smiled at my excitement. "And just think," he said, looking at my bruise without the slightest surprise, "that's just your first one."

A Krampus Christmas

While Salzburg bustled in the holiday spirit, Bertram's apartment remained unaffected. Kept immaculately clean—floors swept every day and not a dirty dish in the sink—no Christmas cards, decorations, or strands of lights could be seen. I quickly changed that. Back home, I had long held the tradition of decorating for Christmas on the first day of December. When it came time to take everything down after New Year's, I pretty much had to force myself and usually waited until February. It was all based on how I'd been raised; in my family, decorations just *made* the season.

I knew that Bertam's place had potential. The four-foot ficus in his living room had particularly caught my eye. On my third day staying with him, I walked to the store while he was at work. I bought a box of red bows; glittering, plastic balls; and two tiny, plush Krampus figurines. After giving the ficus a new, much more seasonal look, I stood back and decided that Bertram would like it much better.

The next time I saw him, his inverted form loomed above me as I woke up on the couch.

"What did you do to my tree?" he barked.

I fought a smirk as Bertram put his fists on his hips.

"I don't know what you're talking about," I protested innocently. The colorful, festive plant glittered just inches away from my feet. I smiled at it. "I think Krampus snuck in last night and did it. It's a Krampus tree!"

He stared down at me. His silent combination of anger and amusement told me that all was well. Plus, the tree was good for him. I was sure of it. I wouldn't learn until later, however, that Austrians don't put up Christmas trees until December 24. This is the night when the Christkind is said to bring the decorated tree to the house, along with the presents. But despite insisting that he hated it, Bertram let the tree stand and only occasionally shook his head while looking at it.

The Throne March

With so many *laufs* running, I was attending shows every two or three nights. Some were in the center of Salzburg, while others required taking buses to surrounding villages. Large *laufs* involved dozens of groups, but I found that smaller shows were much more frequent. Many were held in village squares, where horned, wooly beasts ran amongst a multitude of food and drink huts. Other groups were hired by restaurants to interact with (i.e., *harass*) customers, going from table to table to ruffle people's hair and pretend to take their food. I began leaving Bertram scribbled notes before going to each show:

Mortal,
We tAke GirL. MayBe wE brinG heR back...
Or mayBe wE kEep, haHA!
—Krampus

Eventually, Bertram succumbed to my enthusiasm. He renamed his ficus the *Krampusbaum* and left replies to my notes that I wasn't allowed home unless I had suffered additional bruises. The mark behind my knee remained bright as ever, but fortunately no other beatings showed—though there were several.

But after attending more than a dozen *laufs,* I eventually saw hell unleashed onto Salzburg.

Outside the entrance to Sigmundstor tunnel, I stood bundled in layers. Thermal underwear under my blue jeans and sweatshirt kept me blissfully warm, along with my winter coat, hat, scarf, gloves, and two pairs of socks that slightly bulged my sneakers. I gaped up at Bürgerwehr, the medieval wall within Mönchsberg Mountain, while about a hundred others filled the street around me. Police officers blocked all traffic from the tunnel. I listened to the surrounding German, vaguely disappointed that I couldn't understand a word of it. The dialect sounded nothing like what I'd studied in college. Had it not been for the signs, I barely would have believed that Austrians spoke German at all. But before long, all conversation stopped. A strange noise began to come from inside the deep cavern, making everyone grow quiet and look.

I cocked my head, listening. Whatever was happening inside the mountain was hard to make out. The noise certainly wasn't the dull-sounding Krampus bells that I'd come to associate with *laufs.* It sounded more like a distant, high-pitched scream. After a few moments it repeated,

echoing along the rock until reaching the road. A bright, reddish glow began to glimmer, growing brighter until lighting the entire arch. As the screaming grew louder, a few people crossed the street to get a closer look. I quickly followed, peering into the massive opening while the police attentively watched.

To my amazement, two red devils appeared. Moving slowly towards the crowd, they walked hunched over in apparent effort. Behind them, high flames shot up from a large, wooden chariot, making the tunnel glow eerily around it. The devils drew closer, red from head to foot, with corpselike faces and lips drawn back from cruel teeth. They emerged from the tunnel, and I saw each pulling the chariot forward by long ropes harnessed to their backs. Dark manes fell over their bare chests, their eyes glowed a metallic blue, and their only clothing was black pants torn almost to rags. Behind them, two white, harnessed demons pulled the wagon with equal effort, followed by two large Krampuses guiding it between the wheels. The shaggy creatures resembled so many I'd seen elsewhere, with dark, wooly coats, white manes, and long, pointed horns.

I froze at the spectacle. A leader of the horrid troop stood high on a throne upon the chariot. Long hair fell over his hideous face, which resembled a grinning, living corpse. A red cloak covered his tall, thin frame, and on his head sat a towering crown mockingly resembling a bishop's miter. Crouched before him, a man in a cloak of animal fur threw back his head and let out a piercing wail. I flinched at the sound while keeping my eyes on the scene. Flames shot up along either side of the chariot. The entire edge of the tunnel went ablaze with reddish-orange light. It was unlike anything I could have imagined; hell, it seemed, was coming out of the mountain.

When the flames died down, I heard the familiar sound of dull bells. Five dark, wooly Krampuses appeared from behind the wagon. They ran loose before their captive counterparts, waving branches and animal tails threateningly at the crowd. From above, the gruesome king stretched out his arms. He appeared to beckon us to worship him and all his glory. The wailing continued, now intermixed with loud, dull bells and shooting flames.

I couldn't get over the assembly: Krampuses and devils, horned and horrid, harnessed and free, all revolving around a ghastly leader bringing fire and brimstone to the world of the living. As the carriage moved past, I saw that it was made out of a hollowed section of tree with huge wagon wheels on either side. I quickly ran beside it with the crowd. Not an inch of slack hung from the ropes tied to each devil that pulled it, as the dark procession headed down Getreidegasse.

I had to move fast to keep up. I couldn't help but wonder if pulling the cart was as difficult as it looked, but I quickly lost my thought. An unrestrained, black Krampus appeared beside me. He struck at my leg in an instant. I yelped, feeling an intense sting from the long animal tail, then heard a few people beside me get the same treatment. I immediately laughed afterwards; unlike my initial attack weeks earlier, I wasn't surprised at the fleeting pain.

The procession took us past shops and apartments in the city center. Seasonal wreaths and lights adorned four-story buildings on either side

of us. Large, glowing stars hung from lampposts, contrasting the sudden arrival of evil. From the sidewalks, hundreds of people stared in disbelief. Stopped in their tracks as they held shopping bags and drank from steaming, plastic cups, they gaped at the beasts running straight towards them. The Krampuses crouched threateningly, then struck the occasional bystander on the legs and feet. They ripped off hats and ran away with them, tossing some in the air to make their owners chase after them. Most people laughed at the antics, but I saw some back away and hide. Over the past week, I'd met several tourists who had come to Salzburg for the Christmas markets without ever even hearing about a *lauf*. I could only hope that some of them were here now and experiencing what Christmas in Salzburg *really* entailed: a moving theater of monsters.

Beside me, more people joined the procession. We continued through cobblestone streets and Christmas markets. I laughed as the excitement grew, indecipherable German mixed with the clanking of bells. The fire and ear-piercing wailing ceased in the thick crowds. Horns stood out among winter hats. Glowing eyes glared at the fearful. Quick, sharp thrashes of tails sent people scooting away. I shuffled and ran to keep up, taking pictures while hoping that my flash wouldn't make me the target of a beating. Along every street, police escorts parted the masses to ensure that the chariot could pass. Around one corner, a cart selling hot drinks left so little room in the road that I was nearly pinned against a wagon wheel. I quickly jumped out of the way with a few others and managed to free myself just in time.

But I didn't mind being nearly crushed. And the occasional thrash to the leg was worth it. I was part of something extraordinary. There were enslaved demons before me, a devil leader above, and a dozen legendary beasts running amok through screaming crowds. More people joined in, looking equally thrilled to be part of the ghastly commotion. I had the distinct feeling that, after this, spending Christmas any other way just wouldn't be the same.

A Krampus Interview

A few days before New Year's I sat in Fingerlos Café, eager for the opportunity to have a Krampus interview. After reaching out to the organizer of the Facebook page "Krampuszeit," translating to "Krampus Time," I was referred to Clemens. The tall, muscular man sat across from me and smiled. He wore glasses and had a thin, blond goatee. By looking at him, I never would have guessed that his number-one pastime was portraying an ancient Austrian beast.

"*Laufs* are the age-old story of good and evil," Clemens explained. He spread butter and jam onto two semmel (Kaiser) rolls and sipped a small cappuccino. I listened, drinking from the largest cup of American coffee that the waitress could bring. Clemens' English was fluent with just a hint of Austrian accent, which I found a stark contrast to Bertram's Irish.

"I've been playing Krampus since I was eight years old and I'm over forty now," he said. "And I'll keep on doing it for the next thirty, forty years. Because I'm crazy!"

I laughed. "Does your character have a name?"

"Of course," he said. "My character is named Mente. He's very large, white, and wooly."

I thought back to all the creatures I'd seen over the weeks that matched that description. *Had any of them attacked me?* I wondered. *Should I be on guard around this one... ?* I couldn't remember.

Clemens' group, I learned, was named *Grödiger Krampusse,* translating to "Krampus from the village of Grödig." It currently had thirty-five members ranging from ages sixteen to fifty, as well as several young children. Although the group shared the traditional look of long fur and demonic faces, costume color and mask design varied.

"When I was younger," Clemens said, "actors made their own costumes. They glued fur onto overalls and purchased masks from professional carvers in the mountains. The carvers came from families that had been doing this for generations. But today we buy costumes from professional fur dealers that customize the suits to our bodies. And the bells are often purchased from the same shops that farmers use for their cattle."

"Ohhh, that makes sense," I said. I remembered the first time I'd heard a Krampus before actually seeing one. From the sound of the loud, dull bells, I had pictured a stampede of cows running down the road. "Aren't those bells heavy?"

Clemens chuckled mid-sip from his cappuccino. He smiled and nodded. "Yes, but the costumes are much heavier. My most recent one weighs fifteen kilos from the fur alone."

He looked at me a moment, waiting for a reaction. When he didn't get one, he said, "That's over thirty pounds."

"Oh, wow!" I marveled. "That *is* heavy."

"The belt and bells add more weight, and my shoes weigh a kilo each. The mask weighs eight kilos—a lot of that comes from the sheep horns."

"*Real* sheep horns?"

"Yes," he said with a teasing smirk. "The horns are always real."

"It sounds like being a Krampus is a real workout." I thought back to the characters I'd seen pulling the chariot during the Throne March. I could only imagine how difficult that must have been while wearing a costume and mask that weighed a ton. Even their evil companions had been constantly on the move, chasing people and attacking.

Clemens nodded. "It is, but when adrenaline kicks in, you don't feel how heavy everything is. It's only when it's all over that you're exhausted."

When I asked Clemens about his tactics for "punishing" people during the *laufs,* he told me that he alternated between using a horse's tail and cow's tail. But with a master's degree in psychological marketing, he was more interested in why people choose to attend *laufs* in the first place.

"People want limits," he said. "Especially young people. They don't get that in today's society. But young people want discipline in a controlled, safe environment—from a beast, though, not a human being. A lot of people come to the *laufs* not because of the costumes but to get beaten."

I looked at him in shock. "You think so?" It was hard for me to imagine such a thing; people *not* going to those shows to marvel at horrifying creatures? With their demonic horns and nightmarish teeth, tromping down the streets as if the gates of hell had opened up?

"Of course they do," he said, reading my expression. "It's a local tradition." He put an elbow on the table between us and held up a fist. "I hold the guy in the left hand," he said, "and punish him with the horse tail. Full power. And he's jumping. And screaming. And laughing at the same time. And he's very proud of the wounds. This is a game. That's a cultural game."

I smiled at the passion in his voice. I thought about the picture I'd taken of my own bruise to show my friends back home. I had been proud of it, as strange as it had seemed. It wasn't a mark I had gotten from a random fall or injury; it was a sign of what I'd endured from the legendary creature that I'd come so far to see. I could only suppose that people who grew up seeing Krampus every year would look forward to it just as much. How could encountering something like that ever really get old? But I had also seen reactions from people caught completely by surprise. I remembered some holiday visitors looking at the devils in the Throne March in confusion and fear. They obviously hadn't had any idea what was going on.

"Would you ever attack someone if you could tell they didn't want you to?"

"No," Clemens said seriously. "I can always tell who wants it." He paused, looking at me for a moment as if for the first time. "I can see it in their eyes."

I tried not to blink as he stared at me. I realized that I was unconsciously holding my breath. After a few moments, I brought my coffee mug up to my face and stared at it, avoiding his gaze. *Thank God my jeans cover my lauf bruise,* I thought. "It sounds like it's just as much fun for the actors as it is for the people who watch them," I eventually said.

"Absolutely." Clemens finally leaned back in his chair. I looked at him again and saw that his piercing stare had gone. "Being Krampus allows men—they're almost always men—to portray a creature, a beast, that's permitted to do things not accepted in modern society. They can run and jump, threaten and attack, be scary and intimidating."

I nodded with a smile. I had seen many people enjoying those things in their roles, not just in Krampus *laufs* but at Screamville back in Oaxaca. They had obviously had a great time playing zombies and killer clowns while stalking Ruben and me. It was the same with so many haunters I knew back home. But when I made the comparison to Halloween and haunted attractions, Clemens waved away talk of the American holiday.

"Halloween is just commercial," he said flatly. "Many Austrians think this way. Stores sell costumes and plastic toys, and bars throw parties so they can sell expensive drinks. But there's no meaning behind it. Krampus is about tradition. It's very meaningful to us."

I nodded in thought. I could see his point: to outsiders, Halloween could appear superficial if drunken parties were the extent of their knowledge about it.

"I can understand that," I said. "But I think that part of the reason adults like Halloween is because we remember how much fun we had celebrating it when we were young. It's just like you probably remember playing Krampus when you were eight." Like I'd done with Ruben, I told Clemens about my childhood experiences trick or treating. I described my neighborhood turning into a magical place and seeing my neighbors as funny, dark characters when I went to their door. Clemens listened, appearing to grow thoughtful.

"That *is* different," he said after a moment. "I didn't realize that it had a level of community in it."

"Absolutely," I said. "Most of the time, it's the community that makes it so special. And those memories can really shape us."

As we stood up to leave, I couldn't help but see my new actor friend in a different light. It was hard to imagine an intelligent, normal-looking person behind the mask of a Krampus. The horrifying creature had forever changed my view of Christmas. I wondered how many other actors out there really understood the impact that they could have in their role.

"By the way, were you part of that big *lauf* a few weeks ago on November thirtieth?" I asked. "Maybe I saw you."

Clemens shook his head with a frown. "No. My group doesn't run in big *laufs* like that anymore. We do smaller ones. But we were in town the other night. It started at the Sigmundstor tunnel and we pulled a wooden chariot around town."

My eyes shot open in surprise. "That was *your* group?!"

He nodded excitedly. "You saw it? If you didn't know, the creature we pulled is Kaiser Karl—you may have heard of him as Emperor Charles. He's said to reside in Untersberg Mountain and will one day rise again."

"Oh, I didn't know that. I thought he was some kind of Goblin King..."

Clemens giggled at the thought.

"But the show was amazing!"

He gave a small, cordial bow. "Thank you!" A wolfish smile then came over his face as he leaned across the table with a wink. "I take it you got beaten, then."

Chapter 3

Dante's Florence

"Midway upon the journey of our life
I found myself within a forest dark
For the straightforward pathway had been lost."
—Dante Alighieri's *Inferno*

Fabio in Florence

On January 15, I waited for my new host, Fabio, at the train station in Prato, Italy. It was fifteen miles outside of Florence, my city of destination, and Fabio had offered to pick me up after he got off work. I stood with my duffel bag while dozens of people walked briskly by, all less bundled than the Austrian crowds had been, but not by much. Watching them rush to and fro, I began to wonder how many might be making their way to Florence for the same reason that I was. As the heart of northern Italy's Tuscany region, Florence is world renowned for being the birthplace of the Renaissance. I knew that the city would be filled with architectural masterpieces and sculptures by greats such as Michelangelo and Donatello. But I had come for something else entirely. Florence was also the birthplace of one of my favorite writers: Dante Alighieri.

Since its publication in the mid-fourteenth century, Dante's three-part poem, *The Divine Comedy,* had forever changed the way people envisioned the depths of the underworld. The story's lead character, Dante himself, had lost his way in life through sin. To find his way back to God, he follows a guide, Virgil, through the three realms of hell, purgatory, and heaven. The first part of the trilogy, *Inferno,* takes the two through the nine layers of hell. There they witness the nature of sin and all its horrifying, corresponding punishments. Sinners suffer in cesspools of feces. Others burn in a river of boiling blood and a desert of abysmal sand. They are lashed with whips, blazed in fire, bitten by vipers, and mutilated by demons. Many people have believed *Inferno* to be a true account of what awaits us in hell, in addition to being an allegory for how a life of sin leads us away from happiness on earth. As an atheist, I had always admired the poem's creative imagery and the way that Dante blended Greek myths with the Christian concept of hell. I had also marveled at the story's influence in countless works of literature and art—right down to modern-day horror films and haunted attractions.

In the station, I waited just a few minutes before a man nodded at me in recognition from the entrance. He was tall and well dressed, with short gray hair, and appeared to be in his early forties. A similarly attired man walked beside him. Both wore thin scarves draped over their business jackets and smiled with refined politeness.

"Chris," said the first, holding out a hand, "I'm Fabio; nice to meet you."

I shook his hand, then hugged him hello. "Nice to meet you." I refrained from commenting on my initial reaction: complete surprise over his accent. It was definitely Scottish. Instead, I said, "Thanks so much for picking me up!"

"My pleasure. And this is my friend Enrico."

The man beside him smiled, his short, dark goatee a sharp contrast to his shaven head. "Hello," he said, shaking my hand. "Welcome to Italy."

"Thanks!" I couldn't help but chuckle; Enrico's thicker Italian accent was exactly what I had expected.

The three of us soon sat down at a nearby pizza restaurant. Above, an iron chandelier sparkled from an arched, brick ceiling, giving the place the feel of an enchanted wine cellar. My host and his friend sat across from me, bickering about which appetizer would be my best introduction to Italy. I had to force myself not to laugh through their gesturing at the menu. Fabio and Enrico both seemed to have a distinct, soft pitch to their voice whenever speaking to me in English, but it disappeared entirely the moment they spoke to each other in rapid Italian. As a plate of meats, cheeses, and bread was set between us, Fabio excitedly asked me if my interest in the *Inferno* extended to the horror genre. When I told him that it did, he proceeded to drill me for my opinion on all of his favorite movies and shows.

"Which do you like better," he asked while laying a piece of prosciutto over a slice of white bread, "the 1978 *Halloween* or the remake?"

I followed his lead and topped my own bread with mozzarella. "The original." I secretly smiled, reflecting on the film's influence on haunted attractions.

"Good. Do you like classic Romero zombie films?"

"Of course I do!"

"What about *The Walking Dead?*"

"I've only seen the first episode...."

"Don't watch it; it's crap. Do you like Hitchcock?"

I chuckled, still yet to swallow my food. Fabio didn't seem to even take the time to breathe between questions; from the moment of his arrival at the station, he had moved in a kind of fast forward. "Of course I like Hitchcock. Who wouldn't? He even made *birds* creepy!"

Additional titles came in a constant flow. Thin pizzas were served, crusty and light and complete contrasts to the deep-dish pies I'd always known, while Fabio and I covered the horror genre through the decades. Enrico mostly sat back and listened, having seen almost none of the shows. Two hours later, we headed out and my host casually mentioned that he and his ex-wife had lived in Scotland for several years.

I looked at him in surprise while stepping through the door that he held open. "Oh..." I gave a quick glance back to Enrico behind me. "I thought you two were a couple...."

Enrico flinched in disbelief. Fabio threw back his head and laughed. "Why would you think that?" he asked, following us outside. The street was now completely dark, with quiet apartments above and pedestrians walking quickly by.

I shrugged with a smile. "Well, you both speak pretty softly, and you're both wearing those scarves. So I just kind of assumed...."

Enrico put a hand on his scarf, frowning down at his clothes in confusion.

Fabio only shook his head, chuckling. "It's common for Italians to wear scarves. And men often speak softer when using a second language that doesn't come as natural to them as their first."

"Ohhh..." I thought back to everyone I'd met in Austria and Mexico. I hadn't seen that in either place. But I thought it better to not mention it. "Okay, that makes sense."

After dropping off Enrico at his apartment in Prato, Fabio drove me to Florence. High on a hill, a huge replica of the *David* looked down on a city of gold. I saw a massive dome and towering, elegant cathedral lit almost majestically. Fabio pointed out Santa Maria del Fiore, Ponte Vecchio, Piazza della Signoria, and Santa Croce. I saw love and pride in his face as he named them, while dozens of others admired the view around us.

Moments later, my host sped his small Fiat down old and incredibly narrow cobblestone streets. Parked cars lined both sides of the road, and I watched in astonishment as barely an inch seemed to separate our side mirrors from the cars that we went whizzing by. In the city center, marble statues encircled the Uffizi Courtyard, immortalizing Tuscan greats: Leonardo da Vinci, Donatello, Galileo, and members of the Medici family. I immediately gasped when Fabio pointed to a particular one.

"It's Dante!" I gazed up at the writer in awe. He looked proud and wise in a long cloak and laurel wreath. He appeared to regard the square as someone who has seen more than we ever would.

Fabio beamed at my reaction. He asked about my plans for Florence, and I told him that for two weeks I hoped to see any and all sites associated with Dante. Aside from that, I was happy to just spend time in the very city that had shaped the poet's view of the world.

"I live just twenty minutes from here by foot," he said as we strolled back to the car, "so you can walk to the center every day, if you want."

I lit up at the idea of it. "I will definitely do that!"

"Good..." He nodded in thought. "Because I'll be very interested to see if Florence is what you expected."

"O, you possessed of sturdy intellect..."

Dante Hunting

Fabio left for work early the next morning. He bolted out of his small, tidy apartment after a miniscule espresso had barely enough time to reach his stomach. I took things a bit slower, savoring my diluted, American-style coffee while making up my bed on the foldout couch. When I headed out, I saw rows of yellow stone buildings with red-tiled roofs running along the River Arno. I admired them while briskly walking with gloved hands stuffed inside my jacket pockets. I could barely believe that each house was older than my entire country itself. On Ponte Vecchio, the Bridge of Gold, watches and necklaces were being sold for what could have easily fed a family of four for about a decade. At the domed cathedral, Santa Maria del Fiore, I grew almost dizzy gazing at its massive exterior. Statues of saints and religious icons, looking peaceful, covered every square inch of the white, red, and green marble panels.

But I stopped in my tracks at Basilica di Santa Croce. There before the church stood a massive statue of the heroic storyteller. I stared at Dante's depiction, then couldn't help but smirk at his expression. He scowled beneath his elegant laurel wreath. He looked both intimidating and miserable. But that wasn't surprising. Dante had been in love with his city but forced into exile in 1302 due to Florence's raging political warfare. He was thirty-three at the time—just one year younger than I was. If Dante ever returned, he was sentenced to be burned at the stake. The sentence wouldn't be lifted until 2008.

My statue wouldn't have been smiling, either.

But Dante did what any writer does when dealing with trauma and heartbreak: he expressed himself through words. He began writing *The Divine Comedy* and completed it just a few years before his death in 1321.

Inside the church, I quickly spied a series of marble slabs running along a stone passageway. I gravitated towards the first, then felt my eyes grow wide as a sculpted picture came into view. A winged, three-headed demon held what was undeniably a mass of human flesh. Stunted, curved horns protruded from each of its horrid heads. Additional human remains dripped from sets of razor-sharp teeth. In the background, hundreds of faces filled a seemingly endless sea. Naked, slouching forms resembled half-skeletal ghouls in what was surely a land of death. Only two appeared remotely alive: one man clutching another and tearing out his brain by the teeth. Eventually I noticed a small label below the five-foot slab. *Canto XXXIV*, it read, *betrayers, Lucifero, Brutus, Cassius, Judas.*

I couldn't believe my luck: it was an exhibit of the *Inferno! I'm not the only one obsessed with the story,* I thought. *I* knew *it.*

I remembered Dante describing this very image:

> *At every mouth his teeth a sinner champ'd*
> *Bruis'd as with pond'rous engine, so that three*
> *Were in this guise tormented. But far more*

Than from that gnawing, was the foremost pang'd,
By the fierce rending, whence ofttimes the back
Was stript of all its skin.

After a while I broke my gaze from the beautiful horror and looked to the other slabs beside it. Chained men, weary and naked, screamed in torment. They wailed in a lake that, I knew, was formed from blood. They tore at their flesh and hair. Demons smote them with swords. Serpents twisted round their necks, chests, and arms and squeezed. One viper wrapped its mouth around an entire human torso, reaching up to its victim's neck with horrible fangs. Charon, the "hoary ferryman with hair of eld," beat his ore into the river of pining dead.

I looked at each piece with intense interest, as if I had been given the task of memorizing each one. Each group of sinners from the tale was masterfully depicted: thieves and adulterers, corrupt officials and heretics, suicides and those not baptized, all engulfed in the depths. There were "forests of thick-crowded ghosts," "rocks dark-stained," black air and heavy fog. All was carnage and misery in the endless doom of Dante's imagination.

A few others passed behind me. They regarded each slab for only a moment, then disappeared into a walkway that led to the main church hall. I couldn't help but find their mild interest as incredible as the images. How were they not spellbound by this? How did they not appreciate the accurate, gory detail? But as much as I admired each scene, I began to think about how these images had originally been perceived. *The Divine Comedy* was written in a time when eternal damnation was thought to be an actual possibility, as some still believe it to be today. I could only imagine how such beliefs could affect someone. Fire and brimstone were mesmerizing, but only when it was all pretend. If even a shred of it reflected reality, I imagined life being nothing but a constant state of fear.

That weekend, Fabio joined me in Florence. He translated small plaques on buildings throughout the city that bore quotes from *The Comedy*. In Santa Margherita dei Cerchi, my host explained that the small church was famous for being where Dante had met Beatrice, the love of his life. Although Dante had been only nine years old at the time, he became infatuated with Beatrice and later wrote her into *The Comedy* as a manifestation of the divine.

At the Dante museum, Casa di Dante, a replica of a thirteenth-century home provided a model of the writer's residence. I imagined him sitting at the plain, wooden desk, scribbling with his stylus in his iconic red fur cloak. Reproductions of the *Inferno, Purgatorio,* and *Paradiso* were displayed under thick glass in both Italian and English translation.

Nel mezzo del cammin di nostra vita
mi ritrovai per una selva oscura
ché la diritta via era smarrita.

Midway upon the journey of our life
I found myself within a forest dark
For the straightforward pathway had been lost.

I stared at the words in awe. "This is so cool!"

Beside me, Fabio shot me a condescending smile. "You *do* realize there's a lot more to *The Comedy* than the gruesome images of the *Inferno*. The book is about choices we make in life. We all become lost at some point or another. But it's our actions that lead us to either misery or happiness."

I cocked my head at him, finally breaking my gaze from the text. "Yes, I know that. But I can't help it if his realms of misery are the most visually appealing."

Fabio only shook his head. "Americans are so strange."

"Abandon hope, all ye who enter here...."

Torture in Tuscany

During my second week in Florence, a fellow traveler informed me about a few torture museums outside the city. Supposedly, each contained dozens of replicas of devices used during the Spanish Inquisition. I was thrilled at the idea of it. But when I mentioned it to Fabio during his morning espresso, he only stared at me curiously.

"I've never met anyone who wanted to see something like *that....*" Still dressed in his blue bathrobe, he finished his breakfast in one sip. "Only *you* would want to spend a day in Tuscany going to places about human misery."

I added boiling water to my own coffee. Diluting it was the only way I could stand the taste. "Hey," I said defensively, "those things are educational." I clasped a thin blanket over my pajamas while replacing the kettle on the stove. In addition to keeping me warm, the extra layer made me feel as though I were cloaked for my stay in Florence—resembling Dante in the Uffizi Courtyard. Surely *he* would have understood my interest in the museums. "Besides, it's not like I get to look at that type of stuff back home."

Fabio sighed, then rolled his eyes. "Americans..."

That weekend, we picked up Enrico and headed out for a day of torture. Both museums were located thirty miles outside Florence in San Gimignano. Neither Fabio nor Enrico had ever heard of them. They had also never been to any kind of torture museum before. I had been to several in other parts of Europe, but never in the company of my Couchsurfing host.

We came to Museo della Tortura first. The stone-and-brick building showcased dozens of inventions specifically created for human mutilation. A metal head vise resembled a crude helmet topped with a long, thick screw and handle. Its purpose, I saw, was to slowly crush a person's skull until they confessed to whatever charges had been made against them— more often than not, witchcraft. I stared at the device and immediately felt the way I always did in any torture museum: utter bewilderment over how someone could do anything so terrible to another human being.

In another glass case, four-pronged, metal claws resembled an enormous clamp from an arcade toy machine. A sign below read *Spanish Spiders*. Reading the description, which I was grateful to find in English, I learned that the device was used to lift prisoners by the buttocks, breasts, belly, or head, with additional prongs inserted into their eyes or ears. I flinched in disgust and looked at the tool with new eyes. As repulsive as it was, I found it equally alluring. It provided a small glimpse into Europe's past—one that I couldn't have felt more grateful not to have been a part of. Beside me, Enrico clutched his chin while reading the Italian text.

"My God," he said when he'd finished.

"I know...." I turned to him with a grimace. "How could people have been so cruel?"

"It was a different time back then," he said with a frown. "Punishments like this happened all over Europe. People just saw it as normal."

I shook my head at the idea of it. "That's so sick."

We moved on to a long, metal cooking spoon dripping silver liquid into the cast of a human ear. Its purpose was clear: pouring lead into a prisoner's facial orifice. I imagined a poor soul screaming in agony, no doubt feeling as if the side of his or her face could burst open and probably wishing that it would. Their crime could have been something as minor as saying the slightest thing that was different from the norm.

In another case, an open copy of *Malleus Maleficarum* highlighted Europe's cruel law of the day. The fifteenth-century's infamous "Hammer of the Witches" attempted to provide evidence of people cavorting with the devil. It gave step-by-step instructions on how to prosecute and interrogate them through heinous acts of torture. I looked at the thick, dust-clad tome and felt a rush of contempt at the very idea of it. But after a moment, I began to think about the artwork I'd seen in the *Inferno* exhibit. I remembered admiring its portrayals of agony. I had found them to be fascinating, *beautiful*. But this was different. These hooks and tools demonstrated what had *actually* been done to *real* people. And there was nothing beautiful about it.

While Enrico and I continued cringing in shock, Fabio regarded the displays with only mild interest. He occasionally chuckled over our reactions and eventually smiled at me from a large rack in the middle of the room.

"You like this stuff, huh?" he asked teasingly. He put a hand on the instrument that was roughly the width of a twin-sized bed. The solid wood was cracked and faded. Rusty, metal clamps connected to spoked wheels at either end. It wasn't hard to imagine someone being helplessly sprawled out in the thing and slowly—painfully—being torn apart.

I shot Fabio a sarcastic glare. "Not in the way *you* think, mister."

He shrugged defensively. "Some people do."

"Well, good for them."

"They would have used something like this on *you*, you know," he said, knocking on the wood, "for the types of things *you're* interested in—monsters and devils. You would have been cast out as a witch for sure."

I looked at the monstrosity and considered it. "Yeah, I probably would." I tried to envision what living in those days would be like. I certainly would have kept my love for Dante's *Inferno* to myself. Would I have been fortunate enough to interpret the poem as fiction rather than literal truth? I thought back to my first night in Italy and Fabio's incessant questioning about Hitchcock and zombie films. "Hey, they would have done the same thing to you!"

He chuckled and nodded. "You're right!"

Additional replicas awaited us at Museo Pena di Morte. Metal spikes covered every inch of an Iron Maiden: a man-sized cage made to pierce a prisoner's flesh from head to toe. An Iron Chair provided a similar tactic, with victims enduring iron nails in the seat, back, armrests, and leg rests.

In another room, I quickly turned away in disgust. A naked mannequin hung upside down from a wooden post. On either side of him, torturers tore at his flesh with ordinary farming sickles. Skin from the man's forearm had been completely removed, so that muscle, tissue, and bone were gruesomely exposed. The victim's face was frozen in an eternal, harrowing scream.

Enrico entered the room behind me and repeated my reaction when he saw it.

"Oh my God!" I shook my head, trying to remove the image from my mind. Of all the museums I had been to over the years, I'd never seen anything like that.

Enrico threw a hand over his eyes. "How could anyone look at that?!"

Beside us, Fabio walked casually by. He snickered and approached the display. After a few moments, I heard him call to me.

"You *wanted* to see this!"

From the corner of my eye, I saw him pointing to the ripped flesh.

"I thought misery was visually appealing!" he said.

I kept my attention on another corner of the room. A female dummy had been tied to a wooden stake. The large bundle of sticks at her feet was no doubt waiting to be set to flames. With her skin still intact, she was infinitely easier to look at.

"Well, not so much when it's *real!*" I said. "Believe me—this stuff is making me appreciate the here and now like you wouldn't believe."

I threw a quick glance at my host. I couldn't help but wonder if Dante would have had the same reaction to looking at something so hideous. Evidently we could both envision these types of horrors without the slightest qualm. But staring them right in the face, portrayed in lifelike detail with so much authentic misery and pain? Fabio continued to casually regard the display. For all I knew, Dante would have been able to do it just as easily.

My host eventually stood beside me and folded his arms. "It takes looking at stuff like *this* to feel that way, then, does it?"

I gave him a small smile with a cock of my head. "Well, no," I admitted. "But it's a good reminder."

Chapter 4

Demons of Japan: Oni and Namahage

"Oni wa soto! Uku wa uchi!'"

Taka in Kyoto

On January 31, I waited for my new host at the Kyoto train station. It was my first time being anywhere in Asia, and, for the first time on my travels, I had been a little nervous about going there on my own. I wasn't sure how I would feel being in a place so culturally different from the United States and Europe. But when my new host, Taka, e-mailed me to say that he was looking forward to my arrival, all that changed. I immediately felt as if I was going to meet a new friend. I waited for him in my red, winter jacket beneath the golden arches of the station McDonald's. I began to wonder if some aspects of Japan wouldn't be as alien as I'd envisioned. It didn't matter how many hundreds of Japanese people surrounded me: Big Macs and fries smelled the same everywhere.

It was a demon that had drawn me to the Asian Pacific. In just a few days, the country would be celebrating its spring festival known as Setsubun. Dating back centuries, the traditions involve throwing beans to chase away a Japanese demon known as the Oni. I had read about the custom back in Italy, and it was all I needed to know before booking my flight almost halfway across the world.

After a short while, I saw a man waving at me from across the crowd. He looked to be in his mid-thirties, dressed in a yellow ski jacket and wearing thin-framed glasses.

"Hello, Chris!" he called.

"Taka!" I smiled, recognizing him from his Couchsurfing profile, and gave him a hug. "Thanks so much for meeting me!"

"No problem," he said with barely a Japanese accent. He offered to take my duffel bag, then casually tossed it over his shoulder. "Welcome to Japan!"

A few blocks from the station, I followed Taka's lead and removed my shoes before entering his apartment. I noticed that the custom was unlike in Austria, where Bertram and others had removed their shoes in the foyer. Glancing around, I felt secretly foolish for expecting some kind of ancient, Eastern look to the place; the small kitchen and living room appeared similar to where I'd lived back in Connecticut. The only difference was that the living room also served as Taka's bedroom, which meant that Couchsurfers slept on the floor.

"Do you know about the toilets in Japan?" Taka asked while giving me the tour.

"No..." I felt a flood of panic run through me. *Oh God*, I thought, *please let there* be *a toilet....*

He smiled, pushing open the bathroom door. "They sing," he said. Inside, a pristine, white toilet bore a long side handle with multiple buttons. It reminded me of a help controller for a hospital bed.

"This one plays music," he said, pushing one of the keys. A high tune began to play, sounding like something from a baby mobile. "And this one makes a flush sound—'cause you know... some people want to drown out noise."

"Oh...," I said, a bit confused. I refrained from asking my immediate thought: *doesn't* everyone *make noise on the toilet?*

"This makes it spring water, and this one heats the seat."

"Wow! Toilets back in the States seem pretty behind the times now." I regarded the porcelain seat as though it were a new toy; it was the first time that I could remember looking forward to needing the bathroom.

"I know. After being in Japan a while, you'll really miss these when you're back home. I spent a year in California during college, and I never got used to it."

Since Taka knew that I had come to Kyoto for the Oni devil, he told me the story over dinner. At a nearby ramen restaurant, we sat at a long counter opposite a line of chefs cooking over a steaming stove. Before long, an incredible smell emanated from massive bowls filled with noodles and pork, onion and dried seaweed.

"Setsubun is the first day of spring in the Chinese calendar," Taka said while we ate. "It means 'division of the seasons.' The Japanese believe that bad spirits can enter the world of the living at that time, so they perform rituals to cast them away."

My mouth full of ramen, I felt my eyebrows shoot up. That description sounded very familiar.

"The original story of the Oni goes back to the eighth century," Taka said. "A demon disguised itself as a beautiful woman and visited a young girl. It used a magic mallet to make kimonos for tempting her. But the girl became greedy and wanted to take the mallet for herself. She got the Oni drunk with sake and stole it after the demon had fallen asleep. When the Oni woke up, it discovered what the girl had done and tried to attack her. She grabbed the only thing she could find, which was a handful of soybeans. She threw them at the Oni, and it was enough to make it flee."

"That's really cool," I said, smiling at the story. "And did you know that Setsubun and Halloween have something in common, then? Halloween stems from an ancient belief that spirits can enter the world in late October. And when I was in Austria, my host told me that *their* cultural demon, Krampus, was once believed to keep away evil spirits in the winter."

Taka nodded, looking not at all surprised.

"And before that, I went to Mexico for Day of the Dead. That's based on the belief that spirits return in early November."

"Yeah," Taka said, "it's a common belief across cultures. But the Oni represent evils like natural disasters and illness and misfortune. Banishing them with bean throwing, which we call *mamemaki,* is said to prevent evil from entering the new year. There are huge festivals in town, but people also celebrate in their home. When I was a kid, my father would wear an Oni mask and my younger brother and I would throw beans at him. We yelled, *'Oni wa soto! Uku wa uchi!'* That means, 'Demons out! Fortune in!' You'll hear that a lot in the next few days."

I nodded, trying to memorize the words. They sounded so foreign that I forgot them almost instantly.

"Then my brother and I would eat the beans; it's considered good luck to eat one for every year of your age."

I tried to envision how that might go: casting off demons by simply throwing beans at them. Back in Austria, that probably would have enraged a Krampus. But from Taka's description, it sounded as though the Oni wouldn't pose much of a threat. It was now more than a month since I had to worry about jumping away from a creature that reveled in inflicting pain, but I was more than happy to put those days behind me. Glancing around the restaurant, I noticed that the few dozen others engrossed in conversation barely spoke above a whisper. I had the feeling that, compared to Krampus, even the devils in Japan would seem tame.

Setsubun with Taka

On February 2, Setsubun began. Taka had the holiday off work—a medical lab where he specialized in cancer research—which meant that the two of us could seek out the Oni demon together. We rode bicycles along Maruta-machi Dori Street and passed shops and restaurants ranging from traditional Japanese to much more modern. Embroidered fabric and hand-carved signs adorned wooden buildings beside plain blocks of concrete. I looked at the Japanese characters around me in wonder, completely oblivious as to what any of the words meant. Back in Europe, I had read that Kyoto was a big tourist destination. I had foolishly assumed that that meant multiple languages would be seen throughout the city—one of which being, I hoped, English. But between keeping an eye on Taka in front of me and the nonstop traffic to my left, the only Roman letters I saw anywhere were on street signs high above the roads. Hundreds of pedestrians filled almost every inch of the sidewalk to my right, and only a handful, I noticed, weren't Asian. Of those who were, many wore white surgical masks as if a plague were sweeping through. I enjoyed being in this new part of the world—it seemed exciting and exotic—but it also felt strange to look so different from everyone else. It was the first, and only, time since Mexico that I was the minority.

While taking in the surroundings, I suddenly gasped at something hanging in a shop window. I recognized wide, fat faces, one red and the other black, with broad noses, long ears, and short, sharp teeth. Small holes had been cut inside angry eyes and large, menacing snarls. The plastic Oni masks hung by thin strings. They looked like some kind of anime version of Krampus. I immediately smiled; their design reminded me of the types of Halloween masks that were popular when I was a kid. Instead of superheroes and Smurfs for parties and trick or treating, here was Oni for dressing up at a time when unruly spirits were on the prowl. I glanced at Taka on his bike in front of me. I imagined him throwing soybeans at his father, who wore a mask like that, then eating a few of them off the floor rather than enjoying fun-sized candy bars from a plastic pumpkin pail.

After crossing a few streets, the two of us locked up our bikes beside about fifty others.

"This is the Yoshida-jinja shrine," Taka said. "It has the largest Setsubun festival in Kyoto."

A long, lantern-lined staircase brought us to the smell of cooked fish permeating the air. Steam rose above dozens of wooden vendor huts selling seafood, rice, and vegetables. Hundreds stood in line before piles of tuna steaks and massive fish heads. At Taka's insistence, I tried an octopus ball. He laughed as I grimaced in disgust, then remedied the situation with fish-shaped pastries made out of sweet potato and sugared red beans. Fortunately, the fried desserts removed the taste of the rubbery mush from my mouth completely. At another food stand—the one with the longest line—we bought a nori maki roll: a foot-long sushi roll made specifically for the holiday. Taka brought up a compass app on his iPhone to ensure that we faced northeast, as custom dictated that the maki be eaten facing a certain direction each year. The seaweed-wrapped tuna and rice tasted even better than it looked and ignited an addiction to maki that lasted me the next three weeks.

While savoring it, Taka suddenly pointed into the crowd.

"Look," he said, "there they are!"

I followed his nod. In the midst of the masses, two ogres came into view. Muscular and fat like sumo wrestlers, one was green from head to toe while the other was jet black. They walked slowly through the crowd, wearing only short, tiger-striped pants and casting looks of anger with large teeth curved into terrifying grins. I stared at them, completely transfixed: my first Asian demons. I felt as if I had just crossed a haunting cultural milestone. Even from a distance of several yards, I could see everyone they passed smiling in equal excitement. The demons' costumes were unlike anything I'd ever seen. The masks and bodysuits looked like thick fabric stretched over plastic. I watched a few people carry their timid children slowly towards them, bobbing them on their shoulders while the kids cowered. I feared that the kids would scream out in terror. Fortunately, they only stared, appearing to be just as awestruck as I was.

The Oni waved at them, then continued moving through the crowd until disappearing from sight.

"They look so cool," I said to Taka, turning to him at last. "And the kids didn't seem too afraid."

My host nodded, appearing to contemplate it. "Well, some may be.... Some *will* be."

At the Daikakuji temple, another demon awaited us. Gardens of barren cherry trees and massive pines surrounded Japanese houses with slanted roofs and screen walls. We followed the crowd beside the temple, then entered a seating area before a small, outdoor stage.

"They'll be reenacting the original story of the Oni here," Taka said.

I sat on a long, wooden bench beside him. "Really? Excellent!"

Taka watched me grasp my camera, then pointed to a small sign onstage. The universal prohibition sign encircled the image of a camera. NO PHOTO, it read.

I smiled despite my disappointment—finally, some English.

The show began with the infamous Japanese devil. He was fiercely red from head to toe, and the creature's large, bulbous eyes displayed a frozen countenance of evil. Small, sharp horns stuck out above fire-blazoned hair. Its sharp teeth composed a snarl of fury. In total silence, it draped a golden kimono over its body, concealing its horrid form with the glistening silk. White cloth was wrapped around its head until the demonic face disappeared, leaving only a sliver of its stare. With the transfiguration complete, the devil appeared human at last. It picked up a large, wooden mallet and slowly crept towards a young woman dressed in a blue kimono and kneeling peacefully onstage.

The young woman faced the audience. With a frozen smile painted on her Okame mask, she resembled a living porcelain doll. She gave a start at the sight of her strange visitor, who greeted her through pantomime. With a wave of its magic mallet, the disguised demon presented a shiny, green kimono to the girl. She immediately rose, accepted her gift with a bow, then danced and twirled. The devil watched. It summoned another garment and presented it to the same reaction. But upon receiving a third, red robe, the girl turned her attention to the magic mallet.

Not a movement came from the crowd as the young woman humbly offered a large cup of sake to her guest. I smiled as she bowed in respect, tricking the disguised trickster with drink. Additional cups followed, one after another, while the girl's eyes continued to wander towards the mallet. The concealed Oni grew overcome with fatigue and slowly sank to the floor. The girl lost no time taking the object from its loosened grasp.

I held my breath while she admired it. Everyone around me, I presumed, knew what was about to happen. Unable to blink, I saw the disguised Oni begin to awaken. It peered around the room, slowly regaining consciousness. After a moment, its gaze landed upon the girl. The creature rose slowly, angrily, realizing what had happened. With a forceful motion, it tore at the wrappings around its head. My hand instinctively flew over my mouth as the girl turned to see inhuman eyes, horns, wild hair, and razor-sharp teeth. She backed away in terror, not only caught in her deceit but seeing the hideous thing that she had been dealing with this whole time. The mallet fell to the floor along with the creature's golden kimono, as its true, detestable form was revealed.

The Oni snatched up its mallet in anger. The girl stumbled back, fretfully looking around as if searching for something to protect her. As the creature advanced, poised to attack, she desperately reached for a bowl on a dresser. She scooped up something from it, then threw it at her pursuer. A soft scattering echoed across the stage. It sounded like tiny pebbles skipping along wood. The creature recoiled, shielding its face in defense. Watching it retreat, the girl threw another handful of the unseen, tiny objects from a safe distance. The demon cringed, then turned and fled.

Only when the actors took their bows did I finally breathe.

"That was incredible!" I said to Taka, clapping with the crowd. "Did you like it?"

"Yeah," he said, smiling and applauding. "It was great. I've never seen that show before."

I stared at him in astonishment as we stood to leave. "Really? After all the years of celebrating Setsubun?"

He gave a small shrug. "Well, I've always known the story. I guess I just never went out of my way to see a play about it."

"Oh..." I could barely believe his words. Not going out of your way to see a play about a demon? *My* calendar would have been marked for months! I remembered Ruben in Oaxaca saying something similar; he had never been in a cemetery for Day of the Dead before meeting someone to share it with.

"That's one of the best things about Couchsurfing," Taka admitted. "It gets me out doing new things."

"Well, then," I said with a smile, "I'm glad I got you out here."

"Yeah..." Taka chuckled as we joined the crowd heading back towards the temple. Both of us knew full well that *he* had been the one who had gotten *me* there.

The Demon Dance

With Taka at work for the second day of Setsubun, I headed out solo. My host had given me a map with circled locations of additional Oni shows. Looking at the images of countless temples, shrines, palaces, and gardens, I only wished I had more than a few days in Kyoto.

Rozan-ji Temple stood smaller than the others I'd seen. Japanese lanterns surrounded the traditional arched roof and paper walls. I stood shoulder to shoulder with the crowd, barely making out the sound of monks chanting and holding ceremony inside. I also noticed that, once again, I was the only one there who wasn't Japanese. Despite my excitement about being there, I couldn't help but feel slightly sad. I had the distinct feeling that if I wanted to say even the simplest thing to someone, they wouldn't understand a word of it. *But I've been in this situation before,* I reminded myself. *I'd rarely spoken to anyone in the midst of being clobbered by Krampus.*

Suddenly, a deep drumming began. Slow and rhythmic, it echoed over the grounds, and anticipation seemed to grow throughout the crowd. A shrill wailing followed. I flinched at the sound. I could barely believe that such an ear-piercing noise came from a musical instrument. But the combination of the drumming and wailing created the perfect effect: it was as if a gateway to hell had just opened, and unseen evil was about to emerge into Japan.

As if to confirm my theory, an imposing demon stepped onto the temple's porch. Its short, burly frame was green from head to toe. Short horns stuck out through a mop of dark hair, and a bulging belly extended above tiger-striped shorts. One massive hand clasped a blazing torch, casting bright flames to accompany the thing's approach. A few paces behind, a similar creature followed, as red as fire itself and holding a large sword; then a third, completely black, wielding the legendary magic mallet.

I watched, amazed, as the three marched around the perimeter of the temple. They moved with slow, powerful strides, striking their weapons to the beat of the infernal drum. The dance continued for several minutes. The three stealthily approached the temple, the accursed boom and wail accompanying them, until through the thick of the crowd I saw them crouch their way inside.

I waited, straining to listen. I stood on the tips of my toes, trying to see. The deafening music continued. No one around me uttered a word, looking towards the temple in equal anticipation. I couldn't help but smile at their expressions. So many had come out to see the Demon Dance—the banishment of evil—connected through tradition that's been performed for centuries. I saw the same fascination in their eyes that I, myself, felt. Although they could have seen the show dozens of times over the years, they obviously found it no less intriguing. I scanned the excited assembly with new eyes and felt the loneliness I'd based on our language barrier disappear. I turned back to the temple with a peaceful grin and a sense of being no different from anyone around me.

A monk emerged from the temple. He shot three arrows into the air. "Oni wa soto!" came over a loudspeaker. Several minutes of strained silence followed until the demons finally reemerged. Each moved backwards, flailing its arms in slow, wide circles. The fire, sword, and mallet were still tight in their grips, but they now retreated to the continuous beat of the

drum. As steadily as they had arrived, the three retraced their steps until banished from the grounds.

After emerging from the temple, the monks threw bags of beans into the crowd. *"Oni wa soto!"* they called. *"Uku wa uchi!"*

The masses moved forward in unison, their shyness disappearing at the prospect of getting their hands on magical treats.

With the show over, the three Oni returned. They stepped off the temple porch and walked throughout the crowd. As Taka had foretold, several children cried and screamed at the sight of them. I felt a rush of pity run through me as a man brought his young son right up to the green beast. The boy screamed at the cruel, evil face that glared at him. I thought back to Bertram in Salzburg. I remembered him insisting that any kid would be scared of something so hideous. Although the Oni weren't invading anyone's home like Krampus did in the villages, they still produced quite a shock. After all, there had been near-deafening drumming and wailing to set the scene for this terrifying story. It was, without a doubt, one of the things that had made it so great.

That night, Taka informed me that it was considered lucky to be touched by an Oni.

Poor kid, I thought, frowning at the memory. *Just give him a soybean.*

Hikaru and the Snowy Mountain

I finally found snow in northern Japan.

Pulling back the thick curtain that had kept the bus in complete darkness for the last eight hours, I smiled at the change in landscape. Outside, at least three feet of snow covered the ground in the suburbs surrounding Akita Station. I scanned the gray clouds with seemingly no end, wondering if it had been snowing for weeks. While collecting my bag, I estimated the temperature to be about ten degrees Fahrenheit, but I still reveled in my shivering as I shuffled into the station. It was the first snow I'd seen anywhere all winter. The cold was much more frigid and raw than I was used to, but that was just fine. I knew that nothing would deter me from seeking out the monsters that had brought me to Akita Prefecture: the Namahage.

I had done some research on them a month earlier. Legend holds that these demons once terrorized the people of Oga, a small town in northern Japan. Large and ogre-like, the Namahage came down from the Snowy Mountain to steal away the women. The villagers finally decided to make a deal with the Namahage: if the creatures could build a staircase of 1,000 steps leading up to their mountain peak in one night, they could take their women. But if they failed, they would have to leave Oga for good. The Namahage accepted the offer. As highly skilled workers, they knew that they would succeed without problem. They worked throughout the night to the point of almost completing the task. But as they laid down the 999th step, they heard the sound of a rooster beginning to crow. It was only a trick; a hidden villager mocked the noise from the trees. But the plan worked. The Namahage believed that the sun had come up, and they fled. Today, the creatures are said to return every year to torment not the women of Oga, but the children.

Inside Akita Station, I saw that the Namahage had already taken over. Festival posters covered the walls showing massive, straw ogres. Large, menacing eyes glared out from red, black, or green masks. They had huge, blunt teeth and short horns protruding from long, straw-like hair. Unlike the Oni from Kyoto, the Namahage were muscular but thin. Some carried small, wooden buckets and wielded large chopping knives. Others danced with blazing torches around bonfires in the snow. Walking around the station that doubled as a massive mall, I found souvenirs of the creatures in every gift shop. Photographs showed them snarling on keychains, T-shirts, and boxer shorts, while cute, cartoon portrayals scowled on boxes of candy and cookies. I admired each one, picking them up to touch the image of this new, Eastern monster.

I loved Akita already.

My host, Hikaru, met me at the station a few hours later. While drinking a canned Boss coffee in the waiting area, the snow long since melted off my sneakers, I watched a man in his early twenties approach me in a gray business suit. I had told him to spot me by my bright red jacket. It stood out pretty well amongst the darker colors that, I had glumly noticed, most people wore. The winter coat had been a gift from my stepfather, but I often wondered if he would have chosen a different color had he known I'd be using it to explore monsters after dark.

"Chris?" the young man asked.

"Yes," I said, standing up. "Hello!"

Hikaru nervously extended a hand. I responded by opening my arms for a hug. I knew full well that it wasn't the custom in Japan, but it certainly was amongst Couchsurfers. After we hugged, Hikaru smiled and exhaled.

"How do you pronounce your name?" I asked.

"Hik-*ar*-u," he said slowly.

"Hikaru. Nice to meet you!"

My new host's neighborhood was even grayer than the sky. Gas stations and banks—including the one where Hikaru worked—surrounded plain, cement buildings. In an apartment similar to Taka's, Hikaru gave me the tour of an equally modern kitchen, living room that doubled as a bedroom, and bathroom. The toilet, I saw, was just as toy-like as every other I'd used in the country.

"If you'd prefer a mattress," Hikaru said, "you can take my bed and I'll sleep on the floor."

"That's okay," I said, plopping down my bag. "I'll take the floor. I like to get the full Japanese experience."

"Ahhh. Then we'll have to make rice with my rice maker." He picked up a small, white appliance on the kitchen counter. It immediately reminded me of a Star Wars Storm Trooper helmet. "It sings," he said, smiling proudly.

"The *rice makers* sing, too?" Japan was starting to seem like one big Disneyland. "Does your toilet sing?"

He looked at me in obvious confusion. "Of course it does."

Over dinner on the living-room/bedroom floor—eggs mixed into rice, my own hard-boiled and Hikaru's raw—I learned that my host's fluent English came from spending a college semester in Oregon. Like Taka, his accent was barely detectable. Hosting Couchsurfers allowed him to practice his English in addition to meeting people from around the world.

"But you're the first person who's come to Akita for the Namahage," Hikaru said, sitting cross-legged across from me. "Everyone else was just traveling through Japan."

"Really?" I shook my head at the thought. Despite how many times I'd heard something similar, it never ceased to amaze me. So many people traveled the world without taking the time to look at its monsters. Jim Morrison was right—people *are* strange. "The festival looks like it'll be a lot of fun," I said.

"Yes, but even though the festival's in February, traditionally the Namahage go door to door on December thirty-first. There's a whole ritual to it: they stomp their feet and swing their arms five times on the doorstep to announce their presence. Then the head of the household lets them in, and they shout, 'Are there any crybabies here?'"

I smiled as Hikaru growled to impersonate the creatures. I could tell that he had some personal experience with the ritual.

"When they're inside," he said, "they look for the children—who are usually hiding behind their parents by this time—and pretend to carry them outside. The kids always cry and try to get away."

I envisioned the scene, appalled. I hadn't read about *that* on the festival website. "Oh my God. That's so mean!"

Hikaru shrugged. "Nahhh. It's not like they hurt the kids. The adults ask the Namahage to let them go and say things like, 'Please don't take him. He's been doing his chores; he's been working hard.' The Namahage are there to make sure the kids behave. It was the parents who asked the actors to come to the house in the first place. They don't think of it as mean. It's just tradition."

I continued frowning in shock. "Oh... okay." I envisioned children being dragged through their homes by the ferocious beasts I'd seen in the station. New Year's Eve from my own childhood suddenly seemed so peaceful in comparison. I thought back to watching fireworks on TV with my brother without having to worry about monsters busting in to kidnap us. Sure, something like that would be fun *now*, but not when we were small.

"Then the parents sit down with the Namahage and offer them food and sake. They insist that their kids have been good. In the end, the Namahage leave but warn the kids to stay on good behavior and take their work seriously." Hikaru went on to describe a memory of when he was five. His grandfather had let two of the creatures into their house, then told them that Hikaru was hiding in the closet. After they grabbed him, his grandfather "defended" him until he was released.

"The Namahage aren't considered dangerous or evil, though," Hikaru said. "They're deities and believed to bring a rich harvest for the coming year. *Namahage* means 'peeling off the blisters.' It refers to removing laziness from spending too much time around the fire instead of working hard. Even the costumes are believed to possess luck, and it's good luck to pick up any straw that falls off one."

"Well that's good," I said, determined to find *something* positive about the whole thing. I thought back to the Oni in Kyoto. They were also demons believed to bring good luck. That hadn't seemed to make much difference to the kids who were brought up to them, looking into those large, terrifying eyes only to scream in horror.

I made a mental note to call my father and tell him I loved him.

The Namahage Festival

In the mountains of Oga, dozens of Namahage appeared. Red devils snarled from road signs as Hikaru drove us to the festival. Endless clouds stretched out over the hills, painting a landscape of gray over white. More demons peered out from convenience-store and gas-station windows, depicted as cute, lovable cartoons that, I now knew, could be ferocious to both women and kids. In what appeared to be the middle of nowhere, two enormous statues towered above a snow-covered field. A blue-faced demon posed as if to strike with a massive chopping knife, his red accomplice holding a flag of tattered, white cloth beside him. Both revealed blue sleeves and muscular, very human hands sticking out beyond their straw costumes. At the base of the beasts, tourists poured out of buses to wait in line for taking pictures beside them. Hikaru and I joined them, my thermal underwear from Austria put to good use once again.

We arrived at the Namahage museum two hours before the festival was scheduled to begin. A short documentary showed the types of home visits that Hikaru had described, in all their glory. In horror I watched children aged three to ten scream and cry while being ripped from their parents' arms by straw-covered ogres. I scanned the dozens of people seated all around me, trying to gage if I was the only one regarding the spectacle as atrocious. Unfortunately, the darkness of the theater concealed every expression.

"My God," I whispered to Hikaru. "Those poor kids…"

He waved off my concern. "Nahhh, they're fine."

"This whole thing seems like a lifetime of therapy just waiting to happen."

He gave me a sarcastic smile, barely visible in the glow of the screen. "*Thanks.* You know *I'm* not in therapy!"

I chuckled through my frown. But after I compared what I was seeing to Krampus *laufs,* it was Hikaru's turn to look appalled.

"They would never do that," he said seriously. "Namahage never hit anyone."

A live show at the museum proved his point. Horned demons tramped through the audience: mops of dark hair falling over yellow eyes; large, flat noses above huge fangs. From where I sat on the floor, I could have sworn that the creatures stood about ten feet tall. In reality, I knew that they were barely more than my height of five foot four. They growled at the seated spectators, pointing and speaking harshly to the children. One young boy whimpered as the brute seemed to bark questions at him. His mother only held him and smiled. Others took pictures. I frowned in pity. Onstage, an old man offered tea and food to the deities, bowing in respect while the creatures pointed to the crowd in disapproval.

"The old man is trying to defend us," Hikaru whispered to me. "But the Namahage are saying that we should all be taken away because we haven't been working hard. They say they can see the laziness in our eyes."

He giggled at the idea of it.

I immediately thought back to Clemens in Salzburg. *It seems to be a monster's ability to read the eyes,* I thought.

The show ended with the Namahage warning us all to stay on our best behavior. While the crowd quietly exited, I stood up with Hikaru to stretch. Just like in Kyoto, I couldn't help but notice that I was the only person there who wasn't Japanese. I was used to it by now.

I wondered if this crowd felt a sense of nostalgia about the Namahage. If they had grown up with the creatures coming to their homes every year, I could only presume that seeing a reenactment of it would be meaningful as well as entertaining. My own draw to monsters certainly stemmed from childhood—fortunately without any tears or trauma mixed in.

"That was really cool," I said to Hikaru as we stepped out. "Thanks for translating. I'm glad that none of the kids got too scared."

"That *was* good." Hikaru smiled as we found our shoes on the porch. "I've never seen a show like that. The last time I saw the Namahage come into anyone's house, it was *my* house!"

I craned my head up at him, tying my shoes in a squat while he slipped his on standing. "You haven't gone to the festival before?"

He shook his head.

I smiled. "That's funny."

In a display room, the two of us had the opportunity to transform into the deities ourselves. I felt rough wicker wrap around my arms, chest, and legs as a staff member helped me try on the authentic costume. It felt coarse but light. Looking down at myself encased in straw, I could scarcely imagine trudging through the snow to inflict fear into kids like a young Hikaru. I slipped on a blue, wooden mask, heavy and padded like a hockey mask, with angry eyes and wild, straw hair. Through the small eyeholes, I looked at Hikaru by my side. He had transformed into a red-faced demon.

"I can't believe no one else is in line to do this," I said, gesturing to the empty room with a bristling swish. "Who *wouldn't* want to dress like a monster?"

Hikaru shrugged. "I don't know. Not everybody's into it, I guess."

We posed for a picture. I held a staff with a tattered, white cloth while Hikaru gripped a much more menacing wooden chopping knife. In an instant, I felt a change come over me. I could almost feel the spirit of the powerful, Japanese deity arise. With the mask concealing my face and the straw replacing my ordinary, human appearance, I felt as if I was that imposing creature that could make even the strongest men cower. I experienced the urge to trudge through the mountains outside, leaving deep tracks in the snow as one who dwelled in those rugged lands. I remembered Clemens in Salzburg describing the adrenaline he felt when portraying Krampus. I experienced the same energy now while holding my flag with pride. But despite the change, I felt no desire to terrorize any kids. If anything, I would be more like one of the characters from the Day of the Dead *comparsa*. I would much rather party and dance as

a monstrous creature than intimidate or scare anyone. The only person who would provoke *my* wrath would be anyone who dared take my staff.

As nightfall approached, we followed hundreds into the woods. Snow glistened from glowing lanterns along the trail. The wet, white flakes still fell. I realized that it hadn't stopped snowing since I'd stepped off the bus two days earlier. Before a large courtyard, a row of huts sold cooked vegetables and tea, Namahage masks and toys. People lined up to pray at a small temple and ceremoniously swing a long Suzu rope, bowing and clasping their hands as a bell rang above. *More people are waiting to pray than dress up like monsters,* I thought, watching them. *I really* am *far from home.*

Despite my multiple layers, including two pairs of socks and gloves, I felt my feet and fingers begin to grow numb. While Hikaru seemed completely fine in his black ski jacket and hat, I immediately gravitated towards a blazing bonfire. The temperature had definitely dropped into the single digits. Unfortunately, Hikaru pointed in another direction the minute I reached the flames.

"We need to go there," he said.

I begrudgingly turned around. Across the snow, I saw the crowd assembling at the base of a wooden staircase leading up into the trees. "That's the 999 steps," Hikaru said.

My frozen eyes grew wide. "Okay!" I said excitedly. "Let's go get a good spot."

We found a sliver of space within the masses, then turned towards a male voice coming over a loudspeaker. The Japanese echoing through the darkness sounded as though a story were being told.

"They're telling the legend of the Namahage," Hikaru said, "and the trick the villagers pulled when they built the steps."

I nodded at him, shivering but grateful for his translation.

When the story finished, a Shinto priest approached the base of the steps. Dressed in a red, silk robe and black eboshi hat, he prayed beside a small fire, calling the Namahage to grace us with their presence. Instead, about two dozen men descended the stairs. Each wore a straw costume, but only the leader held a devilish-looking mask before him. A deep drumming began to sound, and the man slowly slipped on the image of a fierce, blue creature. I watched, completely absorbed in the transformation, when an audible rush of awe swept through the crowd. A few pointed to the remaining men on the stairs. I peered through the darkness and rising smoke of the fire and saw that every person on the steps had suddenly become the Namahage. A mixture of red and blue figures emitted deep growls, flailing their arms as Japanese deities in the flesh. I marveled at the spectacle; the horde of mythical spirits had seemingly materialized out of thin air.

With the Namahage's official arrival, the festival began. A series of shows demonstrated their legend as masked performers danced to flutes and drums by the bonfire. A home visit was enacted onstage. A rock band then played drums with the Namahage in a lively concert. I loved the combination of modern celebration with centuries-old traditions. But despite how much I wanted to dance to the beat, I resolved to simply watch. Not one person in the crowd moved a muscle; the "life is short— let's party!" mentality of Oaxaca was evidently not the norm here. But that was okay. I saw the straw-clad creatures onstage express what I'd felt when I had donned that costume and posed for the picture. It seemed that the ancient brutes weren't only about inflicting terror after all.

After two hours, Hikaru translated another announcement from the loudspeaker. "They're saying that the Namahage will walk among the crowd. We can take pictures with them if we want."

I smiled in the dark cold, my lips numb and chapped. "Great! But where did they all go?"

Looking around, we suddenly saw that not one of them was anywhere in sight. Only hundreds of partially visible faces could be seen between winter hats and coats. Then high in the hills above, a small flicker appeared in the darkness.

"Look up there!" I said, pointing to it in excitement. More heads turned towards the flare. Additional flames shot up beside it as slow, powerful drumming filled the courtyard. Within moments, a row of fire bobbed above the snow-filled land.

"They're descending from the Snowy Mountain!" Hikaru said.

I watched, awestruck, forgetting about my numb extremities. The fire trailed downwards to the courtyard, small beacons of light in the dark woods. Hundreds stared at the approach, bundled and frozen with excitement and cold. The Namahage emerged from the trees, growling and trudging through the snow. Adults happily gawked at them. Children reached out from the shoulders of their fathers. I saw them laugh and shiver, looking excited but nervous. The creatures patted each kid on the head, showing ironic affection through their frightening facade. The Namahage weren't here to terrorize or scare them. Whatever they did in late December was over—at least for a while. Here, on the Snowy Mountain, the deities had come to bring good fortune in the dead of winter.

When I finally approached one and asked permission to take a photo, the red-faced demon growled his reply. I stood beside him in the cold, continuing to feel relieved that, unlike in Salzburg, I didn't have to worry about being pummeled.

By the time we made our way back to the car, Hikaru and I were both soaked from the snow. My hands had finally gone as numb as my feet. But it had all been worth it. I still felt grateful to have grown up without brutal ogres barging into my house every year. But I could see that Hikaru was right. The custom hadn't traumatized him. Of the two of us, *he* wasn't the one who had given up everything to go looking for dark creatures around the globe. Perhaps all those Namahage visits had given him enough monster exposure for a lifetime, whereas my own desire seemed insatiable. But it didn't mean that I would have chosen it any other way.

"Hey, look!" Hikaru said, bending down in the parking lot. When he stood back up, I saw a single piece of straw in the grip of his thick glove.

"That means good luck this year," I mumbled, forcing my frozen lips to move.

He handed it to me with a smile. "For your travels," he said. "You might need it, with the stuff you're looking at."

I reached out for it. "Awww... thank you!" I pressed it between both hands, feeling not a thing, then hugged him with the remaining circulation in my arms.

Chapter 5

The Busójárás Carnival in Hungary

"Through making their masks, performers experience their own personal spirit of the Busó come through."

The Mohács Family

On February 27, my train headed to the small town of Mohács at 10:30 P.M. Back in Japan, I had learned about a strange character that would soon be coming to the central Hungarian town. This story in a book about winter festivals around the world had intrigued me. In the sixteenth century, back when Hungary was under Turkish occupation, the Croatian people living in Mohács had defeated their oppressors through some creative measures. The idea had come to them in a dream. In the dead of night, the Croatians were to disguise themselves with fur and masks made with animal horns and painted with blood. Depicting horrid-looking beasts, they then ambushed the Turks and frightened their army away in the 1526 Battle of Mohács. The costumed creatures that saved the lands became known as the Busós. Today, however, the tale is believed to be merely myth; the Croatians didn't even arrive in Mohács until ten years *after* the Turks had fled. But the legend survives, and every year the Busós return for a winter carnival called Busójárás, meaning "Busó walking." Unlike the Namahage and other characters I'd seen over the months, the Busós weren't portrayed as menacing or evil but as friendly, jovial characters who had freed the Croatian people from foreign rule.

My Couchsurfing host, Alexandra, was coming home from college the day after my arrival. In her absence, she had asked a friend to meet me at the station and bring me to her mother's apartment, where I would be staying with the two of them. But when I stepped off the train, I found not a soul in sight—only a desolate, station-less set of tracks stretching out into the darkness.

Hmmmm, I thought, looking around as the train sped off. *I knew that Mohács was small, but I didn't think it'd be* this *small.*

Fortunately, the weather was tolerable. Wearing my winter jacket over multiple layers, I could feel that the temperature was around thirty degrees rather than the single digits of Akita. After about twenty minutes of sitting on my duffel bag beside the tracks, I spied two elderly gypsies strolling down a nearby sidewalk. They looked at me with confused interest as I approached. I showed them a paper with my host's address, then asked through gesture if they could point me in the right direction so that I could walk there. Judging by their looks of recognition, I could see that they knew the area. Through a mix of Hungarian that I understood not at all and pantomime that I understood perfectly well, they communicated that they would walk with me. We traveled through the dark suburbs until the couple finally pointed to a street sign matching the name on my paper. I sighed in deep relief. Before I could approach the old, brick apartment building in front of me, a man rode up on a bicycle. He was in his early twenties, blond, and quite out of breath.

"Chris," he said, "I'm Peter. I was worried about you—you were supposed to get off at the station!"

I cried out in joy. His English was perfect, with a thick, Hungarian accent.

"Oh!" I said. "Sorry, the stops weren't marked and I was the only one on the train. All I had to go by was the arrival time on my ticket...."

He exhaled, then gave a small smile. "No problem."

I thanked my new friends for their help, then followed Peter into an elevator outside the apartment. Its rickety, wire gate echoed loudly in the quiet night, and through the steel cage I saw my gypsy friends wandering back into the darkness.

"That's cool that you came all this way for the carnival," Peter said beside me. He was breathing easier. I could see that a weight had been lifted off his shoulders; finding me meant not having to tell his friend that her Couchsurfer was off lost somewhere. "I've never met anyone outside of Hungary who even knew about it."

"Oh yeah?" I asked as the elevator slowly rose. "I only learned about it a few weeks ago. In Japan, of all places."

His eyes grew wide in surprise.

"It looks like a lot of fun," I said, expecting that response.

"It is. That's why Alexandra's coming home for it. The whole town gets involved, and people come from all over Hungary."

The lift stopped on the third floor. On the other side of the bars, a woman in jeans and a black AC/DC T-shirt stood waiting for us. I found that her short, spiky black hair gave her a striking resemblance to Joan Jett.

"Chris, this is Alexandra's mom, Zsuzsanna," Peter said. "Zsuzsa for short. She doesn't speak English, just a few words."

"Nice to meet you!" I said, smiling with a bow. I surprised myself with the gesture; after three weeks in Japan, it had just come naturally. Zsuzsa smiled and gave me a warm hug.

"I like your shirt," I said after she let me go. I pointed to it and gave a thumbs up. "I love AC/DC."

Her eyes lit up. "I love!" she said, nodding in understanding. She held a hand over her chest, smiling. "'Back in Black,' 'Thunderstruck.' I love!"

Inside the apartment—larger than the ones in Asia—blue, green, and yellow pastels created a peaceful, cheery ambiance. The living room, bedrooms, and kitchen all connected to a long, narrow hallway. Seeing that Zsuzsa and Peter wore their sneakers only in the hall, I realized that the custom was to remove shoes before entering the individual rooms.

After giving me the tour, Peter put my things in Alexandra's room as Zsuzsa handed me something. I looked down at a green, porcelain sculpture slightly larger than my hand. The shining image had large, kind eyes and a wide nose. Short, rectangular teeth formed a jolly smile, and two curved horns protruded from its head. I instantly recognized the face of the Busó.

After Zsuzsa said something to Peter in Hungarian, he translated for me: "Zsuzsa works at an institution for mentally disabled people. The patients made these masks to sell at the carnival."

"Wow..." I looked at the piece of art with new eyes. "What a great idea!"

Zsuzsa gestured to me.

"*Neked,*" she said.

"She wants you to have it," Peter translated. "She bought it for you."

"Oh my gosh..." I held the mask to my chest. "Thank you so much—I love it!" I gave her a big hug, and she immediately smiled and laughed. In an instant I unzipped my bag and took out a gift that I'd bought for both her and Alexandra back in Japan: a box of green tea. Zsuzsa gasped, looking at the Japanese characters as if they were a magical inscription. Despite the late hour, she quickly ran off to boil water.

"I'll keep a lookout for you and Alexandra at the carnival," Peter said as we followed her down the hall. "I'll be walking around, but you won't see me." He smiled playfully. "I'll be one of the Busós."

"Really?" I asked, gasping in excitement. "That's so cool!"

He laughed heartily; I could tell he'd expected that response.

Busós Take to the Town

My official host and I met the next day. A few hours after e-mailing me her arrival time as well as her mode of transportation, Alexandra walked into the apartment toting a duffel bag slightly smaller than my own. I looked at the twenty-two-year-old's wide smile and strawberry-blonde hair and felt suddenly maternal at the thought of how she'd gotten home from Budapest.

"You hitchhiked here by yourself?" I almost barked at her after a hug. "That doesn't sound very safe...." I surprised myself with the words; it was definitely something that my mother would have said.

"It's okay," she replied with a wave. "I always do it. It's really common for people to hitchhike in Hungary."

Her adventurous spirit was reflected in her bedroom. Maps, postcards, and photos of her and friends on vacation composed large collages on the walls. Majoring in world cultures, Alexandra had been to almost a dozen countries. The United States wasn't among them, but it was at the top on her list for after graduation.

"You must have seen all kinds of different things on your travels," my host said after leaving her shoes in the hall and flopping onto her bed. Unlike Peter's, her accent was very minor and reflected regular use of English.

I followed her lead, lounging on the mound of blankets and pillows where I'd slept on the floor. "Yeah, that's for sure. But there are a lot of similarities, too. To me, they stand out more than the differences. People wanting to connect, wanting to share and help, regardless of where they're from or the language they speak."

I told her about the excitement I'd seen in people during shows in Mexico, Austria, and Japan, all marveling at the dark characters I'd gone there to see. I told her about Ruben and the Fabulous Four, Bertram, Fabio, Taka and Hikaru. They had all been eager to share their stories and interests, and they quickly turned a stranger into a new friend.

"I can't wait to do things like that," Alexandra said, looking wistfully into space. She turned to me with a smile. "Though I won't exactly be looking at monsters. How long have you been traveling for?"

I calculated it. "A little over five months."

"Wow, that's a long time to be away from home."

I nodded. "It sure is. I've never been outside the States for this long before. It's a lot of fun, but it'll be nice to be home again."

Before long, a strange sound caught our attention. I felt my muscles tense up as a low, dull clanging noise came from outside. It sounded just like a slow-moving Krampus. A twinge of pain shot through my calf, and I felt the sudden urge to be ready to run. From what I'd read, the Busós didn't attack people. But in my mind's eye I saw the monstrous eyes, threatening snarls, and whipping tails as if the *laufs* had been only yesterday.

"That's them," Alexandra said. She smiled at me without a hint of alarm. "Those are the Busós."

Stepping outside the front door, we saw a half-dozen large, sheep-like creatures strolling down the middle of the road. Elongated, wooden faces, some dark brown and others deep red, smiled wide, goofy grins. Some had a few teeth missing. Large, thick ram horns curved out from the sides of their heads, while others were pointed straight and sharp. White, wooly coats reached down to their thighs over white trousers that, I had read, were stuffed with straw. Knitted, wool socks came up to their knees above leather sandals. The dull clanking came from large cowbells hanging off their belts. Most carried a large, wooden rattler, occasionally whipping it around and producing a loud, cracking noise.

I looked at them in fascination. So these were the creatures that had liberated Mohács centuries ago—at least the stories say. These were the costumes made in the dead of night, turning the Croatians into massive beasts who had frightened off the Turks. It was hard to imagine; all in all, they looked more comical than frightening.

A few women walked beside the wooly creatures. Appearing much more human, each wore a black shawl, colorful skirt, and dark, Turkish mask with a white veil concealing almost her entire face.

"Who are the women with them?" I asked. I hadn't read anything about them in Japan.

"They're called Jankeles," Alexandra said. "They're the keepers of the Busós. Come on, we can follow them into town."

Just a short walk down the road, Mohács's architecture resembled a cross between East and West. Pastel-colored, cement buildings with cupola roofs rose above vendor huts lining the streets. Hundreds of people browsed through tiny, burly sheep men sold as dolls, figurines, and masks. Other images were displayed on T-shirts, coffee mugs, and painted plates. The smell of grilled meat and vegetables wafted through the air. At a food stand marked Kürtőskalács, Alexandra and I ogled a huge stretch of dough spinning around a cone-shaped baking spit. It smelled like fresh donuts cooking over charcoal. The aproned worker rolled the completed funnel cake, about the size of ten donuts on a stick, in butter and granulated sugar. After one bite, I felt a rush of sweetness course through my veins; it tasted as though an entire sugar bowl had been used for making one donut.

In Széchenyi Square, dancers clasped hands and skipped in circles to Šokci music. The guitar, cello, and tambura, an instrument resembling a long ukulele, produced a light, pleasant melody.

"I love being home," Alexandra said with a sigh while watching the show. "I'm so glad they do this every year."

All around us, dozens of Busós walked through the crowds. Some carried flags bearing the name of their group. Others held wooden pitchforks, long sticks, noisemakers, and maces. They waved to the spectators, kneeling down before children and patting their heads. One brown-faced, cheerful beast ruffled my hair before squeezing me in a big bear hug. His long, white mustache stood out against a dark-brown, frumpy mop of wool reaching down to his chest. The costume felt thick and soft against my face, and I laughed at the sight of a tooth missing from his crooked smile. Alexandra beamed giddily after her own embrace, as if she had just shared a tender moment with a living Teddy bear.

The town museum reflected the importance of the Busós in Mohács history. Statues of three soldiers looked proud and strong in their sheep coats and hoods. Each held a different symbol of the Busó: a rattler, pitchfork, and wooden mace. Inside, life-sized figures stood beside hay-filled shacks representing the town during the Battle of Mohács. In a local carver's workshop, Alexandra and I entered what looked like a cross between a monster factory and hunting lodge. Hundreds of sheep horns hung from the ceiling above chisels, mallets, and other carving tools. Masks along the wall reflected changes in styles over the years: round, rectangular, and oval faces frowning, glaring, or smiling, some horned and others hornless. I admired a few that looked almost demonic, painted blood red with thin, black eyebrows and beards.

The carver, Engert Anta, described his work to our group of roughly twenty people. Everyone listened in fascination, keeping their hands warm inside winter coats in his large shed.

"He says he's been a Busó carver for forty-five years," Alexandra whispered, translating the Hungarian. "He says traditionally, masks have always been carved from willow trees, then painted with the blood of animals and given a sheepskin hood."

I nodded in amazement. *Masks painted with blood*, I thought. *That's intense.*

Modern masks, Engert went on to explain, might include horns and menacing faces, but designs from just a few decades earlier were simpler and more peaceful. Men have long portrayed the role of Busós, but in the 1990s, women started taking part in the custom.

Alexandra smiled proudly at the statement. I nodded in agreement.

Engert expressed that, for him, making a mask was a very powerful and personal experience. Through making their masks, performers experience their own personal spirit of the Busó come through. This, he said, is why actors should never remove their masks in public.

While watching Engert speak, I could see his passion for his work. This was his world: one of ancient beasts that were living representations of the heroes of Mohács. Just being in his place of creation felt intoxicating; it reminded me of so many haunter workshops I'd been to back home. Only here, wooden masks replaced those of latex, blocks of wood were substituted for sheets of Styrofoam, and actual blood—out of sight, no doubt, for the sake of his visitors—supplanted artificial mixtures. I thought back to Clemens in Austria. He had shown the same kind of enthusiasm when talking about portraying Krampus. I remembered how I, myself, had felt after trying on the Namahage mask with Hikaru in Akita. I had felt a sudden connection to the mythical creature and a bond to its lands. I supposed that those types of feelings were universal. A powerful transformation takes place behind a mask. It allows us to portray a strong, mighty creature possessing inhuman characteristics that we can't help but admire.

Busójárás Solo

The main day of the carnival was the following day. Every one of Zsuzsa's masks had already been sold. Over coffee at the breakfast table, Alexandra expressed gratitude for being able to stay home.

"It will be *really* busy out," she warned me. I put on my coat and sneakers in the hall, gearing up for another day of Busó mania, while my host sat in her slippers and pajamas: a long T-shirt and sweatpants. "The streets will be *packed*," she said, shaking her head dramatically.

I couldn't help but chuckle. "No problem. I guarantee I've seen worse."

"Okay. I can meet you at the bonfire later. Other than that, I can't stand crowds that big."

I laughed and told her that was fine. *Rookie.*

Once I reached downtown, however, I saw exactly what she meant. Thousands of people filled the streets. Hundreds of horns stood out above the herd. Low bells and cracking noisemakers made the place sound like a crazed animal party at the farm. Busós waved to the crowd, giving high-fives and hugs. I happily swam through the sea of bodies to follow them. Despite barely making it through, I didn't mind the chaos one bit; after three weeks in Japan, it felt nice to blend in.

Perched on a wall overlooking the Danube, I watched a half-dozen Busós on the town ferry lower a coffin into the water. Despite the simplicity of it, I found the ritual fascinating. I knew that it represented bidding farewell to winter, sending away the cold and snow with a symbol of death.

The Busós continued their celebration in a town-wide parade. In hay-covered tractors, cars, and canoes, they waved and sounded their

DRAWN TO THE DARK

noisemakers, feeding off the energy of the crowd. Some rode in decorated wagons as if they worked as farmhands with the gypsies. I thought back to the couple who had helped me when I'd first arrived in Mohács. I could only hope they were here somewhere enjoying the party.

Between taking pictures, I saw one white, wooly creature suddenly point directly at me. I flinched at being singled out as he headed my way. I pointed my camera at him, then saw him lift his mask the moment I snapped a picture. I instantly recognized the face: it was Peter.

"Hey!" I said, waving frantically.

He winked and re-masked, then continued on in the parade.

I could only hope that Engert hadn't seen.

When Alexandra and I finally met up, the sun was beginning to set. A majority of the crowd had dissipated. After hours that felt like days, there was finally enough space to move through the streets. For the first time, I saw a huge pile of wood and debris in the middle of the town square.

"Isn't this *crazy*?" Alexandra asked, looking around at the remaining masses. "You've been out in this all day?"

I laughed. "Oh man, this is nothing. Earlier it was chaos.... But it's good that so many people come out for the show."

She shuddered. "Yeah, I guess."

As darkness fell, two Busós carried what looked like a faceless, naked scarecrow up the massive mound in the square. They set fire to its feet, then hopped down and lit the perimeter of the base. Flames rose up the debris and effigy, popping orange, yellow, and white sparks into the cold air. I stared at the image, mesmerized and grateful for the extra source of heat. An instant later, I felt Alexandra grab my hand.

"Come on!" she said.

I turned from the flames and saw that the crowd had joined hands around the bonfire. They walked in a big circle, resembling moving shadows beyond the roaring flames. I laughed at the sight of several Busós among them. Their happy, wooden faces smiled in the firelight. The crowd pulled faster until Alexandra and I had to run to keep up. We moved quickly then slowly, gravitating towards the flames then backing off again. I laughed with my young host. In her smile, I saw the exhilaration of being back in her hometown. We danced until the fire burned low, and judging by the energy of the crowd, I knew that this was a magical time for the people of Mohács. It was a time that they looked forward to all year, when the entire community could come together, both brethren and beasts joined in celebration.

Budapest's Underground Fear

In a dark basement, I stared at the inhuman thing before me. Its skin looked almost transparent, as if hardened wax covered what should have been its eyes, nose, and mouth. A few hairs stuck out from an equally odd head. Only small, pale ears gave it a somewhat human resemblance.

Pacing before me, the abnormality stood medium height and spoke in a distinctly male voice. I presumed that he was reciting a list of rules for the haunted attraction I had just entered. The actor stepped close to one of the girls in my group, running a hand over her face while speaking in Hungarian. She shivered and laughed, closing her eyes tightly as the monster fondled her. After a few moments, he turned towards me and appeared to stare at me expectantly. As he inched my way, I got the feeling that he had just asked me a question and was waiting for a reply. But I kept quiet and only smiled at him, unsure if he would speak English.

The night before, I had taken a bus into Budapest. The city's haunted attraction, Underground Fear, had come to my attention during an online search. I found it in the theater district. Two large, black signs outside a concrete apartment building vividly expressed what I could expect inside: INTERACTIVE HORROR LABYRINTH, it read in both Hungarian and English. THE PLACE WHERE HORROR MOVIES COME ALIVE WITH YOUR DREAD.

I smiled from ear to ear as I read it; it was perfect already.

After looking at the masked creature a moment, I felt the silence grow thick in the room. Eventually, one of the six others said something to him in Hungarian. He immediately gasped in response.

"Oh, I'm sorry!" he cried. He reached for my face and covered it with both hands, like a blind person trying to make a connection. I laughed as the soft cotton of his gloved fingers slid over my eyes and cheeks. "I didn't know," he said with deep remorse. His hands fell down to my shoulders, then tugged at my shirt. "But what a pity you are wearing too much clothes...."

I cracked up, then heard laughter from the others echo around the room.

"There is no touching the actors inside," the thing said. Like Alexandra's, his accent was only barely detectable. "They will probably touch you, though. And you must do what they say if you want to make it out alive. Okay?"

"Okay," I said, nodding as he stepped away from me at last.

He led us to a large door that slowly creaked open. On the other side, a tall, overweight man stood in a butcher's apron splattered with blood. He sneered at us in loathing, then scanned us with obvious disgust. Moving aside so that we could enter, he exposed a kitchen of filth behind him. Counters dripped with brown and red fluid. Similar stains covered the walls. It all suggested human remains after a recent slaughter. Stepping inside, I heard the masked monster whisper something to the grody butcher. The giant nodded, looked at a girl standing beside me, and pointed to an old, dilapidated refrigerator in the corner.

"*Hozz egy kezet a hűtőből,*" the brute said. He repeated in English: "Get me an arm from the fridge."

The girl laughed and walked to the vile appliance. She timidly opened the door, then cringed at severed arms, feet, and organs oozing blood onto broken racks. She hesitantly reached for the demanded item, quickly shut the door, and handed it to the butcher. He snatched it with a snarl, then pointed to the girl's boyfriend.

"Now you."

The man smiled and took a gallant step. I could only guess the kind of disgusting meal the butcher was planning to prepare—and possibly make us *eat*. But before the brave sous-chef could pick out the next ingredient, the refrigerator door sprang open. A cracked, mangled hand reached out. Hollow, white eyes stared from a face streaked with blood. The living creature hissed as the young Hungarian leapt back, laughing. In an instant the actor retreated into the fridge with a slam of the door.

Our waxy-faced guide led us away from the grime down a long, empty hallway. In a seemingly ordinary bedroom, a young woman lay tied to a small bed. Knotted cloth bound her wrists and ankles to the frame. She struggled against them in desperation, pleading to us in Hungarian. I smiled at the scene. It was a standard horror-film scenario: an imprisoned victim with no hope of escape. Who wouldn't love it? Beside me, I saw similar looks of recognition in my groupmates. But our strange guide quickly threw up his hands for silence. Visibly nervous, he looked back to the door where we had just entered. Slow, booming footsteps sounded in the hall.

"Quick," the guide whispered wildly. "Hide!"

He pointed and waved to a dresser in the corner. The footsteps grew louder as we followed him, crouched down on the floor and only partially hidden from the other side. Within moments, a bestial man filled the doorway. His face looked as though it was made from contorted, stitched leather. Sagging circles formed crude holes around his eyes. I beamed at the sight of him. It was the infamous Leatherface from *The Texas Chainsaw Massacre*. The monster stomped across the room, dragging metal chains that scraped loudly on the floor. The restrained girl screamed in terror, writhing against her bindings as her kidnapper lifted his weapon to strike.

She's doomed, I thought with a smile.

The killer paused, then turned his head towards us. A deep growl escaped his stitched fabric of a mouth. I gasped, loving the unexpected transition. Beside me, the others jumped back, shuddering and screaming as the leather-faced creature stepped towards us.

"Menekülj!" our guide yelled. "Go!" He jumped up and motioned towards a door on the opposite side of the room.

"That was so cool," I said to one of the guys as we fled down another hall.

He laughed and nodded. "Yeah, cool!"

At the end of the passage, we caught our breath before two large wardrobes. Both, I noticed, could easily fit several people. I had an idea where this was going. Once our guide caught up, he hurriedly opened both sets of doors and motioned for us to enter. I filed in with three others behind me, exchanging smiles until the doors shut behind us. Everything went dark. We stood in silence, straining to listen. After a few moments, I heard the familiar scraping of metal begin to echo out in the hall. It moved closer. I instinctively inched back in the small space, feeling my group do the same in unison.

The metallic scraping stopped just outside. An intense hush filled the darkness. In a moment of almost blinding light, I saw the deranged killer standing before us. He held his wretched, sinister chains, while our masked guide stood calmly beside him. I blinked to readjust my eyes while the two exchanged words in Hungarian. They seemed to come to some kind of agreement, and their gaze landed directly on me. I flinched, then turned to my groupmates beside me. They stared back, their faces frozen in suspense. I felt a sudden sense of peril.

The next thing I knew, I was following our strange guide down another hallway, alone.

"It's okay," he said soothingly, his grip on my hand like a vise. I giggled but looked back, hoping that the others would follow.

We stopped before a narrow door, which my abnormal companion quickly opened. He ushered me inside, then kept his blank, eyeless stare on me while speaking without lips to move. "We put everyone in a tiny room now and they find their way out. Okay?"

I faced him from the closet. I got the impression that I was standing in a huge, upturned coffin.

"You find the key and you can get out, okay?"

"Okay," I said cheerfully. *A challenge;* I smiled, suddenly enjoying the isolation. *This is getting better and better.*

The world went dark once again. In an instant I crouched down to the floor, unable to see a thing. With each wall just inches away, I knew that the key could only be so far. I brushed my hands along the cool concrete. *It's got to be here somewhere,* I thought. *Though how I'll find the lock afterwards, I have no idea....*

After a few moments, I flinched at a sharp burst of light from above. I looked up, craning my neck, and saw the blazing flare of a welder's torch. I wasn't alone; standing directly above me was a man in a white hockey mask and blue jumpsuit.

Before I could react, he growled loudly, staring down at me: "What's your name?"

I instantly cracked up. *The killer speaks English!* I had no idea where he'd come from.... Was it possible that I'd missed seeing him as I was crammed inside?

"Chris," I answered, laughing.

The killer bent down, leaning in close and crushing me against his legs. I laughed harder, continuing to feel around the floor, barely able to move. I finally spotted the key from the glow of the torch. Camouflaged in rust, it was flat against the wall – right between my new roommate's feet. I quickly reached for it, gripping the narrow rim. It didn't budge; it was bolted there.

I laughed even harder. *It's a trap—hilarious!*

"Do you know who I am?" the monster grumbled down to me.

I laughed hysterically. I felt tears beginning to form. The Hungarian actor portraying an American monster was asking an American tourist to identify him. It was priceless.

"Jay—" I tried to get out but couldn't.

"What?!" he barked.

I took a breath. "Jason Voorhees," I finally managed. The killer reached down, lifted me up, and pressed me against him. I could only hope that he wasn't offended by my unabashed amusement rather than expressing any fear at all.

"You will stay with me now as my bride," he sneered. "We will have beautiful children together...."

I pushed away from him, trying to catch my breath while laughing. I could see that the masked creature was enjoying toying with me. I may not have been scared, but he could no doubt tell that I was enjoying the performance. I admired his face, one of the horror icons that I'd grown up with. He was a far cry from the happy-go-lucky monsters that had originally attracted me to Hungary. Not everyone, I knew, preferred to dress as jovial creatures like the Busós. Some would much rather portray the deformed and horrid, playfully inflicting fear on their patrons who pretended to be powerless against them—and the more sinister the performance, the better.

While wondering how I could possibly escape, I saw a small window slide open beside me. Turning, I gasped at the sight of the remainder of my group. They stared at me from the other side of the wall. Our wax-faced guide stood among them.

What?! I felt instantly betrayed at the sight of him. *Was I the only one who got trapped?!*

In the others, however, I recognized genuine concern. It looked as though they were trying to determine if I was having a panic attack. This poor girl who had come here alone and didn't speak a word of Hungarian was trapped in a small space with a crazed killer. And it looks as though she's been crying!

I immediately took advantage of the situation.

I reached through the window, looking at them with an expression of panic. "Help," I cried. "I can't get out!" It was a reaction, I presumed, that most people would have when locked in a closet with a killer.

Two girls took action in a heartbeat. They lunged past their boyfriends, opening a hidden door that could only have been visible from their side. Each gripped one of my arms and yanked me towards them. They reacted so fast that I couldn't be sure they'd even been conscious of doing it. Once freed, I smiled at them in gratitude. But by the looks of their boyfriends, I could see that I hadn't fooled everyone.

We continued to follow our guide, whom I now trusted about as far as I could throw him, through several other scenes. We ran from killers, laughing and screaming together, exhilarated at barely escaping sudden death. After all the celebrations I'd gone to over the past few months, I felt completely elated at Underground Fear. For the first time since Screamville, I experienced an all-embracing rush of adrenaline coursing through me. It was as though I were immersed in some kind of magical, horrifying adventure and—at least so far—was surviving it unscathed. It was the same feeling that I had during any kind of scare show. As much fun as I'd had with the Busós, Namahage, Oni, and Krampus, there was just something special about haunts. Their dark characters created an element of danger within an entire fabricated *world*. They evoked fear based on a feeling of imminent doom with no hope of escape.

Now *that* was a show.

We finally found refuge in what resembled an ordinary living room. Yellowing, plaid couches looked welcoming and safe. Static emitted from a black-and-white, rabbit-ears television. We sat as instructed, looking at each other expectantly, until a phone began to ring on a table between us.

I immediately smiled at the black rotary. I knew the scene already; another classic, terrifying moment in film.

The girl closest to it picked it up.

"Halló?"

Our masked guide stared at her. No one spoke a word as we all strained to hear. I tried to think back to the movie. *What had the voice said on the phone?* I couldn't remember. Despite the deadly silence, no one seemed to be able to hear anything.

Suddenly, a loud gasp shot out from a man sitting opposite me. He pointed to a small room adjacent to our own. Turning, I gaped at a large, stone well set in the middle of it. A dull, grating sound emitted from it as the lid slowly slid open. I stared at the well, transfixed as a pale, ghastly hand emerged from within. A head of long, unkempt hair followed, rising from the circle of stones. Pale arms reached around the rim until a girl in a white nightgown slowly began climbing out. I smiled at her emergence: it was Samara from *The Ring!*

But no one else looked for long. Screaming in terror, the group bolted out of the room. The guide quickly followed. I took my time, only inching towards the exit. The horrid-looking actress, repugnant and sinister, crawled on all fours beside me. Her black, dead eyes stared at me blankly.

Beautiful, I thought, smiling down at her. *A perfect show.*

Chapter 6

Transylvania Monsters

"Welcome to the Dracula land."

Robert in Brasov

Before I began searching for a host in Transylvania, a host found me. One late-February evening I had sent an open Couchsurfing request—an online message that all Couchsurfing members within a specific area can see—to Bran, Romania. I wrote that I would be going to Transylvania to explore sites associated with Vlad Tepes, as well as any incorporating Bram Stoker's story of *Dracula*. I received a reply the next morning. A native Romanian named Robert liked my devotion to legends. He was thirty-nine, spoke fluent English, and was legally blind, with only 8 percent vision in one eye. *You are more than welcome to stay with me,* he wrote. *So welcome to the Dracula land.*

On March 11, I slept curled over a few empty seats on an overnight train from Budapest. Waking up to the sunlight, I stared in awe at the scene outside my window. There was the very country where Bram Stoker had set his nineteenth-century story. My mind raced with the train. True to the Irish writer's description stretched "green sloping land of forests and woods, with here and there steep hills, crowned with clumps of trees." I saw farmers working in fields with horses or bulls pulling their wooden wagons. I couldn't help but feel like Jonathan Harker while admiring them, on my way to meet the infamous count. *I read that every known superstition in the world is gathered into the horseshoe of the Carpathians,*

Harker had written in his journal, *as if it were the centre of some sort of imaginative whirlpool; if so my stay may be very interesting.* I imagined those farmers outside my window steeped in some of those superstitions. I envisioned them racing the sunlight at dusk, holding charms to protect them against the evils of night. Of course, I knew that Stoker's story was a far cry from what people here actually believed. Despite that, magic seemed to permeate the very air.

As for so many horror fanatics, *Dracula* had practically shaped my childhood. Before reading the book, I was already well versed in its films, from the 1922 *Nosferatu* to those starring Bela Lugosi, Christopher Lee, and Gary Oldman. My interest in Vlad Tepes, the fifteenth-century Wallachian ruler, had stemmed from Stoker's fictional, bloodthirsty vampire. While the character from the novel acquired land throughout England and kept himself alive by drinking blood, the historical Vlad had taken his people's land back from the Turks while shedding as much blood as needed in the process. But what really put Vlad in the history books was his merciless mutilation of his enemies. He had people burned alive, disemboweled, boiled, strangled, scalped, or skinned and their sexual organs mutilated. But his preferred practice was impalement. Considered one of the most painful ways to die, impalement was performed by tying the victim's feet to a horse, then forcing a long, sharpened stake into their body, usually by the buttocks, until it emerged through the chest, neck, or mouth. The horse then pulled the stake upright so that it could be planted into the ground. This form of slow, painful death served as an example of Vlad's power. But the horrific punishments weren't only reserved for the Turks; Vlad's own people endured his wrath for disobeying the laws, which could include simply being seen as lazy or living into old age. Since impalement was the ruler's favorite practice, historians dubbed him Vlad *tepes*, the Romanian word for "impaler."

When my train arrived in Brasov at 8:00 A.M., I could barely believe that I was now in Vlad's own terrain. I realized that, for the first time on my travels, I had come to explore a historical figure who had inspired one of the most famous monsters in history.

Inside the station, I recognized Robert from his Couchsurfing profile. He stood alone in jeans, a thin sweater, dark sunglasses, and not one strand of hair on his shaved head. I approached him apprehensively, unsure if he would be able to see me. I had never interacted with a blind person before. I stood next to him for a moment, trying to think of something to say, when he turned towards me.

"Chris?" he asked, smiling.

"Yes!" I exhaled, relieved.

He extended his arms for a hug. "Welcome to Transylvania!"

I smiled, both at the gesture and at hearing a genuine Romanian accent for the first time.

While we rode the bus through town, Robert explained that he was able to see everything immediately in front of him, but nothing far away. He lived on his own and could get around without problem, but seeing after dark was difficult. We walked into a green, six-story apartment complex and stepped onto an elevator at the end of the hall. As the door closed behind us, I had a sudden flashback to Underground Fear. The tiny compartment had just as much room as the closet I'd shared with Jason Voorhees a week earlier. This Romanian version, however, looked more like an incinerator from a fifties mental asylum.

"Sometimes the light doesn't work in here," Robert said, pushing the button for the fifth floor. "And sometimes the elevator just stops before it reaches five. If that happens, push the button for four and take the stairs up."

"Wow!" I marveled at his casual acceptance of the deathtrap. "This thing is haunt-like!"

"Is it?" Robert asked excitedly. "What does that mean?"

"A haunt is a horror attraction," I explained, "a scary house with actors that jump out at you."

"Oh... cool!" He nodded, appearing to consider it. "Haunt-like... It *is* haunt-like!"

Fortunately his apartment didn't suggest imminent death at all. After we toured its two bedrooms, bathroom, large kitchen, and living room of modest decor, Robert told me about how he spent his days. We sat at his small table in the kitchen, drinking coffee that he'd made in an Italian coffeemaker. I was well used to the taste by now; it was the only way I'd made coffee anywhere in Europe.

"I've been running an online radio station since 2011," Robert said, seated across from me. "It's called Romanian Rock Radio. Since it's all online, I can do everything from home. Ever since I was a kid, I wanted to make a station for underground groups so their music could be out there for the public."

"That's a great idea," I said. "I don't know much underground music. It doesn't make it to the major radio stations back home."

"Exactly. This way everyone can hear them. And I don't run commercials or anything, so it's not a job. I just do it because I love it."

I smiled at the passion in his voice. I could tell that Robert was just as enthusiastic about rock music as I was about horror shows. He explained that in the Romanian social system, being legally blind is treated in the same manner as being retired. That meant Robert was able to dedicate as much time as he wanted to his show—and that he was free to join me on my monster travels around Transylvania.

Bran Castle

Our journey, of course, started with Bran.

My host and I stood outside a bus at Brasov station, a long line of quiet travelers stretching behind us. It was considerably warmer than it had been in Hungary, and I was glad to be able to wear just one long-sleeve shirt under my coat rather than three.

"Just keep in mind," Robert said as we stepped on the bus, "tourists are always disappointed when they see the castle. I've brought a lot of my Couchsurfers there. It's not big or scary. It's just a castle."

I grinned at the warning while ducking below about fifty, colorful air fresheners dangling over our heads. "Okay," I said, "I promise. But I guarantee you I'll love it." I plopped down into a red, velvet seat beside him. The chairs and similar-colored curtains on the windows seemed remarkably appropriate; I felt as though we were sitting in a gypsy-themed vampire mobile.

Throughout the twenty miles southwest, green, rolling fields separated clusters of small, shack-like homes. I listened to the people chatting in Romanian around us, secretly finding the language exotic and almost mystical. *How could Bran Castle be* anything *but fascinating?* I wondered. It's the legendary fortress in which Stoker based his fictional count; at the very least, I knew that I'd love it on principle alone.

Quaint white and brown village-style houses marked our arrival in Bran. The bus pulled to a stop along a small and remarkably empty main street. Across from us, I spied a small castle perched above a field of sparse, bare trees. Its Gothic, white-stone exterior shone brightly in the late-morning sun, with red, imperial turrets pointing towards the sky. Although I knew that the fortress dated back to the fourteenth century, recent restorations had given it a very modern look—so modern, in fact, that it seemed to possess more of a Disney-like ambiance than one of horror.

"Do you see the castle?" Robert asked, noticing my fixed stare.

"I see it!" I said, unable to look away.

"It's small, right?"

"It *is* small... and very happy looking! I see why you warned me."

I stared at the image that I had dreamed of for so long. It wasn't exactly the "vast ruined castle" that Stoker had described, "from whose tall black windows came no ray of light, and whose broken battlements showed a jagged line against the sky... above a waste of desolation." I knew that Stoker had actually never been to Romania in his life, but I could still see Bran Castle being a good choice for his novel. It looked like an ideal homestead for someone—either human *or* vampire—to isolate himself in the middle of nowhere. I envisioned the count scanning the land from a concealed window after nightfall, his dark eyes peering out over the tall collar of his cape, anxiously awaiting Jonathan Harker's arrival.

"Do you like it, though?" Robert asked as we stepped off the bus.

"Are you kidding?" I still squinted at it in the sun. "I love it! And you know—I think I see Dracula!"

Robert nodded towards the fortress. "Yeah, probably."

Along a stone pedestrian road, wool shirts, hats, and socks hung for sale from small, wooden huts. Vlad Tepes's regal facade adorned T-shirts, tote bags, postcards, and plates. But unlike the overly crowded festivals that I'd attended over the months, the place seemed completely deserted.

"Where *is* everybody?" I asked, looking around in amazement. The quiet vendors sitting beside their wares returned my gaze with bored disinterest.

"It's March," Robert said. "Not many come at this time."

"Oh," I said. "That's kinda sad."

Suddenly, something caught my eye. Across the road from a stand of cheese wheels, a skeleton bust projected from a large, wooden building. Dressed in Roman armor and helmet, the undead soldier smiled maliciously, holding an ax threateningly before him. A cloaked embodiment of death on a posterboard sign pointed towards the building's entrance, its bulging eyes glaring from a shadowed skull.

I gasped, stopped in my tracks.

"Oh my God," I said. "That's a haunted attraction!" The building resembled a wooden version of a castle, with narrow towers along either side. Not a soul stood outside of it, but by the ghoul's enticing gesture, I knew that it had to be open. "The sign says Castelul Groazei... what does that mean?"

"That means 'The Castle of Horror,'" Robert replied, kindly not commenting on my horrible pronunciation.

I turned to him with wide eyes. "Want to go in there after?"

"Sure," Robert said, looking towards it. "I've never been in there. But it's been around for years."

"What? You've been to Bran several times but never went in?"

He shrugged. "No one has ever wanted to go before."

"Oh..." I couldn't help but frown. "Well, that's not right. Have you been to other haunts?"

"No, I've never been in one."

I flinched in shock. "Then it is nothing less than my noble duty to take you in there." I held a hand over my heart as if swearing allegiance to haunt culture.

"After the castle, though, right?" Robert pointed onwards with a smile.

"Yes." I refocused my attention ahead. "After the castle."

Moments later, I found myself just as taken aback as I'd been on the bus. All around us, a large, stone room shone a pristine white. Sunlight spilled in through small-paned windows. Weaponry and armor, antique pottery and pianos adorned a palace that appeared almost untouched by time. We wandered through an extensive labyrinth of stone corridors, and I noticed that none of it bore any resemblance to Stoker's "gloom-haunted rooms... with moth-eaten furniture covered in dust."

"This is all very different from the novel," I whispered, my voice echoing through the wide, winding stairwell.

Robert's chuckle reverberated off the castle wall. "Yes. All my Couchsurfers have said that."

He quickly added a more daunting feel to our self-guided tour, lowering his voice to a creaking moan and whispering, "Vladddd!" as we continued up the stairs. I laughed hysterically. I imagined the Irish writer smiling with pride from his grave and Vlad Tepes scowling.

"Ahhh," Robert said as we approached the top floor. "I think this is what you were hoping for."

Before us, large, framed posters of Vlad Tepes, Bram Stoker, and iconic Hollywood vampires embellished the room. I beamed at the images, grateful to see the wording on each written in both Romanian and English.

"This is all new," Robert said. He walked to a portrait of Bram Stoker, standing just a few inches away so that he could read it.

I gravitated towards Vlad. According to the text, the ruler had spent very little time at Bran Castle. It was only after his father, Wallachian prince Vlad II, was murdered in 1447 that Vlad III fled to Bran. His alias, Dracula, stemmed from his father. Vlad II had been admitted into the Order of the Dragon for bravery in fighting the Turks. From that point he became known as Vlad Dracul, the Romanian word for dragon being *drac* and *ul* its definitive article. The Romanian ending *ulea* means "the son of," so that Vlad Tepes became known as Vlad Dracula: the Son of the Dragon.

Beside me, Robert pointed to the poster he was studying. "This says that Bram Stoker probably learned about Vlad at the British Museum. They had a woodcut called *Forest of the Impaled*. Have you ever heard of that?"

"Oh yes," I said, smiling fondly. "That's a well-known image." I described the picture that portrayed Vlad casually dining on a battlefield beside hundreds of his impaled victims. Although I'd always found Vlad to be a fascinating character, I certainly felt no respect for him. He had enforced methods of torture that I could scarcely imagine one human being doing to another. But I'd also always found the artwork depicting his rule—just like that illustrating Dante's *Inferno*—completely spellbinding.

"It says there was a paper with the woodcut that read: 'Vlad impaled people and roasted them and boiled their heads in a kettle and skinned people and hacked them to pieces like cabbage.'" Robert stared at the description a moment, looking confused by what he'd just read.

"I didn't know *that*," I said. "Jeez, no wonder he inspired Bram Stoker's monster. What a psychopath."

"But that's not true," Robert said, turning to me. "Vlad didn't *eat* people. He was brutal, but he did it to defeat an enemy that had enslaved Romanians for centuries. Remember those Busós you saw in Mohács? They drove out the Turks, too. Vlad just had a different way."

"But Vlad was completely barbaric," I said, shocked at the comparison. "He didn't just use masks as a scare tactic; he slaughtered people."

"The Turks did the same thing to the Romanians, though," Robert said. "They were just as bad."

I looked at Vlad's image on the poster. He appeared noble and defiant in his red crown and cloak, with hard eyes reflecting determination and strength. It was hard to envision him as someone who would just as soon boil your head and eat it as smile at you. "I didn't know that," I said. "But that doesn't make it right."

On another poster, a pale and ghastly Max Schreck portrayed the fictitious Nosferatu. He ominously peered off camera, unnaturally long fingers curled beside his long, black cloak. "Ahhh!" Robert said, pointing to the poster's headline. "Do you know about *strigoi*?"

"No," I said, intrigued. "What's that?"

My host gave a wicked smile. "Those are Transylvania's *real* vampires!"

I laughed, finding his pronunciation of "vampire" hilarious—stressing the second syllable rather than the first.

"It says *strigoi* are believed to be the evil souls of the undead that rise from their graves on full-moon nights." Robert's finger trailed along the poster as he read. "They were children of women who had left their home without wearing anything on their head when they were pregnant, so the Devil put a red bonnet on them."

I stood beside him, reading the text. The *strigoi* resembled rotting corpses that had dug their way out of their graves. Decomposed and bloated, they were a very different breed from the modern image of vampires that are so often depicted as young and beautiful. Like in many places throughout Europe, widespread diseases such as plague and consumption in Romania were believed to be caused by vampires such as *strigoi*. It wasn't until Bram Stoker's story gained popularity that the ghoul-like creatures turned into beautiful, sensual monsters.

"This says *strigoi* can only be destroyed by digging up their grave," I said after reading the poster, "and having a priest perform a religious service over their corpse, decapitating the body and pinning it to the ground by staking it through the heart."

"Hmmmm." Robert shot me a contemplative look. "That sounds very familiar."

The Castle of Horror

In Castelul Groazei, a skeleton with black, silk wings grinned maliciously above us. Resembling a life-sized human-bat corpse, the creature seemed to slowly descend from the ceiling. I looked around the dark, stone chamber. A skeletal prisoner dangled its legs between the bars of a cage. In a large mural, a decapitated soldier bled from the gaping wound on his neck. I described the ambiance to Robert, who was unable to see in such low light.

"It looks like we'll meet Count Dracula and Dr. Frankenstein inside," I said, reading a billboard painted with dripping blood. "There will be many terrifying surprises to remind us we're in Bran, Transylvania: the land which is haunted by vampires and ghosts."

Robert smiled, his eyebrows rising above his dark sunglasses.

"Now *this* is cool!" I said.

After paying fifteen lei admission each—the equivalent of about four American dollars—we stepped through a black curtain to find complete darkness on the other side. Taking Robert by the hand, I stretched out my other before me to guide our way until a dim light shone ahead.

"There's a graveyard here painted on a big canvas," I said, stopping before it. "Dozens of tombstones are shown in a country field at dusk. There are also a few tombstones made out of Styrofoam here on the floor.

One has a pile of bones in front of it. It looks like someone was hacked to pieces and just left there."

"Maybe it means the dead person was dug up," Robert said. "And eaten."

"Oh yeah..." I envisioned it while looking at the mound. "There's some loose dirt in front of a few other ones, so maybe the dead don't always stay dead."

"*Strigoi.*" Robert nodded ominously. "See? They're everywhere."

I giggled, happy to hear his enjoyment of the show already.

"Here's an impaled victim," I said farther along a dark corridor. "Or at least what's left of him. It's a mangled torso stuck on a tall spike. The person's head and arms have been chopped off and you can see some of the ribs underneath the rotting flesh."

Robert grimaced, then squinted at it. "I can see the red. Ewww..."

"I know, huh?" I stared at the image, intrigued; my first depiction of Vlad's rule in a Romanian scare show. After going through Bran Castle, I couldn't help but feel foolish to realize that *this* was more of what I had expected in Bran. This was a glimpse into Transylvania's darker days, but portrayed through the entertaining layout of a scare show: the best of both worlds.

"Now we're in a stone dungeon with a bunch of prison cells," I said farther along. "One has a skeleton inside with his arms and legs hanging between the bars." I squinted at Robert skeptically. "I wonder how many people Vlad actually imprisoned, though, rather than having them impaled or hacked to pieces."

Robert shrugged. "Well, maybe he was just waiting his turn and they forgot about him. He was lucky. But listen.... Do you hear that?"

I cocked my head. Barely audible in the quiet darkness, cries of anguish seemed to come from off in the distance. It sounded like prisoners being tortured somewhere out of sight.

"We should go help them!" Robert joked.

I chuckled. "I didn't even hear that before."

Additional scenes reflected the types of shows that I knew from back home. Frankenstein's monster performed surgery on his creator. The abomination had strapped the scientist to a table in evident grim revenge, ignoring his master's cries of terror. Neon skeletons later glowed against black walls, smiling and waving and appearing to float. A low, foreboding tune followed as we wound through the darkness. I loved it all; the Castle of Horror had turned Bran into the "cursed spot" that Stoker had written of—the land "where the devil and his children walk with earthly feet." At one point I cried out in surprise as my foot sank several inches into the floor.

"Whoa!" Robert said behind me. He threw out his free hand to steady himself.

I stiffened my legs to regain my balance. The hard wood beneath us had changed to a thick, soft cushion. "You doing okay?"

"Yeah." From Robert's voice, I could hear he was smiling. "I like this. It feels really weird; it completely throws me off."

I laughed, laboriously stepping through what felt like a sea of sand.

"Now we're in a room of old, dusty coffins," I said once we reached light again. "One of them has a corpse sitting up in it. His face is a complete mess, like his skin is rotting away. There's a portrait of a vampire in a black cape above him with blood splattered across it."

"Ahhh." Robert nodded. "Dracula must have just eaten. If this is him, he'll look better in no time."

"Oh yeah, that makes sense." I looked around the room. All was quiet, without a single other patron or actor in sight. Despite the season, I couldn't help but feel bewildered at the lack of visitors. Robert and I had only passed a handful of people in Bran Castle, and evidently none of them was interested in a scare show. "It looks like there are only props in here, though," I said, trying to hide my disappointment. "I guess we don't have to worry about anything jumping out at us...."

I immediately cried out and leapt back. Before me, a werewolf jumped out from around the corner. The masked performer arched his back, then howled loudly.

Robert immediately cracked up.

"Except for *him*!" he said.

Transylvania Explorations

Back in Brasov, the city earned its title as the Jewel of Romania. Medieval defensive walls projected a much grimmer fairytale than the more peaceful ambiance of Bran, though yellow, pink, and light-green stone buildings contrasted the gloom. The Black Church, ironically gray, took up what seemed like an entire block. Gypsies wandered the streets, dark-skinned women in colorful but faded dresses approaching people with cupped hands and sad, tired expressions. Robert explained that the gypsies begged all over Romania and was surprised to learn about the elderly couple who had helped me in Mohács.

"There are definitely good people everywhere," I said. The two of us stood at one of the many one-lei coffee machines all over town. The ATM-sized machines poured cups of instant goodness for the equivalent of twenty American cents. "I think these things are gifts from the gods," I said, savoring the cheapest cappuccino I'd ever had.

Robert agreed, pushing a button to pour hot chocolate into his own Styrofoam cup.

But aside from coffee, I made sure to limit my purchases. Although part of me wanted to buy every Vlad souvenir that I came across, I reminded myself of the need to live on the cheap. Every dime spent was coming out of savings that had to see my travels through to the end. I therefore vowed to spend only what I needed for transportation and food and live as though I were broke regarding everything else. Although I expected the resolution to be difficult, I found that it actually wasn't. I was learning that stuff is just stuff, whereas the experience of the journey was worth far more than any T-shirt or knickknack I could buy—and would then only have to haul around in my bag. Robert condoned my traveling lifestyle and dubbed me "Hobo Zero": a hobo with a budget of zero. But as much as he approved of my wandering ways, I admired his own ambition just as much—living by himself and getting around on his own despite the challenges of being blind.

"Of course," he said when I mentioned it. He held up his hot chocolate and shrugged. Despite his dark sunglasses, I saw his expression strongly resemble what I'd seen in the Fabulous Four back in Oaxaca. It was determination and resilience combined with a sense of absurdity at the thought of living any other way. "I never let my condition stop me," Robert said. "Why would I do that to myself? This is my *life!*"

In the village of Turda, my fearless host and I stopped before a series of images dripping with blood. Carvings of impaled victims accompanied crude inscriptions that I recognized as neither English nor Romanian.

"Do you know Latin?" I asked Robert, tracing some lettering within a wooden door.

"No." He leaned in so that he could see the words. "They're probably warnings."

"Probably." I pushed open the door with a smile. "That's always a good sign."

In Castelul Printul Vanator, a restaurant also known as Hunter Castle, the two of us entered a dining room of carnage. Surrounding a colossal king's table set for twelve, murals depicted Vlad Tepes and his butchering army. Axes and spears flew through the air. Turbaned Turkish captives dangled lifelessly from stakes in the ground. Others hung from shackles in a dungeon or knelt before wooden stocks. In one corner stood a life-sized replica of Vlad himself, with long, dark hair running over a gold chest plate and striped cloak. The ruler gripped a halberd: a massive ax topped with metal spike that appeared as heavy as I was. In his other hand, a shield read *Count Dracula* in bleeding letters.

I admired every inch of the room as we toured it. Skulls and bones were partially concealed within faux stone walls. A dismembered hand bled onto a chopping block. A four-foot, cloaked skeleton held a massive scythe. It grinned malevolently with sharp teeth jutting from its charred skull.

"This place is awesome," I said, marveling at the image of death.

"It's very haunt-like." Robert touched a bleeding pitchfork leaning

against the stone. "This is Transylvania's *real* bloody history: horror and death."

In the town of Piatra Fantele, another dungeon awaited us. A cloaked, female guide led us down a narrow and extremely steep stairwell into the basement of Hotel Castle Dracula. Following the soft glow of her oil lantern, we traveled through the dank darkness until reaching a small chamber about the size of a prison cell.

"This room once belonged to the monster Dracula." The young guide held her light to the wall. Before us appeared a handsome vampire. Tall and thin, the painted image bore a waxen face, aquiline nose, and sharp teeth. His eyes were bold and intimidating, resembling both the real Count Dracula and Stoker's fictional creation. But a long, black cape revealed his true identity to be the latter.

The monster disappeared as the guide removed her flame from the wall. She crossed the room, then held up her light once again. Three women appeared, gazing enticingly from the dark stone. I recognized the swaying, round forms with bright, hard eyes, white teeth, and voluptuous lips as three additional characters from Stoker's novel.

"And these are Dracula's brides," our guide said. She paused a moment while I stared at the image and described it to Robert.

When the seducers disappeared, the guide revealed an old, wooden coffin in the middle of the room. The toe-pincher looked as old as Dracula's story, with a layer of dust covering the faded wood.

"And these are Dracula's bones," the cloaked woman said. "Would you like to see?"

I smiled immediately. "Yes."

Beside me, Robert's low chuckle echoed throughout the room. The guide brought a hand to the weathered lid while the other held her light before it. A slow creak whined as the wood inched open. In a second the candle was extinguished. The room went completely black. I heard a strange rustling from within the coffin and gasped in surprise when a breeze flew past me, as if something had just run out the door.

Robert burst out laughing. The guide relit her lantern with a smile.

"Dracula escaped!" Robert said, clutching my arm. "I saw that coming."

A final show awaited us in Sighisoara. In the birth town of Vlad himself, steep, cobblestone alleyways ran throughout the medieval citadel. Turrets rose above the fourteenth-century Clock Tower. And on Citadel Square, a cartoon vampire resembled Count Chocula outside Casa Vlad Dracul. Bleeding letters highlighted the restaurant's main attraction: "Visit the room where Dracula was born!"

On the second floor, black and blood-red curtains made up the walls and ceiling. I stood beside Robert while staring, stunned, at some kind of vampire version of the Big Top. In the middle of the room, the infamous undead lay asleep in a satin-lined coffin. Garbed in a white, puffed shirt and elegant, black cape, the figure was a perfect replica of Bela Lugosi from the 1931 *Dracula* film. While absorbed in the likeness, I suddenly recognized organ music playing softly.

"Do you hear that?" I whispered to Robert, though we were the only two in the room. "That's Midnight Syndicate. This song is called 'Crypt of the Forsaken.'"

"Ahhh!" Robert turned to me with a smile. "*Now* you hear the music!"

We took a few steps towards the sleeping creature, our sneakers echoing along the hard wood. After paying two lei for entry, we were told that our admission included taking pictures. I captured every inch of the room, admiring the vibrant and sleek colors, then aimed my camera at the well-dressed vampire. I snapped a picture, then immediately leapt back as Dracula rose from his slumber, reaching towards me with a hiss. I shrieked in surprise, making Robert gasp and jump. We burst into laughter and applauded the actor for his performance.

While touring the remainder of the restaurant, we saw additional undead appear. A sunken-eyed, marble vampire glared out from behind the bar. A friendlier, plush creature between silver candelabra smiled to reveal cute fangs. I stopped upon spying a striking mural along the wall: a larger-than-life Vlad bore a hard, commanding expression. He proudly stood with the town of Sighisoara behind him.

"Look at this," I said to Robert, gesturing at the artwork in disbelief. "They have Vlad portrayed like a true hero. I've seen pictures like this all over Romania. I can't get over it. He was a tyrant to his own people. Why would they do that?"

Robert looked at the image; it was so large that he could evidently see it without problem. "Well, remember, Vlad did a lot for Wallachia. There was no order when he came into power; there was only crime and corruption. He changed all that. People learned that under his rule, crimes would be punished. But Romanians mainly remember him as the one who freed Wallachia from the Turks. Don't forget, they were doing horrible things to Romanians then. It wasn't just Vlad who came up with all those punishments on his own. And we don't *really* know that he did all those things they say. Some of those stories could be complete lies."

I stared at the mural, pondering it. "Yeah, that's true...." I could understand Vlad being viewed as heroic for liberating his country, despite twisted methods he used for doing it. But I couldn't help but find his actions unforgivable. To me, he was just as much of a monster as Bram Stoker's fictional depiction of him. I felt somewhat strange to have such conflicting feelings about the person who had brought me to Transylvania in the first place. He had fascinated me for so long—but because of his image as a *tyrant*, not a hero. I began to wonder if my draw to him had more to do with the way he'd been depicted in movies and haunt shows than anything else. Back at Hunter Castle, Vlad and his army had been portrayed within the fun ambiance of a haunt. At Hotel Castle Dracula and Casa Vlad Dracul, the shows had blended his legend with the iconic vampire that I'd always loved. There were similar characteristics in both of them, I realized, in the real and the unreal. Both seemed to possess unlimited power. They were dangerous, terrible creatures portrayed as somehow more than mortal. I considered the many demons, devils, and living dead that I'd seen over the months, from one side of the globe to the other.

I saw those very same features in all of them.

The Climb to Poenari Fortress

Over the next several days, Robert and I relaxed back in Brasov. He taught me how to make polenta: a dish almost exactly like American Southern grits, made from cornmeal, water, and salt. We listened to Romanian Rock Radio constantly, while Robert named off each band as easily as I could list *Dracula* films. Outside of town, we walked winding trails in the Carpathian forest. Mossed, broken stone walls looked exquisite, partially hidden between barren beech trees and pine. It felt surreal to be in the very woods where one of my favorite stories had taken place. I recounted movie scenes in which Jonathan Harker had ridden through the Borgo Pass in his coach, then later escaped through the woods half-mad and blood-drained after his imprisonment at Dracula's castle. Robert's imaginings took us to Vlad leading his army through those lands, heading towards Bran after the murder of his father. Sadly, there would be no Castelul Groazei for him to enjoy during his stay.

For our final Dracula exploration, we decided to visit a place where Vlad's reign lived on. It meant traveling to his homeland of Wallachia. There we could find the ruins of the fifteenth-century Poenari Fortress: Vlad's *actual* castle, which was still accessible within the Carpathian Mountains. Unfortunately, it was well beyond the reach of any buses and trains that we had thus far depended on.

But Robert had a plan.

A few days later, I found myself looking at his childhood friend, who shook his head at me in the rearview mirror.

"I swear," he said, "all Americans are crazy."

I laughed from the backseat at Tibi's exasperated eyes. He drove his black Opel Corsa south out of Brasov, a stubby, brown beard half-concealing his deadpan face.

"I've worked at a couple of farms in Texas over the last few summers," Tibi said, "and you wouldn't *believe* the types of people I've met."

"Oh yeah?" I smiled at his sarcasm. "Like who?"

"Women in bars. When they find out I'm from Transylvania they ask me the *stupidest* questions. They always ask me if I'm a vampire!"

Robert, in the passenger seat beside him, stopped flipping through radio stations. "That's because you *are*!" he said, staring at Tibi from behind his shades. "They can't help that they know."

Tibi shifted his eyes from the road to his friend to the mirror, making sure that he kept our undivided attention. "'Will you bite me?'" he mocked in a female voice. "'I want to live forever!'" He looked at Robert for support. "Can you believe it? They begged me!"

"Oh my God," I said. "Were they serious?"

"They were *drunk!*" Robert turned around to face me. "They would have said anything."

I giggled. I thought back to when I'd arrived in Romania, now a month earlier. I remembered dreaming about what Transylvania would be like, imagining the farmers in the fields fleeing from vampires after dark, and thinking the Romanian language sounded mystical. But as naïve as I'd been about it all, I certainly never wanted anyone to bite me. There's a definite line between fantasy and reality.

"So what did you do?" I asked.

"Well, I wasn't going to *do* it. That's for sure. So I said, 'You're right. I *am* a vampire.'" Tibi put a hand over his chest, speaking as though with deep remorse. "'But I'm very sorry; I have sworn to never bite a human being so that I can break the family curse.'"

Robert and I laughed.

"That's great," Robert said. "And they believed you?"

"Oh yeah. *Americans...*" He shook his head at me. "*Come* on!"

The stories continued as the three of us wound our way up the mountains. Sheep spotted the hillsides with shepherds sitting idly by. Farmers pulled horses hooked to wooden carts. Tibi constantly brought the car to a crawl to get around potholes reaching the length of the street, growling in frustration that the next time he would borrow a friend's car.

The base of Poenari Fortress finally appeared along a narrow, country road. From the backseat, I craned my neck up at the ruins. It looked so far up the mountain that I felt as though we had made a trip to Mount Olympus. Barely visible within the trees were just some of the 1,480 stone steps that I knew led up to it.

"And you're going to climb waaay up there...," Tibi teased. "Have fun with that!"

Robert turned to me and smiled. Both he and Tibi had made the climb twice before and neither, they stressed, had any desire to repeat it. But their bowing out didn't deter me one bit; if there was one thing I never could turn down, it was a hike in the woods.

But something had to come first: food. A single restaurant inhabited the almost-desolate area, and one item on the menu quickly caught my eye.

"What's tripe soup?" I asked, reading the English translation.

Tibi threw me a look of warning from across the picnic table. The three of us sat outside, surrounded by only mountains. "You probably won't like it," he said. "Most tourists don't."

I put down my menu and stared at him in defiance. "Do you guys like it?"

"I do," Robert said.

Tibi nodded.

"Then that settles it; tripe soup it is. That's the rule: if there's something I've never heard of before, I have to try it."

Tibi held up his hands in defeat. "Okay..."

"Trust me," Robert said beside me, "she's always like this."

Not a moment after the waitress brought our orders, I realized that I should have heeded the warning. The thick, creamy soup resembled New England clam chowder, but after one bite I found it tasted more like some kind of odd-smelling paste. Insisting that I did, in fact, like it just fine, I focused my attention on the bread that had come with it and my coffee that tasted like heaven in comparison.

"That was impressive," Tibi said after I finished it. "I don't know many tourists who enjoy eating cow intestines."

I looked at him in horror. "What?!" The empty bowl before me suddenly represented a container of deceit. My previous impression of paste now morphed into a revolting image of animal innards, slowly digesting in some of my own. "Why didn't you tell me that *before* I ordered it?"

"You didn't *ask* us," Robert said. "You 'like the adventure!'" He waved his arms in the air like a child at the playground.

I squinted hard at him. "Well, I'm stronger for it, I guess. *Yuck.*"

Ignoring my nausea, I left Robert and Tibi to finish their lemonade and began my trek to Vlad's awaiting fortress.

"Watch out for *strigoi...!*" Robert said, waving after me.

A large poster of Vlad marked the entrance to the woods. Looking up the trail, I saw not a soul in sight. Long and narrow wooden steps were spaced closely together, allowing for an easy, gradual climb. I hopped up quickly, moving higher and higher, marveling at the dense forest around me. After about twenty minutes of continuous ascent, I finally stopped to take a breather. *Phew*, I thought. *At least that soup gave me strength.*

The stone tower above now appeared much larger with fewer trees between us. While taking it all in, I remembered the history of Poenari Fortress's construction. It was a tale as dismal as Vlad's reign itself. In 1459, he had invited rich Saxons known as boyars to an Easter dinner.

Unbeknownst to any of them, Vlad was well aware that they had caused the death of his father twelve years earlier. Upon their arrival, the ruler had the elderly boyars impaled and forced the young and agile to trek fifty miles and 1,500 feet to a fortress they were ordered to rebuild. As I resumed my ascent, I envisioned the scene happening all around me: traitors turned slaves trudging up the land, growing weak but facing excruciating death should they flee. Some had died before reaching the summit. Others perished from the grueling work of breaking and hauling stone. In the end, Poenari Fortress was completed and used to secure and control the passage between Wallachia and Transylvania.

I finally approached a gate and wooden bridge at the hilltop, then paid a five-lei admission to a man who quickly emerged from a small gift shop. Fortunately Robert had warned me of the fee ahead of time; I imagined that going that far without cash and then being turned away would lead to a wrath that only Vlad could match.

At long last, I saw the fortress standing larger than life. I walked across the bridge's narrow planks, holding rope railings on either side. Suddenly something appeared below the slave-constructed accomplishment. An impaled prisoner faced me. High above the land, the mannequin's blank dead eyes stared, his gray tunic flapping in the breeze. I smiled at the sight. It looked like a gigantic Ken doll with blood streaked over its arms and legs. *A gentler image for the tourists,* I thought with a smirk. *There's no way that any flesh would be left after the birds got ahold of him.*

Beside the staked figure, a gallows was set up on a small platform. The noose dangled in the air, as if waiting for its next evildoer. A set of wooden stocks was beside it, its three holes perfectly carved, and an ax dripped blood onto a chopping block. I admired the scene: horrific and beautiful in depiction and authenticity.

Within the castle ruins, I walked through ancient passageways of crumbling stone and red brick—some walls, I knew, totaling nine feet in thickness. It was all that remained of Vlad's vast fortress. It felt peaceful being alone in the stillness of the mountains. Not even a breeze seemed to sweep over the lands. I leaned against the metal barrier separating me from a steep drop and peered into the treetops below. I remembered a scene from one of my favorite *Dracula* films that was based on an actual moment in Vlad's life. It was here at Poenari Fortress that Vlad's wife had flung herself from the tower. I remembered Wynona Ryder gracefully falling through the air in the 1992 film and crashing into the river below. The leap had been explained as suicide after she learned that Vlad had died in battle. In truth, the ruler had been at the fortress at the time his wife had jumped; the Turks were invading and the woman had chosen to take her own life rather than face the horror that awaited her upon capture. With all the practices of the day, I didn't blame her one bit.

While looking upon the surrounding mountains, thick forests that seemingly held no end, I considered what Robert had said about Vlad being a hero to Romanians. I could understand that view. He had saved his country from foreign occupation and slavery. And he had done what, in his mind, was the only way to bring order to the people of these lands. Robert had been raised to see Vlad's actions in that light, whereas I had always understood them in another. But despite the differences, I was glad that my fellow-adventuring host and I had found a common ground. We had enjoyed all sorts of travels and shows built around a history that captured both of our interests. Even if he hadn't been quite as enthusiastic about climbing 1,500 steps into the woods, we had enjoyed so many other exploits. We had been able to laugh and scream in shows that people from these very lands put together. They combined meaningful legend with farce and fiction. There was room for both, I supposed: the reality and the spectacle. One could always lead to appreciating the other—regardless of which we had been originally drawn to.

Chapter 7

Walpurgisnacht and the Berlin Dungeon

"The devil needs darkness."

Walpurgisnacht

In Thale, Germany, two green-faced witches sat on a boulder by the roadside. Colorful patches adorned their corset dresses, and a once-familiar feline topped a wooden walking stick that had surely aided their journey. The pair waved to people passing by, one raising a plastic cup of bright, green liquid. When I pointed my camera in their direction, the hags immediately smiled at me for the picture.

In late April, my travels had led me to the celebration of Walpurgisnacht, or Walpurgis Night in English. Named after the English missionary St. Walpurga, Walpurgisnacht is known in German folklore as the night when evil thrives on the Brocken Mountain, the highest peak in central Germany's Harz region. I had booked a seventeen-hour trip from Romania on the ride-sharing website Blablacar, after reading about a young couple looking to share their drive for forty Euros—or sixty American dollars. The ride had been gorgeous: fields of yellow rapeseed flowers stretched throughout eastern Hungary, Slovakia, and the Czech Republic and into Germany. After spending the last three months in Japan, Hungary, and Romania, I couldn't help but feel relieved to be back in Western Europe. The drinking witches and statue across from them of a short, fat devil pointing towards the mountains seemed to reflect a culture much more similar to my own.

I had first learned about Walpurgisnacht through the story of *Faust,* the epic poem written by Johann Wolfgang von Goethe in 1808. After growing bitter and dissatisfied with life, old Faust sells his soul to the devil, Mephistopheles, in exchange for regaining his youth and enjoying life's more sensual pleasures. On Walpurgisnacht, Mephistopheles brings Faust to the Brocken Mountain, where witches and devils congregate for magic, dancing, and sex. Today, the story is kept alive through festivals all over central Germany on April 30. To ensure that I'd choose the best show, I had asked advice over a few German Couchsurfing websites. Each reply pointed me to the same place: the town of Thale, where the Brocken is located. This was where witches and devils, or Hexen and Teufel, would gather for a rock concert at 1,142 meters on the mountain peak.

Unable to find a host in the area, I spent my first night in a hotel. The next day, I found the town to resemble a German fairytale. Timber-framed houses lined the streets with the mountains stretching off into the distance. Witches appeared in droves as the day progressed. Young Hexen resembled childlike fairies, with orange, red, or blue hair and black-and-purple cloaks shining in the sun. Others appeared much older with spider webs falling off pointed, black hats and long, crooked noses strapped around green faces.

Horned devils accompanied the magical creatures: wild, red hair flew out from faces painted like flames. Many dressed completely in black with long, red cloaks matching their plastic pitchforks. I smiled at the scene while walking through the crowd. It looked as though a mass exodus had just arrived from the depths of hell. The masses shuffled between vendor huts selling flashing horn headbands and witch dolls flying on broomsticks. For the first time, I was proud that my jacket was bright red; at long last, I fit in with at least half of the crowd.

Although I understood only a portion of the German spoken all around me—significantly more than I ever understood back in Austria—I couldn't help but feel a sense of familiarity at it all. The scene reminded me of so many Octobers I'd spent in Salem, Massachusetts. I remembered strolling its streets of witches and warlocks between parades and ghost tours and haunted attractions. Although Salem's tourism is based on the seventeenth-century witchcraft trials, Germany, I knew, holds an even longer history of witch hysteria. In 1692, twenty Salem residents lost their lives after being accused of consorting with the devil. But in Germany, tens of thousands perished from the same accusation over the centuries. I couldn't help but think of it as ironic that Salem commercializes its dark history with shows running all year, whereas Walpurgisnacht is celebrated solely on April 30.

In Thale's Information Center, I purchased a ticket from a kindly Teufel. For twenty-five Euros, I would ride a gondola lift up the legendary Brocken Mountain. I was relieved to be able to make the transaction in English, but before I could walk away, the devil stopped me.

"Hatten Sie eine schöne Zeit in der Stadt?" he asked.

I stared at him from the other side of the ticket counter. He appeared to be in his early fifties, with short, blond hair humorously contrasting his red horns. I understood him well enough: *Had I had a nice day in the city?* But I replied with my most commonly used German phrase.

"Ich sprecht nicht Deutsch."

He nodded slowly. "Ahhh. *Bist du eine Hexe?*"

I immediately giggled. It wasn't the first time someone had asked me if I was a witch.

The devil laughed with me.

"Nein," I said, *"ich bin keine Hexe."*

I could feel my face grow hot and, glancing around, saw big smiles on a few people standing quietly by. *An American speaking German,* their expressions seemed to read. *How cute.* But after walking back outside, I couldn't help but wonder if my college German courses would have been easier had the professors somehow incorporated creatures from the underworld.

On the gondola, I shared a ride with additional demons. Their orange dresses and glowing horns made me feel as though we were on our way to a Halloween party on top of the world. Below us, the thick wood of twisting trees looked eerie in the dying sun. This, I knew, was the very forest where Mephistopheles had led Faust to witness the vile congregation on the mountain. I remembered reading the story in junior high, then later hearing all sorts of tales based on people making pacts with the devil—the Salem Witch Trials being just one of many. As rows of Thale's red, brick roofs grew ever smaller below, I envisioned Goethe's story. I pictured the devil leading Faust, now transformed to his younger self, to the revelry of sin high on the hills. By this time, Faust had already fallen in love with Gretchen, a young woman who knew nothing of her lover's ominous pact.

I remembered the devil's song:

All is turning, whirling, blending,
Trees and rocks with grinning faces,
Wandering lights that spin in mazes,
Still increasing and expanding!

On the mountain, a gate marked the entryway to the Hexentanzplatz: "the witches' dancing place." Dozens stood in line to have their pictures taken beside stone devils, gnomes, and witches seated upon massive boulders. Other figures drank and danced around a blazing bonfire.

They dance, they chat, they cook, they drink, they court:
Now where, just tell me, is there better sport?

The smell of wurst and bread filled the air. Vendor stands sold fried dough and French fries, coffee and beer. I looked on the scene with heartfelt approval: all the necessities for a night of indulgence. After buying an ice cream, I quickly deduced that some sort of dark magic had certainly been used in making it. The vanilla soft-serve was so cold that it burned my throat like fire. It was painful yet delicious. But that only made sense: there had to be pleasure *and* pain on Walpurgisnacht.

More paraded off the gondola until hundreds became thousands. Witches and devils of all ages formed a colorful array of hair, horns, and dress. I felt worlds away from where I'd spent my previous times in the mountains—first with the quiet Japanese in Akita, then alone in the hills

of Wallachia. I felt much more at home here, surrounded by thousands of excited, costumed partiers; now *this* was a culture that I could relate to.

Once the sun finally set, a rock concert began. Dozens of glowing horns flickered and swayed to tribute bands for AC/DC and Guns N' Roses. I had a sudden wish for Zsuzsa back in Hungary to join me; I got the feeling that she had never experienced her favorite music quite like this. But after a few hours all became quiet as two MCs introduced the main event: a laser rock show entitled *Mephistos Pakt.*

"Der Teufel braucht Dunkelheit," one announced in a hoarse whisper. The stage went black.

I smiled at the assertion. *The devil needs darkness.*

After a few moments, a spotlight landed on a tall platform across from the stage. I stared, wide eyed, at the legendary devil. He was exactly like the poem's description:

> *a squire of high degree,*
> *in scarlet coat, with golden trimming,*
> *a cloak in silken lustre swimming*

Mephistopheles cackled wildly, opening his arms to the crowd below. In devious rhyme, he exclaimed his excitement over Walpurgisnacht. I understood less than half of what he said and realized that his lines were in High German rather than the standard colloquial. But the actor played his role so well that it didn't matter. His suave and sinister demeanor was fascinating to simply watch. He was the perfect embodiment of evil. After a few moments, the booming voice of God interrupted him. Their voices echoed across the dark mountain as they made their infamous deal: Mephisto would be allowed to torment Faust and tempt him into sin, for God was sure that Faust would choose rightly in the end.

Intense rock music erupted and the devil disappeared. In his place, a female dancer threw her arms into the air. Long, cloth scarves flew from her costume, resembling wild flames fluttering as she danced. The music intensified as long streams of light shot from the devil's podium down to the stage. Green clouds formed and swirled in the light. The message was clear: although God had spoken to Mephisto from heaven, it was hell that was now coming to earth.

When silence resumed, Faust appeared. The old man hobbled slowly across the stage with the assistance of a cane. A loud growling noise startled him, until Mephisto appeared high above on another podium beside the stage. Through elegant verse, the devil offered to take the old man to places he could scarcely imagine. But there would be a price to pay. I thought back to Goethe's verse in which the devil had proposed the evil exchange:

Come, bind thyself by prompt indenture,
And thou mine arts with joy shalt see:
What no man ever saw, I'll give to thee.

As I craned my neck up to admire the devil, he sealed the deal, magically drawing a bit of the old man's blood. Additional rock music moved the story forward. Faust became young. He courted the young Gretchen. Angels and skeletons danced and fought, breathing fire and waving blazing swords. The stage became a sea of flaming hellfire as Mephisto led Faust towards a night of chaos on the mountain.

Among this witches' revelry
His way one gladly loses

Red, blue, and purple lights shot into the air like flames from the dancers. Skeletons leapt with horned demons, waving batons bursting with fire. Faust had entered the world of dark thrills on the Brocken. Mephisto's voice emanated from the blackness: *"Du schriebst mit den Teufel einen pakt."* You wrote a pact with the devil.

Dancers spun, waved, and kicked until Faust's fate became clear: he had succumbed to what he'd seen on the mountain, and his life with Gretchen had been destroyed. The world became a fog of green, then blue, then black as Mephisto's cackle echoed through it all.

I could hardly breathe while watching the show. I felt the music and dance move me in a way the story never had. Although it was the first festival that I was experiencing completely on my own, without even a host to discuss it with later, I felt closer to this one than I had with any other. The thrills had made Goethe's story real. Faust was *alive*. Mephisto was a rock star! I cheered with the crowd, now one mass of dancing shadows. From high above, the devil gleefully invited us to indulge in the ecstasy that was Walpurgisnacht. He extended his arms, and I suddenly marveled at his resemblance to another demon I'd seen on my travels. It was months earlier, and the creature had stood high on a terrible throne while being carried through the streets of Salzburg. I remembered hell being unleashed on that cold, winter day. It had been in the height of the Christmas season. And now, somehow, the same wrath of evil had made its way to the mountains of Germany. But in an instant the likeness between the creatures was gone, as Mephisto called down to his worshippers below:

"So lasst uns feiern!"

My eyes grew wide as I deciphered his booming message. It carried easily across the dark mountain. It was something I'd heard elsewhere— even before crossing the ocean to Austria. And I'd heard it at a time when thousands of others had congregated as creatures from the underworld.

So let's party!

The Berlin Dungeon

In the depths of Berlin, a female clown burst through the door. Dressed in old, faded stockings and a flamboyantly colored cap, she arched her back and delivered a high-pitched, maniacal laugh. The noise echoed off the dank walls around us. It sounded as though an escaped asylum patient had found refuge in Berlin's subterrain. When her laughter finally died away, she stared at me a moment, her eyes fixed crazily open, and gave me a twisted smile.

"Welcome to the Berlin Dungeon!" she boomed. "The time has come for you to be immersed in Berlin's most glorious and gruesome history. Once down there, you must keep your wits about you—you never know who is lurking in the darkness...!"

I turned to the five others in my small group. They looked at our strange host in anticipation.

It had been a week since Walpurgisnacht on the Brocken Mountain. After a few days in the German countryside, I had taken a train to Berlin for a new experience. The Berlin Dungeon had opened only a year earlier. Unlike so many American shows, it is like interactive theater. For fourteen Euros (almost nineteen U.S. dollars), professional actors put on a series of skits in scenes so professionally constructed that it feels like going back in time. Now, I followed the lunatic jester through what resembled a dismal underground cavern while the busy streets of Berlin seemed miles away. A short elevator ride had taken my group and me down into the depths only moments before, but I couldn't help but feel as if we had been down there for centuries.

The guide motioned for us to enter a small, dimly lit chamber. Inside, two motionless, robed monks sat before tables of ancient, dusty tomes. Candles dripped wax on either side of an arched, stained-glass window. A third figure stood before it, his dark, cloaked form appearing to be about seven feet tall.

"I am the guardian of this ancient library," the creature croaked. The pale light of his projected, waxen face replaced that of the candles, with deformed eyes and mouth stretching well beyond normal reach. "Once used as a sanctuary for peasants, now, in the year 1576, the pestilence is upon us—upon *you!*"

The monstrous monk warned us of God's wrath, which was believed to be inflicted upon the lands. No man, woman, or child was safe, we were told. When the light of his face disappeared into darkness once again, faint red and blue reappeared from the small window. I spoke not a word but turned to my tour mates in excitement. I had come to the Dungeon alone that day, with my Couchsurfing host outside the city unable to join me. But it was much more fun to wander through the depths with others.

Without warning, one of the seated monks sprang forward from his writing desk.

"Heed my master!" he hissed, breaking the silence.

I immediately jumped back in surprise. Two girls shrieked beside me, then we burst out laughing. Like me, they had no doubt believed the figure to be fake.

The monk pointed towards a large, arched door on the opposite side of the room. "Leave these streets filled with disease," he yelled. "Go now!"

While the door opened by its own accord, I followed the group out, noticing that our boisterous jester friend had long since abandoned us.

At the end of a stone corridor, another cloaked figure awaited. He— or she—stood beside an underground river. I could smell it more than see it, though it silently shimmered in the light of the figure's oil lantern. A large raft brought us down what felt like an abyss well inside the earth, our concealed guide never uttering a word along the way. After a few moments, a man came into view. He stood beside the dark river's edge, wringing his hands while watching our arrival. I smiled at his unusual appearance: he was dressed in a white surgical robe covered with red, ominous streaks. He looked like a doctor fresh out of medical school who was still painstakingly learning the ropes.

"Thank goodness you've made it!" the young physician said once we reached him. He eagerly grabbed onto the raft as our silent guide took hold of a railing. "Come with me, peasants! This way—the plague is spreading fast and you'd better see the doctor!"

I giggled under my breath as we filed out of the small boat. Inside a large, circular room, rows of long, wooden benches faced what appeared to be a surgical station in dismal times. The form of a male body lay beneath a white sheet on a stretcher. Trays of crude surgical tools glistened beside it. A small chair stood half-concealed behind a hanging curtain, and I made out metal restraints attached to its arms and legs. The gruesome doctor continued eying us as we took our seats, wringing his hands until stepping beside the still body.

"Oh my...," he said with a quiver. "You all look so sickly!"

I chuckled at his sincerity, hearing a few others beside me do the same.

"I am the doctor's assistant," our new host announced. "And I regret to inform you that the doctor has recently fallen ill and died of the plague himself." He gestured to the sheeted form beside him. "But you know, it's important to understand the disease if there's any hope of trying to cure it. I will therefore take it upon myself to show you the signs and symptoms." He scanned the crowd before him. "May I have a volunteer to help me? You, sir, what's your name?"

A young man in the front row stood up. "Sam," he said in a soft, Eastern European accent.

"Oh, Sam, you don't look well...." The assistant shook his head with a frown. "You don't look well at all." He shuffled to the volunteer, took him by the hand, and led him behind the surgical table. "Now if you would assist me, we can remove the bits of the doctor here."

The white sheet was pulled back as Sam watched. Everyone stared at the image of a male corpse. Its ribcage had been cut wide open, the deep, red wound clearly visible through an unbuttoned white coat. Sam laughed at the sight. The rest of us laughed at his reaction. Beside him, the assistant thrust his forearm deep into the cadaver.

"As you can see," he said casually, "the lungs have completely rotted. Here, Sam, hold that...."

Sam's expression changed to utter revulsion. He stared at the large, black mass in his open hands. I covered my mouth, shaking with laughter as the unfazed assistant reached back into the body. He pulled out what looked like a red glob of mush. Blood oozed from it, trickling down his fingers. He looked back at Sam, studying him.

"Oh, Sam, you don't look well at all.... I think you may have the plague upon you."

He dropped the organ back into the dead doctor. With hardly a glance, he took the rotten lung from his volunteer and tossed it onto the corpse. His blood-stained hand grasped one of Sam's as he led him to the curtained chair.

"Some say it's God's wrath against sinners that has caused this plague...," the assistant said. He gently pushed Sam into the chair then looked back at his audience. His crazed eyes glazed over. In a flash he threw the metal restraints over Sam's wrists and ankles. "And I see a sinner here. I think we need to remove *his* bits! But first, some anesthetic..."

The mad assistant pulled the curtain around the both of them. Only their silhouettes remained visible through the white sheet.

"One hit on the head should do it...." The assistant's voice had grown hyper. I giggled with the crowd. We stared at the outline of a large mallet in the assistant's hand. He lifted it high above Sam's head, then brought it crashing down. A loud "ooooh!" resonated from behind the curtain. I laughed, picking up on the sound of a hidden recording through the strange pitch of the moan.

"Maybe one more...," the assistant said in a strained voice. The mallet came down again, producing another cry. After a third hit, dark liquid splashed onto the sheet with a loud gushing sound.

I laughed as a few girls covered their ears at the hideous noise. The assistant popped his head out from behind the sheet and gave a sheepish grimace.

"Ohhh... it looks like it was too late for poor Sam." His voice revealed deep regret. "But it's true, the plague *is* punishment for our sins—so you'd better all confess your sins. Go on—go now!"

As we rose to leave, I smiled at the confused expressions of Sam's friends. They looked towards the hidden chair. *Were they really supposed to leave him?* But they quickly shrugged it off and followed the rest of us past the murder scene and out the door.

Our silent, cloaked boat guide walked us down another corridor. Following in the darkness, I felt a permanent smile on my face. Although this was my sixth Dungeon show, I loved going through it just as much as I had my first one all those years ago. The London Dungeon had changed my life—or at least the way I experienced haunts. It was a completely different experience than running from monsters or getting trapped with killers like in other haunts. The Berlin Dungeon characters were as hilarious as they were threatening, and I loved how each skit was based on actual history. Having come from a country fortunately free of the Black Death, I had always found the idea of it to be spellbinding; the fact that a single disease had destroyed almost a third of Europe's population over a few hundred years was almost impossible to imagine.

In the next chamber, a series of metal hooks glistened from the stone walls. Clamps and pliers of all sizes hung ominously beside them. Empty shackles and chains seemed almost eager for future victims. A wooden chair with restraints similar to those in the surgical room stood empty, and in the corner a cage appeared large enough to hold several prisoners. Standing before the horror, a woman faced us as we entered. She eyed us with a scowl, dressed in what looked like rags covered in soot. I took a seat with the others along a wooden bench, estimating the dingy woman to be around my age, though her wretched makeup suggested decades of abuse. She scanned each of us in turn until her gaze finally landed on me.

"You there," she barked. "Are you from France?"

I flinched at the question. No one had ever asked me that before. Did I *look* French?

"No," I said with a grin. "I'm from the United States."

Everyone in the group turned towards me. After months of traveling, I was well used to my accent getting me looks. I had also found that my voice was starting to sound strange even to me. It seemed like a lifetime since I had spoken to someone from home. I was beginning to feel almost alien to myself.

The grimy woman pointed towards the cage. "Get in. No Americans in here."

I laughed and did as instructed. A few people chuckled as I passed. Closing the iron door, I saw the once-deceased Sam enter the room and sit beside his friends.

"Welcome to the Torture Chamber...!" my warden exclaimed. Through the bars, I watched her pace before the group. "This room is all about incarceration, mutilation, and pain. In this year of 1618 there is plenty of confusion in the midst of war, and it is sometimes necessary to gain information." She stopped and smiled cruelly, making herself visible to both the crowd and me. "And that's my job. I am the torturer."

She pointed to a man seated beside the risen Sam and called him to her. He slowly approached.

"Now," she went on, standing beside her victim, "does anyone know what this instrument is for?" She picked up an exceptionally long set of pliers from a table of organized horror, then clicked them together.

The remaining audience looked at each other and shrugged. I smiled from my cage; *I* knew what they were for.

"This is a tongue tearer...," she said, turning the device towards the man at her side. "You, stick out your tongue!"

Almost in unison, the group put their hands over their mouths. I felt my own tongue instinctively retreat to the back of my mouth at the thought. My lips pursed tightly shut in protective mode. But the victim played along. He stuck out his tongue despite the female torturer holding the tool just inches away from it.

"I grip and I twist, twist, twist...." She grunted, jerking her weapon around without actually touching the volunteer.

Groans came from the group. My hand flew over my mouth. Compared to that, I was more than happy to be in my cage. I had seen the instrument in other Dungeon shows, but it certainly never got old. I had a sudden flashback of going through the torture museums in Italy with Fabio and Enrico. I remembered cringing with Enrico at tools just like that one and turning away from a sickle ripping off flesh in a mannequin display. Fortunately, the Berlin Dungeon mixed humor with its horrific history. I found it to be much more enjoyable.

The torturer put down her device and exchanged it for a new one. I felt my mouth relax as she held up a large, glistening hook. The other four spectators retracted their hands as their wide eyes looked upon the new object.

"And where do you think I would put *this?*" The woman thrust the hook towards the crowd.

As each took a turn with a guess, I grimaced in repulsion envisioning the scenarios: a large hook being used on someone's neck, armpit, stomach, or eyes. *If Vlad Tepes were here,* I thought, *he'd probably marry this girl.* But each guess proved incorrect. The torturer instructed her victim to turn around and bend over so that she could demonstrate where the hook would *really* be used. No one blinked. I could see them holding their breath and could only imagine that, like mine, their butts instinctively clenched.

Letting her victim go free, the pain inflictor waved her appalled audience away. "Now off with you. It's time to face justice for your crimes—except for you...." She pointed to me. "You stay there."

My companions crossed the room, grinning at me as they passed. I was pretty sure that the moment the room was clear, the torturer would open my cell and send me off. But there was still time to make the most of the scene. I reached out to them from between my bars with nervous eyes.

"Help!" I pleaded. "Don't leave me...."

The first three chuckled but continued by. The fourth man marched up to my door. He pulled it open without hesitation. I smiled at his defiance; I had seen that look before. I recognized it from the girls who had released me from Jason Voorhees at Underground Fear. Some people, I saw, refused to let one of their own suffer—even in jest.

"Hey," the torturer screamed, "how dare you release my prisoner!"

I thanked my rescuer, then ran out of the room with a laugh. *Saved!*

Beyond the stone cell, we entered an enormous, circular courtroom. A judge sat high above in his dark, authoritative robe and white wig. He scowled down at us. At first glance, I thought that the High Court official had to be about seventy years old, but after a moment I realized that he was probably no more than thirty. Once everyone was seated, he heatedly banged his gavel.

"Silence, all of you!" he yelled.

I smiled at his miserable expression. I also realized that each actor's accent was so undetectable that it was impossible to know if any of them were German. But I could only assume that they were, considering that this was the only show performed in English that day.

"In this year 1679," the judge yelled, "you stand in a sacred court of law! I declare this court in session." He banged his gavel then pointed it directly at me. "The first case is brought against *you!* Approach the bench. The rest of you, boo the sinner!"

I laughed as shouts of "boo!" echoed throughout the courtroom. After stepping onto a slightly raised platform, I looked up at the heated judge.

"Where are you from?" he demanded.

I held my breath at the question. Hopefully my answer wouldn't get me into even more trouble. "The United States."

"And where were you last night?" he screamed.

I tried to think. His mock anger had suddenly erased my memory. Where *had* I been? Where was I now? I wasn't home, I knew that. "I was... ummmm..."

"I'll tell you where you were!" he interrupted. His booming voice filled the room. He would have gotten along with Mephisto perfectly, I was sure of it. "You were seen by multiple witnesses dancing in the streets, tearing at your clothes, casting spells to summon Beelzebub, your lover!"

I laughed with the crowd. Did he know about my adventures on the Brocken? Now *that* would have been hilarious. But as absurd as his script was, I also knew that those exact accusations had once resulted in the deaths of tens of thousands of people around Europe—as well as those from the Salem Witch Trials. The fun farce definitely made learning about those darker days more enjoyable—and memorable, as it happened to *us*.

"You are hereby accused of witchcraft!" the judge proclaimed. "You have two options: you can plead guilty and be burned for your crimes... or you can plead insanity and go free."

My comrades smiled as I pondered the decision. "I plead insanity!" I said cheerfully.

"Insanity it is." The gavel crashed down once again. His Honor looked down at me with contempt. "Now you must prove your insanity to this court: you must repeat for us your actions from last night. Go on then—strip off your clothes and dance for Beelzebub so we can all see."

I gasped in surprise, then looked to my group. The girls burst out laughing. The men only waited.

"Oh... ummmm..." I looked up at the judge innocently. "You know what? I forgot—I *am* guilty!"

For an instant I saw a smile break His Honor's face. "You *are* guilty?" he repeated, then forced back the grin. "Oh, well then—you are hereby sentenced to burn for your crimes!" He slammed down the gavel. "Step down. Boo her!"

Our onward journey led to additional horrors. We wandered through more streets of plague, and encountered the ghost of the White Lady said to haunt Berlin, before ending up outside what resembled a ramshackle barbershop. A woman in heavy makeup greeted us. Her low-cut top, black corset, and short, tattered skirt looked right out of the nineteenth century. She warned us against the dangers of wandering the streets alone then invited us to meet her friend and "customer" Mr. Großmann.

"Come on in this way," she said, as we stepped across a creaking porch. "He's *dying* to meet you. Just have a seat and make yourselves uncomfortable."

Tall, wooden thrones formed a semicircle within a large, dark room. Mr. Großmann, we were told, would soon be joining us. As the owner of the town's sausage store, Großmann was said to be particularly handy with a knife. In a flash we were left in darkness, as our coy guide extinguished the light and disappeared. The six of us sat in silence, until I heard a man whisper in my ear.

"What have we here? Lots of pretty ladies, I see."

The voice was deep and brutish. I smiled at its thick, London accent. It appeared to come from just inches away.

"My name is Mr. Großmann," the man continued in the darkness. Heavy footsteps echoed around the room. All of it, I knew, came from a hidden speaker in the back of my chair.

"I can cut, chop, and slice the choicest pieces of meat from any animal you put in front of me—dead or alive!"

As he spoke, quick flicks of his blade seemed to move across my neck and ears, caused by slight whiffs of air that I knew came from secret blowers in the seat. I heard the girls beside me shriek from the simulated touch. I laughed at their excited panic. As much fun as it had been to see the story of Faust performed on the Brocken, there was definitely something to be said for a psycho killer playfully threatening to hack you to pieces.

"Relax...," the voice growled, "I wouldn't want to spill any blood—yet."

The growls finally ceased as a blast of air shot across my throat. Everyone screamed in the darkness, then burst out laughing.

When the lights came back on, our prostitute friend had returned.

"Ahhh, still alive, huh?" she teased. I looked around the room with a peaceful grin. Everyone giggled, hyper about their near-death experience. We had all just had a close encounter with one of Germany's nineteenth-century serial killers. I had never read about him before, but I sensed that whatever I might have learned, it wouldn't have created quite the same impression as feeling the flick of his blade in the bowels of the city.

"Well, you'd better get out of here now...," the woman warned, gesturing towards the exit. "But consider yourselves lucky—for *this* time you survived the Berlin Dungeon!"

Chapter 8

Ireland's Mystical Dead

"You lie there... shivering... screaming...
gasping for breath...."

Thomas in Dublin

"Be afraid.... Be very afraid."

I quickly withdrew my finger from the buzzer and looked around to see if anyone had heard. Large, lavish homes along the dark Dublin street stood quiet at midnight. Spying not a soul, I felt my breath come a bit easier.

I had fulfilled my promise. My new host, Thomas, had specified that he would only stay awake for my arrival should I speak those exact words over his apartment intercom. With that behind me, I could relax. I had finally made it; after eight months of travels, I was in a native English-speaking country at last. My host even hailed from the motherland. A loud click soon came from an electronic latch in the door, and I gratefully pushed it open.

Inside, a lean man in his mid-thirties smiled coyly in a Trinity T-shirt and sweatpants. "You followed your orders perfectly," he said with a London accent.

With a loud sigh, I heaved my bag across the hall to where he stood, then whispered in the late hour: "Thank God nobody heard... I would have died!"

The man shook his head. Six-foot-three with short, brown hair, he loomed over me and welcomed me with a hug. "No way, that would have been hysterical. Come on in. I'm Thomas, nice to meet you."

Inside stretched a room of elegance: sheer drapes covered elongated windows reaching to a towering ceiling. Silver candelabra adorned a solid-wood table that ran from one pristine, white wall to another. Along a perfectly lined bookshelf, I scanned titles about business marketing, psychology, and philosophy.

"This is where you'll be sleeping." Thomas motioned to a small alcove branching off the living room. On the floor, a pile of brown and gold blankets lay between adjacent loveseats, with a half-dozen silk pillows thrown haphazardly about.

"Wow," I said, admiring it all. It felt like a Turkish coffeehouse inside a Victorian mansion. "This is great, thanks."

I plopped down my bag as Thomas walked across the bed mound in his socks, then stretched out on one of the loveseats. I removed my shoes and repeated the action across from him. After my long day of airports, planes, and buses, the cushions felt as soft as clouds. My new host discussed his move to Dublin to attend Trinity, where he'd studied business and psychology, and his current work in business marketing.

"But you must be pretty sleepy," he said after a long while.

"Very." I rubbed my eyes. "But thanks so much for staying up to meet me."

"No problem. Ever since I saw your Couchsurfing profile, I've been interested in what you're doing. Traveling for so long to look at scary shows... I've never heard of anyone doing something like that."

"Well, I love scary shows and I love traveling. It's amazing to see all kinds of characters in different parts of the world. There are more similarities than I was expecting. And the haunted attractions are almost always good in their own way."

"But *that*, of all things..." He looked at me intensely. I suddenly felt like an alien life form being studied with scientific fascination. "Have you ever thought about why you're so... almost *obsessed* with it all?"

I chuckled. "I don't think it's an obsession. It's more of a passion. I like looking at the different ways people conceive of what's scary."

"What's the scariest thing you've seen?" He smiled at me in anticipation.

I thought about it. My mind searched through foggy memories from the past few months. He was obviously hoping for something remarkable.

"Well... I wouldn't say I've seen anything *scary*. But the shows I've gone to are really good."

I described Krampus wailing on spectators in the streets without mercy and being trapped with Jason Voorhees at Underground Fear. I laughed over patrons getting threatened with torture devices in the Berlin Dungeon while I watched from the confines of my cage. Thomas nodded, listening patiently.

"But you know, they're not *scary*," I said. "At least, not to me. They're just fun."

"Have you ever *really* been scared?"

"On the trip, or ever?"

"Ever."

I tried to think back. "I accidentally locked myself in the attic once when I was a kid—other than that, not really." I gave a tired blink at the memory. "I guess it made me realize that there were no monsters waiting for me up there, so I could pretty much rule out that they were waiting for me anywhere else."

"That must be pretty disappointing, though." Thomas cocked his head at me, resembling a therapist delving deeper during a psychotherapy session. "Going to all those shows, and they don't even scare you."

I laughed slowly. "It's not about feeling scared. I like looking at all types of monster characters. I like to see what people *envision* to be scary. There's a lot of creativity in it—in portraying the strange and running elaborate shows about it. But there's nothing to be scared of when it's all fake."

"So you like the aesthetics of it all."

"Yes, and the theatrics of it."

"But you only seem to be interested in the ones that are scary." Tired but intrigued, Thomas regarded me. I got the feeling that he would not rest until his new puzzle was solved. "The people I know who like those types of shows actually want to feel *scared*."

I rested my head on my arm. I smiled at the memory of my tour mates back at Underground Fear. I remembered them running in panic as Samara made her slow descent from the well. "Oh yeah, I see plenty of that. But I'm drawn to anything that's scary *themed,* dark but magical and kind of mystical, you know?" I reflected on gazing down at Budapest's well-dweller crawling across the floor; she had looked devious and beautiful in her ability to frighten without saying a word. *What an art.* "To me, that's what makes a show exciting and fun."

"I think you'll find that Ireland is more mystical than scary." Thomas slowly pulled himself up off the loveseat and stretched. "People here are more likely to tell you a joke than throw you into a cage or whip you with an animal tail."

I laughed, waving goodnight as my host headed off to bed. "Okay, good. I'll be sure to let you know which ends up happening."

The Dublin Ghostbus Tour

I spent the next day exploring Dublin. Flowers and potted plants splashed color onto brick and wood buildings along cobblestone and pavement streets. Flags of every nationality hung above pubs. Clover-embroidered sweatshirts and leprechaun dolls hung in the windows. I walked the spacious sidewalks, smiling at every chalkboard sign advertising drink specials. Newspaper headlines, magazines, and posters looked equally beautiful, each written in my sorely missed, native English.

All around me, conversations from the crowds was music to my ears:

"Do you want to stop for a bite to eat?"

"Let's go to the Guinness factory!"

"I think it's this way. Let's ask someone...."

Irish and British, Scottish and American accents were everywhere. Each sounded fascinating in its own right. I made chitchat with people as I passed, eagerly saying, "Good morning! How are you? Nice day!" I loved every reply and fought the desire to hug everyone. Heads no longer turned when I spoke. No one shrugged in confusion, grinned, then walked away when I talked to them. Communicating felt as natural as breathing, and at last, my own voice no longer sounded alien to me.

And then when I reached my destination, Dublin Bus Headquarters, the Grim Reaper appeared.

Along O'Connell Street, a gigantic, looming phantom emerged from a sea of purple mist in the night. Surrounded by about thirty tourists, I gaped at the double-decker bus pulling up to the sidewalk and the cloaked creature painted along it. It looked as if Charon from Greek mythology had chosen a new method for transporting souls to the underworld. As soon as the hell-on-wheels pulled to a stop, a man in black hopped out.

"Welcome to the Dublin Ghostbus Tour," he bellowed, motioning us over.

I eagerly got in line, gave the man my name, and watched him check it off his clipboard. I had never taken a ghost *bus* tour before, and after a long day on my feet, the combination of ghosts and sitting sounded perfect.

Onboard, long-deceased passengers wasted away on web-strewn benches. Rather than the typical rows of seats, a small space composed a waiting area for the dead. I admired the bulging eyes and skeletal frames before me, each looking terror-stricken in anticipation of reaching their final destination. I loved the bus at once.

While I marveled at the scene, two girls in their early twenties stepped onboard behind me. They giggled at the skeletons, immediately snapping me out of my stupor. I crossed the space and passed through a thick curtain to find an expansive cell beyond it. Walls of stone resembled a dark dungeon deep in the belly of the city. I stood admiring it, suddenly finding it hard to believe that I was actually inside a bus. In a dismal corner, a skeletal card player smiled eerily from a table shaped like a coffin. Long-eroded lips exposed huge, yellow teeth. White hair fell past shadowed, sunken eyes to his dusty dinner jacket. In his hand, yellowing playing cards composed a royal flush. I stared at the figure, drawn to its red pupils and a painted skull on the death-framed table beneath him. This was the dark, mystical ambiance that I had tried to describe to Thomas. After a moment, the two girls behind me caught up.

"Wow, look at that," the taller of them said. "He's cool."

"That's from the Hellfire Club," said her friend. Both sounded Irish. "You know that place, right? They say the devil used to go there and play poker for people's souls."

"Looks like this guy lucked out," I remarked, motioning to the cards.

The taller of the pair chuckled. "Yeah, I wonder how often that happened!"

Across from the dead, a frail woman sat hunched inside a small, iron cage. Appearing alive and terrified, the prop wore only a dirty blanket for clothes, her gray shroud wrapped around little more than skin and bone. Barely an inch came between her and the bars, and I estimated the cage to be about a tenth the size of the one that I had been in thrown in back in Berlin. These hanging cages, I knew, were used to suspend prisoners to starve and rot on high for the world to see. It was a horrid way to go— and a rather tight squeeze for scare shows.

Turning a corner, I caught the gaze of additional dead eyes along a hall of portraits. I studied the first graven image—a sneering, undead zombie dressed in his finest—as the girls walked closely behind. Suddenly, a roar of sliding wood filled the corridor. The three of us jumped and gasped. The framed undead before us disappeared. A black-hooded head took its place. A high-pitched scream reverberated from the void where its face should have been. I felt a shiver rush through my body as the horrid sound broke the silence. The girls clung to each other and cried out. In a flash, the framed image returned. I turned to the pair beside me. Their wide eyes looked back. We immediately burst out laughing as the mysterious phantom lay concealed behind the wall once again.

"I love those!" I said after catching my breath.

The girl who had known about the Hellfire Club nodded. "I knew that would happen!" She fell against her friend in laughter.

"Ugh," the other said. "*I* didn't!"

At the end of the hall, a winding staircase brought us to the bus's second deck. A Victorian theater stretched before us. Over a dozen rows of deep-red seats faced a small stage in the center of the bus. Some seats that would have normally faced front had been repositioned backwards.

Velvet, tasseled curtains covering the windows concealed all of O'Connell Street, which now seemed oceans away. The rows closest to the stage were already filled, with low light giving the appearance of parlor guests awaiting an illusionist. I slipped onto a soft cushion towards the back, wanting a good view of everyone's reactions as well as the show itself. My new friends sat behind me.

"Isn't this place incredible?" I asked, turning to them excitedly.

The shorter of the two seemed to match the gleam in my eye. "Yeah! I've done this tour before, but it's my girlfriend's first time. I take all my friends on it when they come to visit me."

"Really?" I felt a sudden sense of envy; I immediately wished that *I* lived in Dublin. "That's a great idea."

Once the remainder of our group had boarded, the man in black hopped up the stairs and leapt onstage.

"Welcome, friends, to the Dublin Ghostbus!" He eagerly scanned his audience while clasping his hands before him. His subtle Irish accent projected clearly through a wireless microphone headset beside his ear. "My name is Vincent and tonight we are being led by our demented driver, Frances. Say hello, Frances!"

When he leaned over the railing and looked down the stairs, two beeps sounded from the deck below. I laughed with the crowd, smiling at the girls behind me.

"Friends," Vincent continued, "tonight we are going to embark on a series of stories to transport you back into Dublin's history. Scenes," he said, now glaring mysteriously at those before the stage, "which become vivid in the dark...." Howling wolves began to sound as if off in the distance. I giggled under my breath as it grew steadily louder, as though we had suddenly entered a dark, sinister wood. "Listen to them...," Vincent said, his eyes growing wild. "The children of the night—what sweet music they make...!"

I laughed at the *Dracula* reference. I had the distinct feeling that Vincent would have gotten along great with Robert back in Transylvania. As the bus gave a slow bounce, I knew that we were pulling away from the curb and beginning our journey.

"Dublin has incredible stories of its horrid past," our host went on. "The first person I'd like to tell you about is a nineteenth-century doctor named Samuel Clossey. Here's a man who would rather have your dead body over a slab in his classroom than in a graveyard, resting in peace."

Vincent pulled a white doctor's coat from below a table by the stage. He draped it over himself as casually as a pro preparing for a plague examination.

"Dr. Clossey purchased stolen corpses from body snatchers and used them in his lectures to medical students." With a quick move of the hand, our guide revealed a life-size, plastic torso. He held the human remains in front of him as though it were still alive and standing upright.

"Dr. Clossey would take the corpse like so," he went on. "To give a thorough demonstration of the human body, he would prize open the skin, then plunge deep into the oozing gap...." Vincent stuck his hand into the plastic cadaver. A look of concentration fell upon his face, as though he were fumbling for just the right contents inside. "The doctor would yank out handfuls of organs, guts, and bile...." A tangle of gray intestines hung from his fingers as he withdrew them from the prop. They looked soft, sleek, disgusting. I shut my eyes, shaking my head with a shudder and a laugh. The girls behind me giggled.

"He, then, would say these words to his students," Vincent continued. "'This, gentlemen, is what you are....'" He held the handful of innards to a young woman close to the stage. She cringed into her seat with a contorted smile. "...And it is *all* you are.'"

I laughed, loving both the grim scene and its existential reference. *Well done, Clossey.*

The bus soon pulled to a stop outside the Royal College of Surgeons. Vincent instructed us to open the curtains next to us so that we could see the buildings. This, we were told, was where the gruesome doctor had taught.

"Could the spirit of Dr. Clossey still be here?" the guide asked with an air of mystery. A slow, eerie tune began to play as we looked over the white columns and gray stone. "Students say this building has a memory.

They hear footsteps and a strange whistling when no one is around.... Perhaps it's the lonely doctor, forever searching for his next victim."

Glancing back, I chuckled at Vincent's crazed eyes and mad grin. He reminded me of the female jester back at the Berlin Dungeon. Like that show, the Ghostbus was an excellent combination of dark humor and sinister history.

"If you'll look outside the bus now, friends," Vincent later announced, "you'll see a small house where Bram Stoker once lived."

I lunged to my window with a gasp. Along terraced, white-paned windows and doors, a black, oval plaque stood out from the brick. *Bram Stoker 1847-1912,* it read. *Author of Dracula lived here.* I stared at it in awe. I suddenly wished that my vampire-hunting companion back in Brasov were with me. I remembered standing with Robert beside a bust of the Irish writer outside Hotel Castle Dracula, then walking in the dank basement and feeling Dracula's bones flying past us in the dark.

After a Ghostbus Horror Quiz in which we had to identify horror films from clips of their soundtracks, the bus pulled up to a tall, iron gate. With a devilish smile, Vincent asked us to join him for a tour in the burial grounds. A wide, paved path led us around sparse, stone markers spread throughout a well-kept garden. We followed our guide to an enclosed, stone ruin, where ivy and moss covered the remains of an ancient chapel. Hundreds of demolished gravestones lay scattered in pieces at our feet, resembling broken fragments of sidewalk after a massive earthquake.

"This is the oldest section of St. Kevin's Cemetery," Vincent announced. He set down a large, black satchel that he had taken off the bus. "It dates back to the nineteenth century, a time when body snatching raged in Dublin." Folding his hands solemnly, he cast a devious gaze around the group. "Nightly patrolmen guarded graveyards like this one against body snatchers and thieves. They were looking for jewelry, teeth,... and bodies they could sell to doctors like Samuel Clossey."

I smiled at the story. I had heard about legends of body snatching since I was a kid. It felt almost surreal now to be in a graveyard where it had actually taken place.

"Body snatchers had to be quiet," Vincent continued, "but quick. Once they dug down and reached the newly buried coffin, they had a particular practice for removing its contents. Chris!" Our guide opened his palm to me. "You'll help me with this, won't you?"

I froze at the sight of his wild smile. This, I realized, would be the price I'd pay for recognizing the most horror movies during our Ghostbus quiz. I slowly walked towards him in trepidation, then followed his instructions to turn around and face the crowd. From behind me, I heard a rustling in the mysterious black bag. An instant later, a large, metal hook appeared just inches from my face.

"After breaking through the head of the coffin...," Vincent said, stepping behind me, "the body snatcher would put his hook below the skull of the corpse."

I didn't blink as the gleaming metal moved towards my chin.

"He would then tug...."

I felt my head move instinctively backward as the tiny, sharp point pressed against my skin. I didn't breathe. *Not even the torturer back in Berlin had gotten* this *up close and personal.* My gaze sought out the girls who had sat behind me on the bus. My eyes felt about as wide as the coins for Charon's payment.

Why do I *get the hook...?* I tried to ask the girls silently.

I suddenly missed my cage.

The girls only giggled.

"You okay there, Chris?" Vincent asked. The back of my head now rested against his chest.

"Mmmm-hmmmm." I dared not speak. When the hook was finally removed, I eagerly bounced back to the crowd, breathing easily once again.

Back on the bus, additional ghost stories followed. We periodically opened the curtains of our Victorian-style stage show to glimpse sections of Dublin that I knew I never would have seen otherwise. We drove by St. Patrick's Cathedral, where Vincent explained some practices used during times when premature burial was a common fear. He described the living writhing in their coffins deep underground, mistakenly pronounced dead

when they had actually suffered from narcolepsy or slipped into a coma. All the poor souls had to depend on beneath six feet of dirt was a single string tied to their finger. It connected to a bell beside their grave marker above and, with any luck, the slightest movement of their hand would cause it to ring.

"Now I want everyone to close their eyes," Vincent said after the story.

I did as he instructed, shutting out the elegant theater and my many companions.

"I want you to all to imagine," his voice continued in the darkness, "how it would feel to be six feet under the ground in a coffin... buried alive...." His voice dropped to a whisper. "How would it feel?"

I felt my shoulders rise in silent laughter. I could tell that Vincent enjoyed his work enormously. But that wasn't surprising—who *wouldn't* want to do something like this?

"It would be very, very dark...." Our guide's voice stayed low and ominous. "Pitch black... and cold, icy cold..."

I envisioned the scene. Blinded, now from being underground, I imagined lying in a hard, wooden coffin deep within the earth. I felt cold and alone, telling myself that no one knew I was still alive.

"You lie there... shivering... screaming... gasping for breath...."

I felt my breathing become strained. The air seemed thin. I imagined that, should I open my eyes, the blackness around me wouldn't disappear. I would eventually die here, alone. But as I had described to Thomas, there was nothing really to fear. It was all just a story. But it was an exciting one. It was a game that Vincent was making based on pretending that we really *were* in danger, that we really *could* die right here and now. And it was a game we could all enjoy together. We could look death and fear in the face—we could feel it, see it, hear it—then come right back again completely safe and sound. And everyone around me, each lying in their own grave, knew it.

"Then perhaps you feel on your face," Vincent whispered, "a wet sensation...."

I heard a woman scream from the opposite end of the bus. A burst of laughter followed. I smiled, keeping my eyes pressed shut despite wanting to see what was happening.

"A big, fat worm," Vincent continued, "pops onto your cheek..."

More screams followed, growing closer and closer to my seat.

"...looking for some fresh flesh to devour...."

A sudden chill ran threw me as drops of liquid splashed onto my cheeks and forehead. I giggled, wiping them away. Not a moment later the girls behind me shrieked, then exploded in laughter.

An unexpected twist, I thought. *Nice touch.*

Castle Dracula

The next adventure brought me a few miles outside Dublin to the area of Clontarf. Hopping out of a city double-decker, sadly without even a single chained corpse or skeleton inside, I headed towards Westwood Gym. As intrigued as I'd been about a ghost tour taking place on a bus, the Castle Dracula magic show sounded even more incredible. According to their website, it was held inside a large gym complex. I couldn't wait to see how this would be pulled off. As an avid runner, I refrained from my usual draw to rooms filled with treadmills and aerobic machines and instead followed a group of thirty up an empty stairwell. On the second floor, I immediately forgot about the dozens of exercisers below and the seemingly normal world outside.

A dark, stone corridor stretched before me. Framed posters of Hammer *Dracula* films from the fifties and sixties glowed eerily red along the walls. I followed instructions to line up against them, then saw Bram Stoker's birth and death certificates behind additional panes of glass, along with sections of his original *Dracula* manuscript. After a few moments, the sound of a strange voice came from the end of the hall.

"Oh my, who has entered my master's castle...?"

I leaned past the row of spectators. There in a striped prison uniform stood a man chained at the wrists. He was short and quite thin, and his pale face looked worn and dirty as he gaped at us in delirious wonder. "Visitors...," he said in a high-pitched, British accent. "More visitors, oh my..."

The odd character began shuffling down the hall, his hair in disarray. A dull scraping sound accompanied him from a second chain binding his ankles.

"My name is Renfield," he said. "I have been a resident of this castle for quite some time. Now that you've come you'll have to mind yourself— you'll have to be careful at every turn...!" He paused, then jerked his head and looked around anxiously. "Mina! Mina, where are you?"

After a moment he turned back, as if suddenly remembering we were there. I smiled at the perfect rendition of Dr. Seward's "pet lunatic" from the *Dracula* novel. He was just as morbidly excitable as the writer described. I could envision him consuming insects in an asylum somewhere with the mad hope of strengthening his powers for his master.

"But you won't be going through the castle alone, oh no...." Renfield giggled. "Dr. Van Helsing will guide you. I would stay close to him, if I were you! You might be safer... but I wouldn't be too sure." He turned away from us again, moving down the hall and calling in hysterics: "Mina! I'm coming, Mina."

As his voice echoed away, I chuckled to a young woman beside me. I knew that he was calling to Jonathan's love interest in the story. "He was awesome."

The young woman laughed. "Yeah, he was really good."

Chuckles ran throughout the crowd until a tall, robust man appeared where the lunatic had vanished. Dressed in a blue laboratory coat, he held a burning oil lamp before him and leaned against a crude walking stick. His eyes were barely visible behind a mop of shaggy, brown hair, but I could still see him staring at us with deep interest.

"What have we here? Some strangers have come to the castle...?"

His calm, Dutch-accented voice was a stark contrast to Renfield's mania. He held his pale light up to a young couple beside him. They immediately giggled and backed away. The large stranger shot them a queer look, as if pondering their own mental state after enduring our previous host.

"But why on earth have you come here tonight?" he asked. "This is not a place for the faint of heart, you know...."

"My name is Dr. Abraham Van Helsing," he said after a pause. He slowly proceeded down the hall, peering at each person as he passed. "I don't know why you've taken your life in your hands by coming here, but it's your funeral now, isn't it?" He stopped, leaning towards a man beside him and widening his eyes as if demanding an explanation. When he didn't get one, he moved on.

"I guess you'd better stay with me, then. I'll take you through this castle and show you just what we're dealing with here. You might be able to help me and could do with learning a thing or two. Just stay close, very close, and maybe you'll survive to see the sunrise."

I giggled silently as he cast an ominous gaze down the hall. Everyone remained quiet, smiling at the legendary vampire hunter, until he motioned for us to follow.

Along an equally dark corridor, hundreds of bats hung above us from the ceiling. Seemingly alive, reptile-resembling mammals hovered in midair. Others stood against the wall with their scaly wings outstretched, as if ready to take flight. One large creature resembled a bat-like man with a gray, skeletal face, pointed ears, and gigantic wings folded over a bare chest. I recognized the figure from the 1992 film *Bram Stoker's Dracula.*

"Everyone, this way, in here...," Van Helsing called from the head of the line.

We followed him into a large, stone chamber. Inside, a faded, wooden coffin lay on top of a cement slab. Across from it, a red-stained sheet covered a seemingly humanoid monstrosity beneath. In a small alcove, an exquisite Dracula replica lay inside an open, black coffin. He was wrinkled and bald save for thin, gray hair above the ears. Blood trickled from either side of his mouth, matching the bright red satin lining his resting place. I admired it; it was the perfect depiction of the aged count from when Jonathan Harker had first explored the castle.

"This is the vampire's lair," Van Helsing said. He motioned for us to join him beside the plain, wooden casket. "If you want to be a true hunter, you need to see what we're dealing with. But first I'll need two volunteers. Do we have any strong men here?"

I couldn't help but smirk as every man in the group looked at each other questioningly. Compared to Van Helsing's proportions, no one seemed eager to pronounce themselves strong.

"How about you, sir...?" Van Helsing pointed to a tall, well-built man, then another of similar stature in the back. "And you, sir. If each of you could take one end of the lid and carefully place it here on the floor."

They did as instructed. I stared, intrigued, at the pine box with a thin, red cloth draped inside it.

"Now..." The hunter scanned the group. "Who would like to volunteer to get inside the coffin?"

A few girls giggled. Surely, I thought, he was joking. But Van Helsing only waited. Seeing that he was serious, I immediately wanted to raise my hand. I'd been in several coffins in Halloween displays over the years, and there was always, as the saying goes, room for one more. But with greater interest in taking a picture of the person inside it, I forced my hands to stay still.

"No one?" Van Helsing prodded. "It's important to understand your enemy, you know; to get inside their head. I guarantee you: Dracula is already inside yours." He paused, continuing to look around. "No one wants to get inside and lie like a vampire?"

"Okay, I will!" a young woman said in an Irish accent. She raised her hand, her black leather jacket shining against dark leggings. "What the hell!"

"Very good." Van Helsing aided the woman as she stepped into the hexagonal box that stood level to her knees. I watched with a smile, spying others do the same. She casually lay back and folded her hands over her stomach, then laughed when I took her picture.

"Is this your first time in a coffin?" Van Helsing asked, looking down at his volunteer curiously.

She giggled. "Yes."

He smiled coyly. "It won't be your last."

The woman cracked up with the rest of us. After all the Dracula-based shows in Transylvania, I loved how this one was the most interactive and built around humor. It also seemed to take place in the actual "gloom-haunted rooms" of the "wild and uncanny castle" of which Stoker had written.

"A big round of applause, please, for the young woman for being so brave."

After helping her back out, the tall doctor beckoned for us to gather around the covered form across the room.

"Now if you want to be true hunters," he said, "you need to learn the proper way of destroying a vampire. That means staking the creature through the heart. Who wants to give it a try?"

Several men threw up their hands. I couldn't help but be surprised at the sudden change in participation. *Why do men always volunteer to destroy things?*

Pulling a stake and mallet from his side satchel, Van Helsing handed them to a new volunteer.

"You place the stake here...," he said, centering the sharp, ancient-looking tool over the sheeted creature. "Then hold the mallet like this. We'll all count to three...." He lifted the mallet high into the air then slowly brought it to a mere inch above the stake. "And on three, you strike. Okay?"

The man nodded and took the weapons. As he studied the creature he was about to destroy, I thought back to the novel. Van Helsing had taught the heartbroken Arthur Holmwood how to destroy his bride-turned-vampire Lucy with a stake and hammer. Whatever lay hidden before us now looked much bigger than the frail Lucy and much more muscular than the bloodthirsty count. But the new slayer-in-training seemed not to care as he slowly lifted the mallet.

"One...," we all began to count.

A roar immediately came from beneath the sheet. The volunteer jumped back and gasped, his hand frozen in midair as the undead bolted upright. It extended two muscular arms as if to attack whoever had dared threaten his life and, perhaps worse, disrupt his sleep.

Wow, I thought after the laughter died down. *That is one trusting actor!*

The covered creature resumed his slumber as we followed Van Helsing out into the hall. A set of spiral stairs brought us to a small alcove where a man sat huddled in a straitjacket. His eyes were fixed in a deranged, delirious stare. Chained to the wall beside him, a muscular creature seemed to resemble a cross between the Hunchback of Notre Dame and the Elephant Man, holding a human brain in one large, twisted hand. Both were only props: still-life versions of other inmates from Dr. Seward's asylum.

Spiked, cracked skulls formed a fence along a narrow passageway above. Their hollow eyes and frozen screams composed an image that I thought would have made both Bram Stoker and Vlad Tepes proud. After descending a second set of stairs, I saw a dozen horrid faces glaring out from framed portraits along a dismal hallway. I walked timidly with my group, finding the scene to be rather familiar.

"Right this way; come along...!" Van Helsing called from the front. The next thing I knew, the image of a sickly, skeletal woman came crashing down beside me. It disappeared into the wall, and a loud growl bellowed from within the blank space. A young woman ahead of me screamed. I jumped back from the piercing noise that made my ears vibrate. In a flash, the ghoulish creature resumed its place on the wall. I laughed with the group, thinking back to the same tactic back on the Dublin Ghostbus.

Two intriguing figures awaited us in another corridor. A tall, cloaked specter glared at the strangers before him. Bloody, gaping holes around his eyes and mouth suggested that his skin had been removed and stitched back into place. Beside him, metal wrist restraints bound a man to a large, wooden chair, a black hood covering his face. Both remained perfectly still until the mysterious specter forcefully pulled a lever by his side. A loud electric buzzing erupted, causing his seated companion to spring to life. The bound prisoner writhed and pulsated in his chair, muffled screams mixing with sharp cracks and whining pops. The lever was eventually released and the prisoner sat lifeless once again.

That's odd, I thought. *I don't remember anyone being electrocuted in Dracula.*

But before I could question it further, an explosion of sound ripped through the silence. I jumped and turned around. There before me stood a stitched face of contorted flesh. The creature held a chainsaw streaked with blood. Despite recoiling at the deafening noise, I found myself smiling in recognition. It seemed that Leatherface from *The Texas Chainsaw Massacre* had somehow found his way to Dracula's Castle. But the enthusiasm from my group mates was much less nostalgic. A pandemonium of screams and shoves surrounded me as the killer

advanced towards us. He revved his weapon of destruction, holding it up before an apron smeared in human misery. Van Helsing quickly stepped aside and let the frenzy pass him. I slowly followed, glancing back at the infamous monster in approval.

Silence resumed in a graveyard. Faded and mossed stones sank behind an iron fence. Beyond it, a small stage at the end of a large chamber resembled a Gothic church. Winged, horned gargoyles crouched over stained-glass windows, eerily glowing in low, blue light. I recognized the old, ruined chapel from Stoker's novel. It was also, I saw, where Castle Dracula's magic show would take place. After everyone followed the vampire hunter's instructions to take a seat, the lights were extinguished. Long moments of silence passed in darkness. Eventually, a male voice came from the stage.

"Welcome to my Graveyard Theater," it said. "And to my castle. I trust that you all arrived here safely."

The blue lights slowly returned to reveal a phantom before us. He stood dressed in a dark suit, top hat, and black and red cape. An expressionless, white mask concealed half of his face.

"My name is Ronan MacGabhann," he said. "Here in the birth town of Bram Stoker, you may have already come across a vampire or two in this castle. And with the help of Dr. Van Helsing, you may have mastered the art of how to destroy such a creature. What you're about to witness tonight may lead you to believe that I, too, am a vampire. I will leave that to you to decide."

With a smooth gesture, he removed his mask. The man scanned the crowd. He appeared remarkably young, with pale skin, shining eyes, and light brown hair, though I could hear from his voice that he was a few decades older than he looked.

For the next hour, the mysterious Ronan performed a series of acts with help from the audience. He read our thoughts. He communicated with the dead. He predicted our actions before we even knew what was happening. Each act resembled a magic trick that I had seen performed elsewhere, but never through the portrayal of a sinister trickster with seemingly demonic powers.

"So you see," Ronan eventually declared, pacing the stage after his final act, "I have demonstrated many abilities beyond human understanding. You may be led to believe, therefore, that I truly am a vampire." He extended an open palm towards us with a smile. "Perhaps you will never know."

A short intermission followed. I raved about the show to Sam, the young woman who had enjoyed a quick rest in one of Dracula's coffins. After everyone had time to wander the Graveyard Theater, the show resumed with magician Nevin Cody. I looked at his tall, burly frame dressed in slacks and a sweater and couldn't help but find his physique to be a little familiar. Unlike Ronan, Nevin based his show on comedy. Card tricks and disappearing acts were accompanied by music and help from the audience, each so hysterical that my face soon grew sore from laughter.

Once the performers took their bows, I was happy to meet the cast. Magicians Ronan and Nevin introduced scare actors Lorcan and Brendan McIvor, who had played the roles of Leatherface and the executioner. I praised their show until the other guests had left and told Ronan about my reasons for coming to Ireland. His face lit up.

"Your project sounds fascinating," he said. "Tell you what: if you'd like to come back for our next show, we'd love to have you in the haunt as one of our scare actors."

Still shaking his hand, I felt my grip instinctively tighten.

Act? I thought. *In front of* people? I couldn't blink. The thought of it made my stomach instantly morph into solid rock. My only previous haunt acting experience had involved dressing up as the Grim Reaper. Years back, I had stood outside a Connecticut attraction, silently manning the entrance without having to scare anyone. It had been fun only because it involved very low exposure—with the added bonus of pretty much zero chance of screwing up.

But Ronan and Nevin smiled broadly. *An American writer working in our show,* their beaming faces seemed to say. *How exciting!*

I didn't want to let them down. And how could I pass up such a kind offer—an offer to be part of a Dracula show in the very town where Bram

Stoker had been born? *If the writer knew that I feared the very thought of it, he would crawl out of his grave to haunt me for sure.*

I smiled feebly, trying to hide my panic. "Okay," I forced out. "I would love to."

"Great!" Ronan clapped me on the shoulder and squeezed it gently. "We'll see you in two weeks!"

Irish Travels

To get a sense of Ireland outside Dublin, I spent the next week in County Cork. My host, Tony, was a retired college professor. Always jumping at the opportunity to meet new people and show them the countryside, Tony drove me through mazes of rolling hills, lush and green, with so much livestock that I dubbed it all "The Invasion of the Sheep." His love for teaching was evident as he recounted the history of English occupation in Ireland, deciphered the Irish language on road signs, and discussed fighting between Catholics and Protestants in the north.

The following week brought me to Limerick. My host, Carl, was a second-year medical student. In his late thirties, he had moved to Ireland from London for college. After reading my Couchsurfing profile, Carl was interested in discussing any connections that scare tourism might have in allowing people to come to terms with death.

"That's the main reason I decided to become a doctor," he said almost immediately upon meeting me. Carl was easy to spot at the bus station. He sat at a table buried in binders and piles of highlighted notes. "For me, I'm looking at death and trying to stop it," he said. "But it looks like all the shows that you like are about poking fun at death."

I sat across from him at the table and nodded. Although both of Carl's parents had come from India, my new host sounded just as English as Thomas had back in Dublin.

"Yeah, they kind of poke fun at it," I said. "But that's a bigger theme for Day of the Dead in Mexico. That's where you'll find people dressing like skeletons with fancy clothing and jewelry. It demonstrates that everyone shares the same fate, whether we're rich *or* poor. But it's also about remembering people after they're gone. I think that for a lot of people, the main reason they fear dying is because they're afraid they'll be forgotten."

Carl nodded, listening intently. I could see that the subject was a big concern for him.

"But the other types of shows I've been looking at aren't based on teaching anything about death or dying. If anything, they poke fun at *fear*—the idea of being afraid of *anything*, really. Devils and monsters and all these creatures pretend to be frightening and make people feel like they could be hurt or killed, but of course there's really nothing to be scared about. We're the ones psyching ourselves out about it all. But I guess you could say that about anything—it's not just limited to scare shows or death."

"So there's never a question of *why* people have to die?" Carl sat on the edge of his seat. I got the feeling that he was asking me a question he had posed to himself and others for a long time. Maybe someone like me, he thought, who was fascinated with shows and characters reflecting death, would have the same questions—or, better yet, an *answer*—if he had yet to find one in all those binders of notes.

"Well," I said slowly, "for me, there isn't a question of *why* people die. Or why *anything* dies. I think it's like Camus's definition of absurdity: you're looking for meaning in a situation where there is none."

He exhaled and sat back in his chair. "Hmmmm... maybe."

"But many people believe that facing death helps us come to terms with it and allows us to appreciate life even more. It's like what happens when we let ourselves get scared: we face it, then can overcome it and feel better afterwards. That's kind of like anything—the more you confront it on some level, the more natural it becomes. So see?" I gave him a reassuring smile. "All this stuff is very healthy!"

Perhaps it was the contemplation of the bigger issues that made Carl decide to take a day off studying. He drove us to the Cliffs of Moher, and we walked the ancient rocks along the Atlantic while the waves crashed peacefully below. I felt humbled before the vast ocean, stretching far out of sight, and immersed in the beauty of nature. It could have cleared anyone's head.

Back in Limerick, I took Carl's advice and visited St. Michan's Church—or, rather, what lay beneath it. For four euros, the church's groundskeeper brought me through a dank, stone passageway below ground. A burial vault awaited us at the end. In a small room, four lidless coffins revealed centuries-old, decomposed skeletons. I didn't hesitate when the guide invited me to enter the dark, musty chamber and touch the hand of one of them. I crouched over the remains, staring at the ancient thing before me. Dirt covered the ribs and vertebrae. Staring at the faceless skull, I found it barely distinguishable from countless plastic ones I'd seen over the years. It felt almost surreal to think that I, too, was something like that: a collection of connected bones, animate for the time being only to one day be reduced to nothing else. I brought my finger to the pale, brownish bone and found that it looked suddenly vibrant pink and orange in comparison. It seemed to almost glow beside a lifeless twin. I felt my skin suddenly feel remarkably soft and warm against a texture of smooth rock that held no temperature at all. *This is real death,* I thought, grazing it. I became more aware of my own breathing. I felt my lungs expanding in my chest, filling with the stale air. My guide, whom I estimated to be in his late fifties, quietly watched me as I pulled my hand away. I could only imagine the reactions he had seen in people after touching the dead. I looked back at him and realized that we shared the same priceless gift: the good fortune of simply being alive.

The Return to Castle Dracula

On June 6, Van Helsing met me at Stephen's Green Shopping Center—or, at least, Nevin Cody did. The magician who had played the mysterious doctor at Castle Dracula had kept in touch with me during my weeks in Cork and Limerick. After learning that I'd be staying with a Couchsurfing host upon my return, he invited me to stay with him in Kilkenny.

Nevin's house perfectly reflected what I would envision for a magician. Expansive rooms with antique furniture appeared to be right out of the 1963 film *The Haunting*. He smiled when I made the comparison. Looking through his library of books on magic, psychology, and mental wellness, I told him about my stay with Thomas and his questioning my love of scare shows.

"Are you sure that staying with these people is safe?" Nevin asked. His face contorted with concern. "These 'hosts,' as you call them? It all seems a bit risky."

I cocked my head with a smile. "Yes, I'm sure. I wouldn't stay with someone who didn't have references. But it's funny: Couchsurfers never ask that. It's only people who have never done it who do. Most hosts just want to connect with the person staying with them, that's all—and learn from them, if there's something about them or their culture that they don't understand."

"Just as long as you're safe," Nevin said.

I smiled with a nod. "I am."

Secretly, I couldn't help but find my situation amusingly paradoxical. I felt completely at ease staying in the homes of people I had just met and being in countries I was visiting for the first time. But the idea of acting in Nevin's haunt—portraying the type of character that I loved so much in a show I'd come so far to see—terrified me. I kept those thoughts to myself, though.

On the drive back to Clontarf, I praised Nevin for his role as Van Helsing and his magic acts on stage.

"I like to make active participation a key part of my show," he said.

I nodded at him, sitting on his left in the passenger seat.

"Of course, it's all based on the power of suggestion," he said. "All magicians do that. Making people laugh puts them into a more comfortable state of mind. They feel better about themselves when that happens. In this day and age, it's almost sad how so many people seem to need permission to have fun." He turned to me with a small frown. "A lot of us actually lose the ability to have fun with childhood."

"I think that's also one of the main reasons that people like Halloween," I said. "I know plenty who love to dress up in crazy costumes when they go to parties, but there's no way they'd feel comfortable doing that if they didn't have the excuse of the holiday."

"Exactly. Whereas kids love to do things like that anytime just because it's fun. In my show, I give people *permission* to let loose and have fun. It lets them enjoy the show more and also enjoy *themselves* more. And they take that with them when they leave."

I grinned at the philosophy. "I think that's the most inspiring mentality about an act I've ever heard."

He smiled. "Thanks. If I can make someone happier, I know I've put on a good show. It's as simple as that."

Back at Castle Dracula, I was thrilled to see the cast again. Brendan and Lorcan—the robed executioner and Leatherface who, I also learned, were father and son—gave me the tour. The bat corridor, insane asylum, and vampire's lair seemed quiet and peaceful without a large group wandering through. I remembered taking pictures of Sam inside the coffin and Lorcan chasing us away from the executioner scene with his chainsaw. With his mask now off, the twentysomething-year-old looked remarkably sane and human as he pulled masks and capes from a large bag of costumes in the Graveyard Theater.

"What kind of character do you want to play?" he asked. "A werewolf? Or a mental patient? Or a vampire?"

I looked at the latex masks as he handed them to me. I felt immensely grateful that any of them would at least hide my face. Playing a werewolf sounded fun, but I knew that no such creature made an appearance in Stoker's story. Dracula had transfigured into a dog in Whitby, but I wasn't sure if a werewolf mask would get that across.

"Well, what kind of character do you think you need?"

Lorcan thought a minute. "We don't have anyone working the asylum on the stairwell."

"That sounds good." I studied the grayish face in my hands. It resembled an old, crazed man with chapped, shriveled lips and huge, jagged teeth. A short, stubby nose was barely noticeable between black, hollow eyes and strands of hair sticking out from behind wolf-like ears. "Will you show me what to do?"

Lorcan handed me a black trench coat and leather gloves, then led the way up the winding staircase. The crouched lunatic sat huddled and lifeless on the floor, with the Hunchback/Elephant Man figure chained to the wall behind him. I stepped over the low, iron fence separating the alcove from the stairs and gestured to a lone, dusty chair between the props.

"I could sit here?"

"Yeah, that's good," Lorcan said as I plopped down into it. "Maybe you could stay really still so that no one knows you're real, then after a few people come up, kinda lunge out at them."

I envisioned how that might work. Playing the role of a lunatic like Renfield, I could see how the inmate might rush towards people in a frenzy. But with stairs involved, that could end badly.

"Uhhh, I don't want to make them so scared that they fall, though...."

"Oh yeah." Lorcan turned and looked down behind him. The dozen steps winding out of sight could have easily become a deathtrap. "Good point."

"But if I move slowly, they'll just kinda get creeped out instead of startled."

I thought back to the *Ring* scene from Underground Fear. I remembered Samara's eerie emergence from the well, slowly crawling towards her audience as we stared at her in disbelief. I tried to imagine a similar creature. Slightly slumping into the chair, I hung my head lifelessly. I gradually rolled it towards Lorcan as if I had just come to life. I let my upper body fall slowly forward, then dropped my hands to the floor and began crawling towards him like a wildcat on the prowl. I reached for his feet, twisting my hand into a grasping claw over the stairs. My anxiety about acting immediately disappeared. I was no longer Chris; I was a psychotic asylum patient craving human life.

"That's good!" Lorcan said, smiling down at me. "And if you want, use those chains by the hunchback. You could wrap them around your feet and that can be why you move so slowly."

"Oh yeah!" I said, picturing it. "Okay."

I repeated the action. A loud scraping sound followed me as the chains dragged along the floor. The noise brought me back to another scene from the Budapest haunt. I remembered watching a crazed killer peer over his captive who was tied to a bed, then later stalk me and my group mates while we hid from him in a wardrobe. I imagined myself being just as sinister, with my own chains as potential weapons.

"Perfect," Lorcan said, nodding. "Good job!"

For a second scare, my haunt trainer suggested that I work the drop panel in the portrait hallway. It would mean hustling down the stairs after the visitors passed the asylum and running through the vampire's lair before they entered the hall. We tested it out and agreed that it would work.

Back in the asylum, we waited for the show to begin.

"How long have you worked here for?" I asked. I sat in my chair, holding my soon-to-be psychotic visage with gloved hands. The long trench coat reached down to my feet, with only the tips of my sneakers poking out from beneath it. Lorcan sat on the steps beside me, now dressed in his bloodied apron and twirling his leathery mask before him.

"Two years. I love it here. I wish we had shows every night. It's fun making people scream."

I chuckled, nodding. It was something that my haunter friends back home often said.

"Yeah, I can see how it would be."

But as the minutes passed, I felt my muscles grow tense. I envisioned how my acting might look in the eyes of visitors. I saw myself crawling as a psycho patient towards a big group, only to have them look at me in confusion. I imagined expressions of: *What the hell is* that *thing?* and *Was that supposed to be* scary? I saw scowls and heads shaking in disappointment. Beside me, Lorcan suddenly appeared like some kind of superhero: able to face crowds without the slightest apprehension.

I remembered going through Screamville with Ruben, watching him nervously gape at zombies as they staggered after us while I regarded them all in admiration. It had been the same at Underground Fear: I smiled at the psycho killers and their unique scare methods while my group mates ran away screaming. The blank, crazed face staring lifelessly from my hands began to feel ironically alien. I felt as if I should have been playing the role of a psychiatrist in the asylum rather than one of its inmates.

"I hope I don't screw up," I confessed. "I would hate to do something stupid and ruin the whole show."

Lorcan turned to me and shook his head. "You won't. You'll do great. I was nervous before my first show, too."

I looked at him with a glimmer of hope. "Really?"

"Oh yeah." He crossed his arms in thought. "Terrified, actually. But remember, people won't be seeing *you* in here—they'll only see your character. Just do what we rehearsed and they'll love it. And just think: if you totally screw up, they'll never know the difference, now, will they?"

I gave a short laugh. It was good logic, and I found it funny that Leatherface was trying to calm me down.

"Good point. Thanks, you're a great trainer."

His eyebrows shot up, and he grinned. "Really? You're actually my first trainee. This was pretty cool."

Our attention soon turned to a familiar, high-pitched voice from below. Ronan's desperate cries for Mina echoed as the crazed Renfield welcomed the night's visitors. Brendan, now cloaked as the executioner, poked his head up the stairs to signal that the show had begun. Lorcan pulled on his mask. I did the same, looking at the star of *The Texas Chainsaw Massacre* through two small, rubbery holes. The monster gave me a thumbs up, then hopped silently down the stairs.

Alone with my stationary inmates, I heard Renfield's ravings die away. I felt my stomach once again harden into rock as Nevin sarcastically teased his crowd. My hands balled into fists inside my thick gloves while I listened to the whimsical Van Helsing below.

"This way, watch your step," my new host soon said from the bottom of the stairs.

I slid down into the chair, staring blankly ahead. I tried not to think about a hundred things I might do wrong. The sound of my heart beating began to intensify as shuffling on the stairs grew closer. *There goes my theory of feeling more comfortable behind a mask,* I thought.

But as Nevin's large frame came into view, I forced myself to stop imagining the worst. I let my mind go blank. I was now lost to the world, over-drugged by Dr. Seward and his fellow doctors, while a line of patrons approached me as if in slow motion. Van Helsing kept quiet while leading the troop. I remembered his words: *I give people* permission *to let loose and have fun. It lets them enjoy the show more and also enjoy themselves more. And they take that with them when they leave.*

"Mind the inmates of the asylum...," the vampire hunter said as he passed me. "They won't bite you. I don't think...."

Once he was out of my vision, I slowly turned my head. Through glazed eyes I saw a group of twentysomethings smiling at me. I felt eternally grateful that their reaction wasn't one of disappointment—or, worse, flinching backwards and falling. Seeing that all was clear, I let myself fall forward from the chair. The group watched my every move, as if looking away might cause me to pounce at them at any moment. My chains scraped loudly as I crawled across the floor and reached a thick, dark hand towards a man's calf. He shrieked and laughed, backing and shrinking away. Those behind him shuffled to the edge of the stairs to avoid being touched by the strange inmate. I grasped for additional legs and feet until the last person in line, about twenty in all, hopped giggling out of sight. Once he was gone, I pushed the chains off my feet and dashed down the stairs.

I did it! I thought, running past the coffins in the vampire's lair. *The asylum monster lives!*

Above, Nevin could be heard leading the crew down the second set of stairs. I raced to what resembled a closed window along a dark, plywood wall. I grabbed a small handle at the base of it, silently waiting until muffled voices came from the portrait hallway on the opposite side.

"Right this way; come along...!" Nevin said, just inches away.

I moved in a second. Yanking the handle with all my might, I lifted the drop panel and screamed into the open space. Through the tiny holes of my mask, I recognized the same man whose leg I had reached for just moments before. He instinctively jumped back, turning towards me in alarm. I knew that look; I'd seen it on countless group mates during my tours through haunted attractions. And it was no doubt the same look I'd had from the scare in the Dublin Ghostbus. In an instant I slammed the window back down, before my victim could recognize the lunatic who had somehow escaped his chains. Then I heard an explosion of laughter come from the other side of the wall.

"Holy s—...what was that?!" asked a male voice.

"Ha ha, he got you good!" a female friend teased.

I chuckled silently at additional remarks in Irish accents. *Was it their first time in Castle Dracula?* I couldn't help but wonder. I bet they never would have guessed that some of its inhabitants come from across the pond.

With the group out of sight, I pulled off my mask. The air felt refreshingly cool on my skin. Although I had only worn the latex for about five minutes, it hadn't taken me long to start sweating inside of it. *I did it!* I thought, exhaling. *That wasn't so bad—that was actually pretty fun... and they* liked *it!*

Buzzing and cracks of the electric chair soon erupted. I used a secret entrance to slip into the portrait hallway, heading towards the sound of screams and Lorcan's chainsaw. Outside the Graveyard Theater, I approached the bloodied killer from behind as he turned off his weapon. The two of us watched the group disperse, then relax in the safety of the stage.

"How'd you do?" Leatherface asked.

"It went great!" I whispered excitedly. "Woo hoo!"

"Excellent." A black glove rested on my shoulder. I turned to see the hooded Brendan behind me.

From the last row of the theater, the three of us watched our vampire leader mystify his new audience. They stared in disbelief at his enchanting, inhuman powers. They laughed and clapped as he read their thoughts and spoke with the dead, volunteering and taking turns to be part of the show. Ronan's magic wasn't something to simply sit back and watch, I realized; it needed to be experienced to be believed—to be participated in to truly enjoy. I smiled with my fellow psychotics, the homicidal maniac and cloaked executioner who had welcomed a new lunatic to their castle. Like Nevin, they knew what led to Ronan's "abilities beyond human understanding": the wonderful, though sometimes terrifying, act of engagement.

Chapter 9

The Horror Games of England

"No one's coming for you...!"

ScareCON Haunt Conference

"We're here to celebrate a love for scare attractions."

I smiled at the introduction. It was the best opening for a haunt conference that I'd ever heard. In a large and surprisingly pristine barn, haunt owner and conference organizer Michael Bolton welcomed more than two hundred attendees to ScareCON: a scare-attraction conference being held in Crawley, England.

"ScareCON," Michael continued into a handheld microphone, "is a gathering for small, professional haunters to learn from each other, help each other succeed, and expand the scare-attraction industry."

I found myself instinctively nodding. All around me, the crowd listened, eagerly engaged, from rows of folding chairs packed within the building. We had gathered at Tulley's Farm, which would later transform into Shocktober Fest Scream Park in October.

"We're joined today by people from Scotland, Wales, Ireland, America, and even Australia."

I was touched when he glanced at me with pride but felt lucky to have arrived there at all. In my infinite wisdom, I had neglected to check the address of exactly where the conference was being held. After taking a ferry from Ireland to Liverpool, I had purchased a bus ticket to Victoria Station, with the vague recollection of ScareCON's website saying something about south London. But when I called the hotel where I would be staying, the woman at the front desk sounded understandably confused when I asked her how to get there from the station.

"You need to take a *train*," she said, annoyed, "to Crawley. We're not in London."

I might as well have asked her how to get there from Connecticut.

I had the pleasure of attending ScareCON with a friend from home. Dick Terhune, also known as the infamous "Voice from Hell," was attending as America's haunt-advertising expert and guru. I had contacted Dick from Salzburg back in December, threatening to hound him on a weekly basis until he booked his flight. The two of us had attended conferences together for years, but this, I stressed, would be our first international haunt adventure.

I got to the hotel a few hours before Dick arrived. I was already nervous. I had agreed to give a talk at ScareCON about my first six months of travels. To ease my nerves, I decided to do a dry run. I loaded up a PowerPoint presentation I'd made on my laptop, feeling the same rock in my stomach that I had before acting at Castle Dracula, now three weeks earlier. Similar anxieties arose. I envisioned myself standing before a large group only to forget everything I wanted to say, or people wondering what in the world I was talking about or finding my presentation so boring that snores emanated from the crowd. But I forced myself to ignore those thoughts. I faced the mirror in the hotel room, ready to practice, when I realized that I barely recognized my own face. With wide eyes, I stared at arms remarkably thicker and jeans significantly snugger than they had ever been back home. It was my first glimpse in a full-length mirror since before I could remember, and my steady diet of cheap food—which almost always consisted of sugar and fat rather than fruits and vegetables—had definitely taken its toll.

Surprisingly, my first reaction was to laugh.

"Oh my God," I said, pointing to myself. "You're so *fat!* What in the hell have you been *eating?!*"

I was as taken aback by my reaction to how plump I'd become. A year earlier, I certainly would have been mortified at the change, but it was more amusing than anything. My encounter with the skeletons in Limerick had really helped put things into perspective. Compared to the gift of simply being alive, a few extra pounds hardly seemed like anything to stress over.

Fortunately Dick was polite when he arrived and claimed that I didn't look any different at all.

Now *that's* a friend.

But as I sat at ScareCON, all those thoughts were behind me. I felt as exhilarated to be with my friend as I was to be around so many others who shared our passion for dark shows. A full day of talks involved haunters describing their scare attractions. They explained how they had built their scenes and trained their actors, how they advertised their shows, and some of the funniest reactions they got from their patrons.

"Actors are the most important thing in a scare attraction," one speaker noted. "We're very careful to make sure our actors are well trained so that they know exactly what they're doing."

"With the basics of human psychology," said another, "you can better plan the scenes, know what you want to do, and ensure that people enjoy the experience of being scared without being traumatized by it."

"We had a twenty-year-old go through and whiz herself and a two-year-old go through and laugh his head off," one haunter recounted.

"Some of our scenes got more and more disgusting until one night we actually had someone throw up," said another.

Absorbed and inspired, I listened and laughed, feeling an instant connection to everyone around me. I also couldn't help but marvel how, unlike me, the speakers seemed to have no fear about either public speaking *or* acting.

My talk followed lunch. I paced the barn like a prisoner awaiting execution until Michael introduced me. But when the tall, British haunter put the microphone in my hand, I found myself slip into immediate ease. I described the festivals I'd attended in Mexico, Europe, and Japan. I flipped through pictures on the projector screen, explaining that each monster-themed show was about more than fun celebration. The Day of the Dead traditions had allowed people to remember their loved ones and accept death as a natural part of life. The Krampus *laufs* and Namahage festival provided opportunities for people to either portray or encounter a seasonal demon that's been part of their culture for centuries. Walpurgisnacht turned classic literature into widespread events that entire communities could enjoy together. Each show involved creative expression and the potential to make people feel more connected to their communities—features, I stressed, equally inherent in scare attractions.

That afternoon, a haunt actor complimented me on the talk. Dom, a thirty-year-old business owner from Wales, had been playing the role of a zombie for years. The two of us walked through a small building on the farm where vendors promoted zombie camps, haunt-building companies, professional makeup, and horror-themed photography. I told Dom about my acting experiences back in Ireland, and he nodded in understanding.

"I get nervous before all my shows, too," he said.

I flinched in astonishment. "You do?" I never would have guessed it to look at him; he casually stood beside me with his hands in army-pants pockets and dreadlocks reaching down to his shoulders. "Even though you love playing a zombie?"

"Sure," he said with a shrug. "I think about all the ways I might totally screw up. And that everyone would just hate it."

I threw up my hands in exasperation. "That's exactly what it's like for me!"

He nodded with a grin. "But as soon as the show starts, it goes away. I guess because I'm not thinking about it anymore. I'm just doing it."

"Yeah, I've noticed that, too." I thought back to the panic I'd felt just hours before, waiting for Michael to introduce me in the barn. It had disappeared so quickly once I started talking that I felt somewhat silly for ever being nervous in the first place. It was the same change that had happened as I crawled after people at Castle Dracula. I scanned the tables all around us: posters and photos showed rotting creatures wearing the latest in makeup and red and black contact lenses. These businesses were based on helping actors look more authentic and professional in their horrifying performances. The shows were supposed to be scary for the *patrons*, not the actors. But I supposed that, sometimes, it could be scary for both.

"I guess I was just psyching myself out about it, more than anything." I stuffed my hands into my jeans pockets, staring down at a table selling liquid latex.

Dom picked up a small jar and studied it. Green flesh fell off a screaming zombie on the label. He read its contents while I admired the image.

"But it's always worth it," he said, turning to me. "I love every show." A wolfish smile suddenly spread over his face. "And it's fun to make them scream."

Johan in Worcester

On July 3, I prepared to get my butt kicked.

The more relaxing shows were behind me: casually walking through scare attractions, lazily enjoying a ghost tour from a bus, even speaking before a crowd at a haunt conference. What lay before me now was physical, brutal. I needed to get tough. This was Zombie Boot Camp.

My new host picked me up from the National Express bus stop in Worcester. After reading my Couchsurfing message about coming to the area for a half-day course on how to survive a zombie apocalypse, Johan not only accepted my request but signed up to take the course with me. I was grateful to find a fellow zombie fan. He was my age and had recently moved to England from the Netherlands. I could only assume that, like me, he had seen all the zombie movies, from *Night of the Living Dead* to *Zombie Land,* and was excited about being able to step into one of his favorite films. But as he got out of his Honda Civic, I saw that an interest in monsters probably wasn't the reason he signed up.

At six foot three, Johan reminded me of a Navy SEAL. He held out a hand for me to shake, and I saw an arm that could no doubt bench press three times the weight of any zombie actor. I returned the gesture with a hug, knowing full well that he could crush me to a pulp if he wanted to. Fortunately he didn't.

"I go to the gym every morning before work," he said with a strong Dutch accent. He showed me around his apartment, spotlessly clean with few items beyond basic furniture. Opening a few cupboards, he revealed barrel-size tubs of protein powder and a fridge packed with food for mixing in his blender: berries, peaches, yogurt, oatmeal. "I like to have a protein fruit smoothie for breakfast and usually a vegetable one for dinner," he said. "Beet smoothies are my favorite. Want one?"

I stared at the items in his small kitchen, hoping to God he was kidding. I was all about trying new foods, but beets are bad enough to *eat*. Now he wanted me to *drink* them?

"Okay...," I said, trying to hide my revulsion. I supposed that, at the very least, I could think of it as Boot Camp prep. Miraculously, it didn't taste bad; the conglomeration of beetroot, yogurt, and protein powder produced what looked like a bright-red alchemical experiment. It tasted like a thick, sugary V-8.

"It's pretty good," I admitted. "I can see why you like them."

Johan shrugged. He sat beside me on his small couch, one of the few items in his living room. "I wouldn't say I exactly *like* them. But they're a quick way to have your vegetables for the day. I'm usually watching a movie or something when I have dinner, so it's not like I even taste the meal. I'm more focused on the show."

I frowned at this mentality. "You don't enjoy your food? That's no way to live.... Don't you find it better to *like* the things you eat and drink?"

He cast a disinterested gaze around the bare walls of the room. "I don't know...."

"I always make a conscious effort to enjoy what I eat," I said, "even if it's a bowl of rice and glass of water. And believe me, sometimes lately, that's all it's been."

I smiled without a hint of qualm over my recent lifestyle. Johan chuckled. Fortunately, he didn't comment on the fact that someone who *really* lived on rice would have been several pounds lighter.

"I mean, if you're not enjoying it, what's the point?" I took another swig of my drink. It really did taste pretty good. "Life's too short for that!"

Zombie Boot Camp

The next morning, the two of us pulled up to a man standing guard outside a large business complex. He turned to us without expression, dressed in camouflage clothing, military hat, and boots. The sign beside him read *Rushock Training Estate.*

"Is this the right place?" Johan asked me from the driver's seat.

I looked around, seeking out any signs that might contain images of the undead. "I'm not sure...."

The officer approached Johan's window. "Can I help you?"

I leaned forward from the passenger seat and smiled. "We're here for RAM Training...?" I said with a hint of question. I didn't dare say "Zombie Boot Camp" and risk getting a strange look if we were in the wrong spot. Better to remain cryptic and stick to the company's name.

The uniformed man nodded. "The carpark is on the right."

In the lot, a few things caught my eye right away: the three dozen or so people standing around their vehicles all appeared to be in their twenties and thirties, and they were all men.

Oh God, I thought as we stepped out of the car. *I'm gonna get killed.*

Before I could confide my worry to Johan, a woman stepped out of the passenger's seat of a small truck across from us. My face lit up immediately. When she saw me, she smiled back.

A waiver was quickly passed around in which everyone had to agree that RAM was not responsible for any injuries incurred during Boot Camp. I signed it, wondering what in the world I was getting myself into. We were instructed to pass through a "secured" tent and pat ourselves down with white powder to "prevent infection." We strapped on shin guards, knee-, and elbow pads in a large briefing room, along with bulletproof vests that Johan had to sort through before finding one that would fit him.

After finalizing my new soldier facade with a visored helmet, I sat beside the woman from outside.

"Can I just say," I ventured, "thank God you're here!"

She laughed and nodded. The entire troop now sat in rows of folding chairs facing a large white board.

"I know," she replied as Johan sat down on my other side, "that's exactly what I said to *him!*" She motioned to the man next to her. "'Oh, good, there's another woman here. I'll stick with her!'"

The couple, I learned, was named Catherine and Tom. Both were in their late thirties and originally from Liverpool. Tom had gone through Zombie Boot Camp a few weeks earlier during a stag party. I noticed that neither of them appeared any buffer than I was and certainly didn't have the beetroot-protein-shake-diet look that Johan did. Scanning the group, I saw that no one did—not even the instructors.

"All right, everyone," a sergeant called from the front of the room. The crowd grew quiet as he faced us expectantly. He wore similar attire to the guard outside and stood with his hands folded behind his back. "You've been called here to deal with an outbreak that has occurred at Rushock. RAM specializes in these situations, and now we need your help to eliminate the problem."

The man introduced himself as Alan, the owner of RAM Training, along with a fellow instructor Jack: a tall, red-haired officer standing off to the side. Alan motioned to a sketch on the white board behind him. A schematic showed another building on the property and its surroundings.

"What we're looking at here are zombies," he said with a steady gaze. "They have invaded the compound, both inside and out. Now one thing you have to understand is that these zombies are *fast.*" He paused a moment to let his point sink in. "These zombies are not from *The Walking Dead.* Those zombies are typical Americans: slow and lazy."

He stopped as a few heads turned towards me and chuckled. They had no doubt heard me talking with Catherine.

"Sorry back there," the sergeant said to me with a nod.

I gave him a wave. "No problem."

"Our zombies," he continued, "are more like those from *28 Days Later:* fast and powerful."

I thought back to the movie. I remembered seeing it in the theater: red-eyed undead plowing down lingering survivors of a virus outbreak. They had moved with as much speed as Olympians in training. *Not quite Romero style*, I had thought, *but a nice, alternative depiction.*

We would have two trainings, we were told, combat and armory, followed by two missions out in the compound. All RAM sergeants had gone through the British military, so we would be learning actual military techniques. I cast a nervous glance at Catherine beside me. I was excited to take a stab at being one of those survivors from a bloodbath horror film, but I had never done anything even remotely close to combat. Catherine mirrored my expression. On my other side, I saw Johan studying the instructors with interest.

After splitting us into two groups, mine fortunately including my three new friends, Jack ordered us out into the hall to begin.

"In this training you will learn how to use riot shields." Our instructor eyed his cadets as we faced him from the wall. "You will also be given a baton. You are *not*, under any circumstances, to use the batons on *each other.*" He looked hard at a few of the men at the end of the line. "You will learn how to group up...."

He stopped suddenly and pointed to two people mumbling.

"You two: ten pushups. Now."

I turned to the men in shock. They immediately grew quiet, then sighed loudly.

"No speaking out of line." Jack pointed to the far wall. "Ten. Go."

I felt my lips purse shut while watching the effortless reps being done on the floor. I knew that if I were over there, I could probably do about two.

In a large auditorium, I stood in line and took a long, black baton from a table of weaponry. I couldn't help but feel like a nineteenth-century bobby holding it, gearing up to hunt out Jack the Ripper in the streets of Whitechapel. While the rest of the group picked up large, rectangular armadillo shields, Jack directed Catherine and me to smaller, circular snatch shields. I held mine awkwardly, watching Johan handle his with pride. He looked born for the role, ready for action, with the thick, plastic guard extending from his shoulders to his knees. My own seemed miniscule by comparison. The circle barely covered my torso. I looked at Catherine by my side, now my mirror image as a padded, armed soldier about to face a horde of lightning-fast zombies.

I gave her a manic smile. "We're gonna die."

She hunched over in laughter. "That's *exactly* how I feel."

Tom grinned. "You'll both do fine."

Following Jack's orders, half of us "grouped up" in the center of the room, connecting our shields side by side to form a single unit of protection. Catherine and I stood at either end, our two small circles making the assembly look like a deformed Q-Tip. The remaining men were given the role of attack, facing us with neither shield nor weapon. I felt strange preparing myself to fight off my fellow recruits. I tried to imagine them as the zombies that I would later face, out for brains and blood and stinking of rot. I smiled at the image, finding it much more exciting.

"Visors kept up during combat," Jack called from beside us. He motioned to the wide guards above our helmets. "And when you strike, you will only do so on the *legs*—not the chest and *never* the head."

I stared at the offense cadets across from us, gripping my baton and holding fast to my shield. Scenes from dozens of zombie movies flashed through my mind: soldiers ambushed by roaring creatures, decaying flesh and biting teeth coming from all directions. A moment later all those thoughts disappeared as a vested, padded opponent came straight towards me. He held his arms out before him, ready to force himself against my tiny shield. I felt two strong sensations immediately arise: the need to fight or *run*.

I ignored my instinctive preference for the latter and forced back my baton to strike. A second later I strained to steady myself against the crushing weight of the man as he pushed against my small circle of protection. He was barely taller than I was but seemed about fifty times as strong. His goofy smile told me that he felt even stranger attacking a girl than I did having to endure it. I gently struck at his legs while hearing much more forceful whacks and thuds come from the battle all around us. I was pushed farther and farther backwards but couldn't help but laugh the entire time. No matter how hard I hit, it didn't seem to faze my would-be-zombie opponent at all.

Jack eventually blew his whistle so that everyone could swap roles. Before I could recount the episode to Catherine, the instructor nodded in my direction.

"Don't be afraid to hit them," he said. He gestured towards the window, indicating the outside world beyond it. "Out there, they won't hesitate when they come at you like these guys will."

I immediately felt myself blush and cringe. I was already out of breath and starting to sweat under my padding and helmet. *If I did this every day, at least I'd lose those extra pounds.*

"Okay," I said. "Sorry." I grimaced at Catherine. She immediately chuckled.

The opposing team got into formation, and I stood ready for my new role in offense. I felt much more comfortable without a weapon; if I had to attack someone as a monster, it was nice to have my hands free. It's what I'd seen hundreds of haunt actors do over the years—if only in pretense. Knives and chainsaws were the rarity—*real* evil means being able to tear someone limb from limb by our hands alone.

When the signal was called I ran towards my victim. I chose one of the smallest guys in the group, ramming into his shield with all my might. I saw surprise and amusement flash across his face. He chuckled a moment, then struck me several times on the thigh. I was amazed to find that it didn't hurt at all, despite having no padding over my jeans. I had the distinct feeling that had a Krampus actor been here to see this, he would have burst out laughing.

"That wasn't so bad," Catherine said after the drill. She stood with her hands on her hips, breathing as heavily as I did.

Tom smiled at her enjoyment. "See? Nothing to it."

I glanced at Johan, standing quietly by. He had the look of a soldier who had just reluctantly obeyed orders to retreat from the heat of battle.

"The drills could have lasted a bit longer," he said.

I frowned at him in sympathy. "Don't worry; I'm sure there'll be plenty of zombies to pound on during the mission."

A gleam seemed to come from his eyes. "That's true."

The next drill made him much happier. Back out in the hall, I watched my host hold a new weapon with such confidence that he could have been cast in the next *Predator* film.

"Each gun is equipped with a splitter," Jack called. He walked the line before us, ensuring that everyone had properly flipped off their safety clip. I watched Tom demonstrate the action to Catherine, only vaguely understanding how I'd done it myself as Jack nodded to me in approval. "You will be firing at close range so only short blasts of paint will be emitted on impact."

I regarded the massive device in my grip as though it were a bomb. I felt awkward even holding it. The last time I'd handled a gun was at a firing range when I was ten. The lesson with my father had lasted only a day, after I showed absolutely no interest in handguns or rifles. I knew that guns were an essential part of surviving a zombie outbreak but could only hope that no *real* injuries would occur in our little game about one. *What if I accidentally hurt the zombie?* I grimaced at the thought. *That would be terrible.*

In a second gymnasium, I maneuvered like a soldier with my new weapon. Partnered with Tom, I fired at large, metal plates propped up against mounds of sandbags in a winding maze. Green paint splattered over existing blue, orange, and yellow. We cleared each room and shouted when other teams could pass. While crouched in my gear, a thick visor now covering my face, I realized that I liked this training even more than the combat. I felt as though I was going through a videogame—with the added bonus of not getting physically beaten at all or actually hurting anyone I "shot."

But once our trainings were through, the *real* undead awaited.

A short van ride brought us to the site of the zombie invasion. Half-crushed cars wasted away outside a dilapidated, steel-framed building. Faded tires and sandbags lined a dirt path surrounding it. I scanned the area. It reminded me of Screamville back in Oaxaca. I remembered going through the show with Ruben, passively wandering through sets, marveling at the gruesome creatures that only pretended they were going to attack. What was hidden here, I knew, was different. Here, I was a member of the SWAT team: an enemy of the zombies whom they would ambush without mercy. I instinctively stepped closer to Catherine, holding tightly to my almost nonexistent shield and club. Johan, Tom, and the others, I saw, examined the perimeter with heads held high.

"All right!" Jack shouted, looking over the group. He lacked any weapons himself, and I realized that he would be giving orders from the sidelines rather than joining us in battle. "Everyone in formation. We'll be walking the perimeter of the compound. You will wait for my orders to break. When you do, you will strike *only the legs*. Once all the zombies have fallen, I'll instruct you to regroup, which you will do immediately and continue forward. Everyone understand?"

I nodded with my fellow soldiers. I tried to visualize the scene that he had described so casually. It all sounded so complicated. *Thank God I'm not doing this alone.* All around us, everything seemed unusually quiet—*eerily* quiet—as the threat remained hidden.

The troops quickly formed a line. They stood from one side of the path to the other, their full-body shields creating an impenetrable wall before them. With no room for our assigned spots at the ends of the line, Catherine and I walked behind, following the sound of grinding, hard plastic. I scanned the trail as we moved forward, observing cars, tires, and steel sheds along either side of us. I saw countless spots that would be perfect places for actors—*creatures*—to hide. I held my little, round shield before me as though it contained magical powers and remembered the words from our briefing, just over an hour ago but what seemed like weeks earlier: these zombies would move *fast*.

After about ten paces, I saw movement within the rubble. Three young men staggered out from behind a doorless, collapsed car. I stared at wild, matted hair and bloodstained, camouflage jackets and pants. Grime covered any previous living complexion of their skin. They moved slowly at first, glaring at our troop from beside a windshield spiderwebbed with cracks. Directly in front of me, every helmet faced them. In a split second, the creatures sprinted forward. Jack ordered us to break formation. More green-clad attackers came from the sides. And our impenetrable wall, separating Catherine and me from the charge, was penetrated.

Hell broke loose. The zombies flew into shields all around me. They crashed into them with full force, pushing and shoving. The soldiers retaliated, beating mercilessly at bloodied legs. There were seven or eight zombies now, grunting and fighting against my fellow cadets. But the chaos seemed to freeze as one of them looked directly at me.

My heart seemed to stop. I stared, motionless, at the blood-covered thing before me. Everything else disappeared. But I wasn't paralyzed from *fear;* I saw lifeless eyes and hideous flesh reflecting the perfect embodiment of death. I admired the once-blond hair, now clumped with ooze, and the reddish fluid streaming from his chin and neck. He had that allure of a bloodthirsty creature fresh from the grave. He was the perfect monster: sinister and deadly. But as his vile mouth curled into a crooked, teasing smile, I quickly reminded myself that I would have to hit him, and that if I didn't, my role in our game of life versus death would be over.

In an instant he charged. I felt a force ten times as strong as my fellow soldier back in training had produced. I went hurtling backwards and crashed into a mound of tires. The creature crawled on top of me in a second. I struck at his tattered, gruesome leg with my baton. The thing only growled and smiled, completely unaffected.

"You're gonna turn...!" he mumbled.

I burst into laughter. The last thing I had expected was for the zombies to speak.

"No one's coming for you...!" he said with a low gurgle. I hit him harder as he pressed against me with all his weight. Based on the clashing and thumping all around us, he was no doubt used to much worse.

Between the grunts and strained breathing, I heard Tom's voice yell in my direction. It sounded muffled and distant, as though it were coming from a fading dream.

"Man down!"

After continuing his fight, the zombie rolled off me and went lifeless by my feet. I heard the sounds of struggle die away in the distance. Looking towards the others, I saw my fellow recruits standing throughout the path. They panted with their shields held firmly before them and batons down at their sides. All stared at the creatures they had apparently just battled that now lay sprawled at their feet. Tom ran over to me and extended a hand. Catherine raced to join him, catching her breath. I steadied myself after being helped up, feeling suddenly about fifty pounds lighter with no one trying to force me into the ground. From across the path, I saw Johan nodding to a soldier beside him. I could only assume that he had saved his fellow cadet from getting destroyed.

"Oh my God!" Catherine said with a huff. "That was crazy. I really had to whale on that guy!"

I gave an amused groan. "But he didn't throw you *down*, right?" I asked, shaking my head in embarrassment.

Tom clapped me on the shoulder. "It's okay. Another guy was thrown down, too."

I exhaled and rolled my eyes. "Ugh, I guess that makes it a *little* better...!"

"Back in formation!" Jack bellowed from ahead. Tom took off to the front of the line. Catherine and I followed, laughing and panting.

We continued the march. Around a corner, more cars, sandbags, and barrels appeared. But no one's attention stayed ahead for long; we all knew that our assailants were behind us. We took only a few paces before the seemingly defeated creatures began to move. They clambered to their feet, then slowly began to stalk us. In an instant they picked up speed. Jack yelled for us to break once again. The living corpses plowed into our plastic armor, loud crunching erupting from the impact. The soldiers fought back, grunting and striking with what looked like godlike fury.

I remained unchallenged but saw a zombie run straight towards Catherine. He plowed into her shield with a violent growl. She fought against his strength, hitting his legs and hips. I watched for only a moment, then felt my previous fascination with the creatures vanish.

No one attacks my friend...!

With a rush of adrenaline, I lunged at the assailant. I struck at his legs with more force than I knew I had. He spun towards me and plowed into my shield. Catherine came at him even harder, striking at one leg while I beat the other. The zombie roared, then collapsed onto the path between us.

"Thanks!" Catherine said, trying to catch her breath.

I smiled at her. "No problem." We looked down at the creature by our feet. He lay motionless with his arms and legs sprawled out in the dirt. I exhaled and felt any lingering anxiety I'd had about combat leave my body. "That was fun!"

Catherine laughed. "I know!"

We resumed formation once all the undead had collapsed. As we continued around the path, we glanced back at the actors, knowing they would reanimate before long. I excitedly held on to my shield and weapon. After defending myself—however unsuccessfully—and saving a friend, I felt ready to face a hundred more if need be. Catherine marched by my side, looking equally elated.

It wasn't long before the next attack. My fellow female soldier and I were immediately targeted. I held fast against a living corpse in a bloodied gasmask pushing and trying to force me backwards. I beat against his legs, steadying myself while trying to keep a distance from heavier blows beside me. The thing went down within seconds, as did Catherine's attacker. We looked for fellow recruits in need of aid, then ran off to ambush more growling creatures. Once they were all conquered, we resumed formation, walked the perimeter of the compound, and returned to the van.

Back in the briefing room, we recounted our exploits. I noticed Johan smiling much easier, having saved several others from the furious undead. We reveled in the sweet comfort of the air conditioning while the second team headed out on their mission. My clothes were now soaked with sweat. It must have been eighty degrees out in the sun, but I somehow felt the effects much more *after* the battle. I could only imagine what it was like for the poor actors.

But the next time I armed myself against them, it was with the gun.

"Visors down!" Jack bellowed at us.

We stood outside the steel-framed building once again. I looked at the large weapon in my grip. I kept it pointed safely towards the ground after wrapping its thick strap over my shoulder and back.

"Remember that you will only shoot the zombies in the *chest*," Jack stressed, "never in the *face*. And you will only fire at close range. Remember your guns have splitters that only reach out to four meters."

My nerves quickly revived. Horrible thoughts ran through my mind as I followed orders to line up before the entrance. *What if the splitter doesn't work? What if I trip and shoot someone in the face?* I envisioned actors clutching their eyes in pain after any number of freak accidents. But I forced myself to shake those thoughts. *The zombie movie continues,* I told myself. *I won't actually hurt anyone.*

I glanced back at Catherine while lowering the thick plastic over my face. She smiled in assurance while crouching in line. The first pair ran in. The rest of us waited, silently, until the sound of muffled gunfire made its way outside. Jack ordered in a second team, then waved for Tom and me to enter after the room was announced clear. I ran behind my partner, keeping low with my weapon aimed at nothing but ground.

Inside, a chilling silence took over. An expansive, concrete room felt cool and remarkably dark away from the blazing sun. I scanned massive sandbags covering every inch of the floor. They looked almost cloudy through my thick visor, like an army-green, lumpy desert. In an instant I saw a camouflaged figure sprawled out over them, close to a doorway on the opposite side of the room. I followed my partner, carefully stepping over the rough, uneven plastic, while never taking my eyes off the seemingly dead.

After only a few steps, the creature jerked to life. He looked even less human than his counterparts had outside. A thick pair of goggles covered his eyes with several spots of red and blue paint splattered over them. He appeared more like a color-speckled alien than a bloodthirsty zombie. The thing growled, fumbling over the bags and moving in our direction. Tom fired, sending a blast of blue paint onto the creature's chest. I hesitantly aimed my gun. I wasn't sure about how the force of the blast would feel on a *person* rather than a metal plate. After a few seconds, I willed my finger back on the trigger. I felt a slight jolt as the gun fired but presumed it to be more from nerves than from the blast of the weapon. Yellow paint sprayed over the actor's chest, covering small sections of Tom's blue. Judging by how far it spread, I knew that the impact had been much more subtle than I'd feared. It was probably barely felt at all. I watched, relieved, as the creature fell backwards and collapsed onto plastic flooring.

I exhaled while observing its demise. *Whew!*

A hanging tarp marked the entrance to the next room. Huge stacks of wooden crates tilted across the cement floor. Tom scanned each corner, then dropped to one knee. I copied the action by his side.

"Room clear!" he shouted.

Additional firing came from the room we had just left; the fallen dead had evidently revived. Catherine and Johan emerged through the tarp then shuffled past. Tom tapped me on the arm and gestured for me to follow.

Additional reanimations waited throughout the compound. Zombies charged from dark hallways. Creatures growled and foamed at the mouth while plowing us down, each wearing thick goggles concealing inhuman eyes. Tom immediately fired. I followed, no longer nervous about hurting anyone. The things went down—camouflage clothes crashing to the floor, each splattered with blue, yellow, and red—while muffled gunfire resounded in the distance. In the midst of the maze, I crouched with my weapon aimed at the next charging fiend while a second grabbed my ankle from behind. I turned to face the hissing dead frantically pulling me towards him. I couldn't help but laugh at the face of colorful goop while trying to jerk my leg free. *This is definitely like a zombie movie,* I thought. *Gore, sweat, and frenzy with no time to* think, *let alone* fight!

Beside me, Tom fired at what charged us head on. The attacker collapsed onto the floor. My partner then blasted the thing with the death-grip on my foot. I threw a hand over my face, trying to shield myself from his ammo, but it was too late: a shot of thick slime ricocheted under my visor onto my eyes and mouth. I cringed and groaned as Tom gripped my elbow and heaved me back up.

"You all right?" I heard him ask me.

I was blinded by paint. "Yeah, I'm good," I said, wiping the mess off with an arm. I suddenly felt like a slimed Ghostbuster. "Gross!"

Back in the briefing room, Catherine and I collapsed onto our chairs. The entire troop looked exhausted. I laughed with my new friends over our missions. Paint covered our arms and legs. Sweat stains marked my knees as I pulled off my padding. I felt ten pounds lighter with the plastic stripped off me at last, and that, somehow, we really *had* saved the world from a zombie apocalypse.

After the second group returned from their mission, Alan applauded everyone's effort.

"But one person deserves a special acknowledgment for going above and beyond," the sergeant said. He paused a moment, holding a piece of parchment before him. "He was quick to announce whenever zombies were approaching and when soldiers were down. Tom," he said with a decisive nod, "if you would please come up to receive a Certificate of Excellence."

I clapped with the crowd. My partner walked to the front of the room, looking surprised and touched. I remembered him calling to the others when I'd first been ambushed in battle. I remembered him helping me up not once, but twice, and blasting my raving attacker in the compound. Beside me, Johan applauded his fellow soldier. It seemed that both of them would have made excellent Navy SEALS—as well as zombie-elimination officers.

After a few claps, Catherine cupped a hand to her mouth. "Shoot him!" she called with a smile, chuckling.

Alan immediately pointed at her. "You. Back of the room. Ten pushups."

Zombie School

With the world saved from zombie outbreak once again, Johan and I relaxed at a cafe on site. We wolfed down sandwiches and chocolate milk after saying our farewells to Catherine and Tom. The meal tasted nothing short of exquisite after a full morning of beatings and gunfire. I could also only hope that Johan found it to be at least *slightly* more enjoyable than a protein shake.

"I liked Zombie Boot Camp," he said, sitting across from me at the table. "It was really cool."

I slumped back in my chair after devouring my sandwich. It was hard to fight off the urge to order three more. "Me, too. I've never done anything like that. I was nervous at first, but once I realized that no one would get hurt, it was a lot of fun."

Johan mused at the thought. "I didn't mind the violence. That's what I liked about it."

I shook my head at him and chuckled.

"What?" he asked without a blink. "That's why most people like this kind of stuff. It's an outlet for aggression—you know that, right? That's just instinct."

I thought back to watching my fellow recruits whale on each other without mercy. They had certainly seemed to love it—so much, in fact, that Jack had to constantly yell at them to take it easy on each other. I could only hope that the zombies hadn't ended up limping out of the compound, bruised and sore, to empty aspirin bottles backstage. They had definitely gotten more of a beating than we had.

"Yeah," I said, "I can see that. Well, one thing's for sure: running around fighting zombies is way more fun than going to the gym."

Johan smiled as he crumpled his napkin. "I'll agree with you on that."

"Well, there's still some time if you want to join me for a second adventure." I glanced at a clock behind him on the wall. "Zombie School starts in twenty minutes. And it should be nice and relaxing, not like Boot Camp. What do you think?"

My host shot me a puzzled look. "What do you mean, 'relaxing'?"

"Well, you know, it's *school*. It'll probably be sitting in a classroom learning about zombies from the movies and stuff and how to prepare for a zombie apocalypse before fighting in one." I grinned at the thought. It all seemed so peaceful compared to what we'd just endured.

"Chris," Johan said, shaking his head, "that's not what it is. Didn't you read the website description?"

My eyes glazed over. I had read it back in Ireland when researching zombie camps around the UK. It seemed like ages ago. "I forget."

"They teach you how to *be* a zombie! They put blood all over you and you have to attack people."

I felt my eyes grow wide in alarm. The image of a quiet afternoon suddenly vanished. "What?! Are you sure?"

"Yes," he said flatly.

My shocked brain went blank. I tried to recall just what I had read online a month before. Had I not understood that it involved acting? Had I not known that that acting also meant getting beaten by men with batons and shot at with paintball guns? Where was the analytical, more cerebral experience of the undead?

"So you have fun with that," Johan said, interpreting my terror. "I'll pass."

Back in the carpark, I counted three dozen new twenty- and thirtysomethings filling the lot. The male-to-female ratio was similar to that morning: one woman and the rest men. There with her apparent boyfriend, the girl quickly locked eyes on me. I remembered that look. I could only hope that she was there for Zombie School and not Boot Camp. But after Johan drove off and I went to Alan for my orders, I found that I had no such luck; I was the *only* one there for Zombie School.

"That's okay," he assured me. "It isn't always as popular as Boot Camp, but you're in good hands."

Moments later, I found myself following a kid in his late teens through a side entrance of the building. I recognized the red-splattered gasmask around his neck from one of my missions. *Had he taken me down? Had I taken* him *down?* I couldn't remember. So many of the undead had come at me in such a short amount of time, it was all blurring together in a whirl of rotting flesh and camouflage. I took a final glance behind me and saw the lone woman give a crestfallen frown.

I can't get too attached, I thought, turning my attention to my new trainer. *The next time I see her, she'll be the enemy.*

My new teacher introduced himself as Phil. In a room down the hall from Boot Camp's briefing room, five similar-aged men sat before a large mirror. They quietly dabbed "blood"-soaked makeup pads onto their faces and necks. I vaguely recognized each of them from earlier. I presumed that they had washed the colorful gunfire off their skin and now created fresh scabs and scars with latex and paint. Their rumpled, military clothing also appeared clean but showed several old, red stains, which were no doubt permanent additions. Bottles scattered around the makeup table were as dirty as their users, spilling thin, red liquid between brushes, pads, and what looked like hunks of human flesh.

"Everyone, this is Chris," Phil said beside me. "She'll be doing Zombie School with us."

The crew turned and exchanged hellos, then proceeded to dab black, green, and yellow paint onto their fingers. They applied it over the scabs, watching their reflections begin to rot and ooze.

"Great job during Boot Camp," I said from the doorway. "That was a lot of fun."

One actor quickly turned to me. His thick, greasy Mohawk and blackened eyes made me envision an undead biker. "Are you from America?" he asked in a French accent.

"Yes," I said. By now, I was well used to the question.

"That's so cool!" he exclaimed, beaming. "I love America. It's my dream to live there!"

"Of *course* she's American," a kid said beside him. "Can't you tell by her accent?"

The excited kid shrugged. "I couldn't tell; I'm French! You all sound the same to me. I'm Freddy," he said, eagerly extending a now-multicolored hand.

I smiled at his enthusiasm. "Nice to meet you."

In an adjacent room, Phil took me to what looked like a clothing store for those fresh out of the grave. Military clothing, gloves, and plastic padding were neatly organized, with stains of liquid humanity adorning each piece. The actor pointed to a tidily folded stack of everything I would need for the afternoon: a pair of army pants, shirt and jacket, leg pads Velcroed to a plastic belt, kneepads, elbow pads, a camouflage hat, plastic goggles, a thin pair of gloves, and thicker, biker-style gloves. He returned to the makeup room to give me privacy and I proceeded to strap on my new gear. With each layer, I felt as though I was preparing for war. It all felt very different from just slipping on a latex mask, as I'd done back at Castle Dracula. Here, I had to prepare to not just scare but to endure a wrath that I would evoke by doing so. Once everything seemed to be in place, I sought out Phil.

He looked at me blankly beside his fellow actors. "Great, good job."

I peered down at my attire. "Are you sure?" The leg pads and belt seemed a bit odd over my army pants. The others stared at me from the makeup table. I suddenly saw a sign behind them taped to the mirror. *All Padding is Worn UNDER Army Pants!* it read.

I felt my shoulders rise in embarrassment. "Oops..." I pointed towards the sign.

Phil waved it off. His own knee guards, I saw, were worn the same way. "It's okay; I always wear them like this. Anything goes here. Come on—I'll do your makeup."

A blond-haired actor hopped away from the mirror and lounged on a sandbag across from it. I took his seat while Phil picked up a small bottle of red liquid. He carefully tipped it over a fresh makeup pad, then studied my face a moment. The young actor resembled a professional artist looking for inspiration on a new canvas. He leaned towards me with a new brush and I felt wet goop touch my nose. My eyes instinctively slammed shut and my nose scrunched in protest.

Beside us, the lounging actor spoke up.

"Is it true that people in America can just walk around carrying guns? 'Cause that's cool."

My eyes reopened at the question. Still concentrating on his work, Phil bit his lip.

"I don't know," I said. "It isn't that cool when you see how easy it is for kids to bring those guns into schools." Phil nodded but kept quiet.

"I didn't even like using the paintball guns on you guys. I was afraid you might get hurt."

"Nahhh." Freddy leaned past Phil to watch my face undergo monster metamorphosis. "Those things are harmless; they have splitters on them. I get shot in the face all the time, and it doesn't hurt."

My eyes froze as I looked at him. "You guys get shot in the *face?*"

Phil laughed.

Freddy smiled. "Oh yeah—just wait, you'll see!"

Once Phil concluded that my zombification was complete, I looked at myself in the mirror. My eyes now appeared sunken into the sockets. The skin above my cheekbones was a mixture of purple and red. One eye trickled blood. My nose gushed from a dark wound painted on the bridge. A gash drawn below my mouth oozed down my chin.

"Wow," I said in admiration, "it looks great. Thanks!"

Phil bowed with a smile.

We remained backstage while the new Boot Camp recruits underwent trainings in the adjacent rooms. Jack shouted the orders. Loud whacks of batons thumped against plastic shields. Paintball guns blasted through the training maze. I occasionally admired my new corpse look in the mirror, feeling much happier on this side of a zombie outbreak. If my choices were between being a flesh-hungry creature or a soldier who had to beat and shoot at one, I realized that I'd take the former any day—if only for the appearance alone.

When the time came, Alan drove us to the compound for the first mission. Phil handed out water bottles. and as we stepped out of the van, I understood why. It felt about ninety degrees. The intense sun made my additional layer of clothing, padding, and hat feel as if they weighed thirty pounds. I vaguely remembered being hot in my gear as a soldier; the memory of it seemed almost laughable now.

"The recruits will be here in a few minutes," Phil said. He and Freddy led me down the dirt path running beside the building. "Hide over there for now and you can come at them when they get to you."

I looked at the small shed where he indicated. I felt a familiar wave of panic begin to arise. I suddenly longed for the peaceful asylum of Castle

Dracula. I remembered how nervous I'd been waiting for the patrons to make their way up the stairwell. Back then, all there was to fear was that my performance wouldn't be eerie enough. I longed for such a trivial fear now. Compared to the thought of being whaled on by strapping, young men, simply crawling around and growling seemed extremely preferable.

I turned to Freddy, trying to hide my fear. "How long should I wait before falling dead once they hit me?"

Freddy shrugged. He casually stood with new, bloody corrosions gleaming on his cheeks and neck. "Just let them hit you a few times, then drop down somewhere out of the way where you won't get stepped on. And curl into a ball—that always helps."

I nodded. I immediately wished that I hadn't just *asked* Johan to do this with me but *begged* him.

My monster trainers crossed the path and crouched behind a lopsided wreck of a car. Freddy waved. I waved back, forcing my grimace to resemble more of a smile. In my mind, I saw that zombie education class that I'd hoped for earlier. I pictured sitting in a quiet, comfortable classroom, watching slides that showed the evolution of zombies in pop culture. I imagined learning about legends in places such as Africa and Haiti, where zombies are said to be resurrected corpses used for slave labor. I saw myself watching clips from the 1932 *White Zombie* to more recent films—those portraying the undead moving suddenly, *painfully,* fast. Instead here I was, dressed in what felt like eight layers of army clothes in the stifling heat, about to get pounded on by guys eager to use their new baton toys. I had to give my new actor friends their due: these guys were tough.

A soft crunching on gravel marked the van's approach. Across from me, Ray, the actor who had confessed his gun obsession, joined the others behind the bashed-up car. I decided that my plan would be to attack the recruits just after the more experienced actors did. Judging by their knowing grins, I presumed that they already knew my tactic.

Jack's voice came after the van door clicked shut. "All right, everyone in formation!"

The familiar snapping of plastic shields followed. I envisioned the single wall of defense slowly making its way down the path. I wondered if the lone woman was in this group. I could only hope that she was having fun. But as the dozen soldiers came into view, I saw that she wasn't with them. Smaller, shorter men held two snatch shields behind the others as the troop advanced. Within moments, Ray, Freddy, and the others slowly emerged from their spots. The soldiers watched. I saw the same resolute expressions that I'd seen in my own group that morning. My fellow creatures charged. The soldiers broke formation. They scattered throughout the path, holding their shields firmly before them. The forces collided: bloodied undead using all their weight against very-much-alive soldiers. The recruits struck hard with their batons, using a level of force that I was sure would hurt a lot more than anything that I had done that morning.

After what felt like a year, I staggered out from behind my shed. I locked my gaze on the smallest mortal I saw. He held a snatch shield before him, watching the ambush that he had just been spared from suffering. He turned to me in an instant and instinctively drew back his weapon. A second later he flinched. I had seen *that* look earlier, too: *I have to hit a* girl...?

My panic increased at the thought of what I might do, but I forced myself to stop thinking. Instead I threw up my arms and ran straight towards my victim. I rammed into his shield and pushed against him with all my might. He didn't budge. Instead, a small smile grew on his face. Not only was he being attacked by a female zombie, but she wasn't very strong. The soldier regained himself, then hit me softly on the thigh. I immediately laughed, both at his expression and from feeling what was no doubt about a tenth of his strength. I forced myself to turn my reaction into a growl. The cadet's strikes gained in power. After a few hits, I flopped down onto the ground and curled up my legs. My would-be victim ran off to join the surrounding sounds of a much more aggressive battle. A moment later, I heard a familiar voice.

"A little more aggressive next time!" Alan said with an amused tone.

"Okay..." My muffled voice escaped through my arms shielding my face. "Sorry!"

Through partial vision, I watched my fellow zombies push and plummet into the man-size shields. They suffered retaliation of grunt-filled force. Each waited until he had been beaten long enough, then dropped to the ground as if dying a second time. Jack called the recruits into formation. The ensemble continued down the path. Only after the other actors began to get up did I start to move.

Freddy bounded over to me. "You all right?" he asked with a hint of alarm.

I laughed. I could only hope that he hadn't seen my pathetic performance on the battlefield. "I'm fine."

He waved for me to follow the shuffling army. *This time will be better,* I thought with gusto. *Remember, you're not a soldier now—you're a monster back from the dead!*

I targeted my next victim. I stared hard at the man holding the second snatch shield. While Freddy ran towards a larger, Johan-proportioned cadet, I noticed Alan standing on top of a sandbag beside the trail. He was taking pictures. *Oh, God,* I thought, freezing at the sight. *Had he been doing that this morning? Was I too busy avoiding the kill to notice?*

It changed everything. I couldn't be a cowardly zombie on camera, not when I knew that the members of this SWAT team were going to look at those pictures later. They would want to remember their glory days of battling the undead. And I could help with that. I charged my new victim at top speed. I pushed him back several feet, trying to break through the armor that stood as the only thing separating me from his flesh and blood. He fought back, harder than his teammate had, while I strained to force him to the ground. *A much better picture,* I thought while keeping cadet mutilation on the brain. *This feels much more like what I've seen in the movies.* The purpose of Zombie School became crystal clear; there could be no passive classroom learning to truly understand the undead. Learning about zombies meant *being* one, and the last thing they are is cerebral.

I eventually fell by the soldier's feet, who remained unshakably upright throughout my attack.

While the living army advanced, I trailed behind with the others for our third and final ambush. I no longer waited for my trainers to make the initial move. I ran towards a man-sized armadillo shield at full force. I suffered his long stretch of thrashing and blows, then fell defeated as my comrades did the same. All but one—Ray had pinned his victim against a sandbag wall. Jack ordered the soldiers back into the van while the conquered mortal strained to free himself.

"Do you want to turn into a zombie and get the others?" Ray asked his victim as the van drove off.

The kid stopped struggling. His white T-shirt and jeans were now rumpled canvases of dirt and dust. "Sure!"

Ray hopped up, then extended a hand to his victim. "Awesome."

With ten minutes before the next group's arrival, our newest addition joined us at the starting point. Phil smeared thick, red gore across his chin and neck from a secret stash of makeup along the trail. The fresh zombie smiled at himself in a handheld mirror. I matched his reaction, marveling at his excitement about it all without even a hint of apprehension.

We used the same techniques for the next group. Our newest member of the undead showed just as much gusto as the more experienced killers. I couldn't help but wonder if it was aided by the fact that he probably knew at least some of the soldiers he lunged after. But his enthusiasm was inspiring. I saw the female cadet at long last, sticking close to her male friend the entire time. I let Freddy and the others take their turns with the duo, preferring not to jump into the ambush. After the final bout of combat, Freddy approached me while catching his breath.

"Okay, now they'll be coming back with paintball guns."

I stared at him, unblinking and soaked in sweat. "Okay."

"You ready?" He studied my face. "Having fun?"

"Oh yeah..." I forced a smile, trying to hide my new horror. "You bet."

We grabbed our goggles and headed into the large, steel building. I recognized the room with sandbag flooring. The cool and dank concrete felt even better than air conditioning. I immediately sighed in gratitude.

"You'll be with me the whole time," Freddy said. "Just remember: never take your goggles off. They won't mean to hit you in the face, but they still will."

I shuddered at the thought. I had already been hit in the face that morning. I remembered it feeling utterly disgusting, but fortunately it hadn't hurt at all.

"They come in here first," Freddy explained, stepping across the sandbags with ease, "then go through here...."

He led me on a tour through the tarps and corridors, winding through a maze of confusion. I ran to keep up. We would have to maneuver through hidden entrances several times to catch the cadets off guard. I began to feel like a rat trying to make its way to the cheese in some warped science experiment.

"Does all this make sense?" Freddy asked in the final room. I could hear Phil, Ray, and the others taking their places behind the surrounding walls.

"Yup," I said, remembering almost nothing. "I'll be with you the whole time."

Freddy chuckled. "Exactly."

Back among the sandbags, we got ready for the first group's arrival.

"I'll lie down over here," Freddy said. He flopped down onto the floor midway between the entrance and exit, his goggles dangling from his hand. "You lie down over there, past me. When they come in, start crawling towards them. As soon as they shoot you, go down."

"Okay," I said, fumbling over to my spot.

"Okay, you can put your goggles on now—and don't take them off!"

The familiar crunching of the van's approach sounded from outside. I wrapped the thick, plastic frames around my head. Everything immediately blurred. The walls became gray vapors. Freddy turned into a large, vague outline lying on top of green clouds. I heard the door of the van open and Jack's voice follow. Freddy's fuzzy, gloved hand gave me a thumbs up. I slumped back onto the plastic, feeling like a soldier mentally preparing for execution. I rolled my head towards the door, staring vacantly towards it like a Romero-style zombie. But I thought back to Alan's words once again: *these zombies are fast.*

Within moments, two soldiers entered. Each held a paintball gun before him that, somehow, looked more dangerous than a real one. I watched Freddy immediately lift himself off the floor and charge. The men stopped in their tracks. They aimed their weapons and fired several shots. Frozen, I watched Freddy flop facedown with a loud crunch. The soldiers resumed their advance. As their visored attention turned in my direction, I forced myself to become that zombie that I had been just minutes before. I bolted upright and leapt onto my hands and knees. I crawled and growled towards my enemy—these mortals whose blood and flesh were mine and no one else's. I stood up to sprint as they fired. I felt dull impact on my chest. Red and blue splattered onto my face, wet but painless, and fragments shot onto my goggles. I threw myself back, acting as though the hits had been a hundred times more powerful. My arms collapsed onto the rough plastic as though I'd been instantly destroyed.

From the corner of my glazed eyes I saw the soldiers maneuver past. They disappeared through the tarp. Moments later, voices came from the adjacent room.

"Room clear!"

Two more entered. Blurry forms stepped cautiously towards Freddy. The entire room was now streaked with red and blue. It quickly became foggy from the heat in my goggles. My fellow monster repeated his pounce and ran towards the new soldiers. He crashed to the ground after they fired. I clawed to my feet, now too energetic to crawl, and lunged towards the enemy who awaited my attack. They held fire until I was almost upon them. In a flash I recognized the small frame of the female soldier. She stood behind her taller, broader partner and shot at me just moments before I could reach her. The ammo struck my chest with the slightest force, but I threw myself backwards as though it had gone clean through me.

She is *having fun*, I thought. Reopening my eyes, I saw that the room had become one big mixture of bright colors. *Good for her!*

More shuffles of feet passed until I heard Freddy hustle over.

"All right?"

His man-shaped form helped me up. I saw nothing beyond the vague outline of green camouflage. "Come on," he said. "We have to follow them!"

I wiped off my goggles. Thick goop smeared onto the fingers of my gloves, and the walls and my trainer reappeared. *How could anyone see in this?*

I ran after Freddy through the tarp separating the rooms. He bolted at full speed, screaming at gun-bearing soldiers as set on their destruction. I charged past him after he fell to the floor. More paint splattered onto my goggles, chest, and neck. I threw up my arms to block my fall, while the kneepads softened any impact from the concrete. Freddy's hand appeared seconds later.

"I can barely see!" I said as he hoisted me up.

"I know!" From his voice, I could tell he was smiling. I wiped off more goop, then saw that his own goggles were equally sullied. He obviously was used to the blindness.

We continued our hunt through the maze. No longer afraid of the gunfire, I hurled myself at my victims as though ready to tear their limbs from their bodies. I could also only hope that my arms would help shield my face from the blasts. It didn't work; wet, sticky globs sprayed over my nose and mouth, ricocheting off hits to my chest. My padding aided every fall as I flung myself backwards. I could vaguely make out the colorful concrete that had become the world around me.

After the first team completed their mission, Freddy and I returned to the sandbag room.

"How can you guys see through all the paint?" I wiped a wad of blue from my mouth and spat some of it onto the floor. I had seen only fleeting glimpses of Phil, Ray, and the others throughout the compound, but the gunfire from every direction told me they were never far off.

"Yeah, it gets hard to see," Freddy said, nodding. "But it's fun, right?"

I looked at him. I was covered in paint and far sweatier than I ever could have fathomed back in Boot Camp. But I was also running around like a monster. I was growling and screaming and attacking survivors of a zombie outbreak. It was something I had only seen in the movies, and even the most realistic of haunts had never put me on *both* sides of the story.

And that was pretty damn cool.

"Oh yeah," I said, crossing my feet on the lumpy floor. "It's wicked fun. Thanks for showing me the ropes."

Freddy looked at me blankly. "The ropes?"

"It's an expression. It means, thanks for showing me how to do things."

He lit up while flopping down onto his death spot. "Is that an *American* expression?" he asked. "Great! You're welcome." He leaned back and stretched out his arms and legs. "Where else would I get to do all this and get *paid* for it?"

He laughed towards the ceiling in utter bliss.

I laughed with him.

"Who *wouldn't* want to do this?" he asked. "I mean, really!"

The next day, I checked my e-mail from Johan's apartment. Alan had sent the pictures from our combat missions. I laughed at the image of my Couchsurfing host, Catherine, Tom, and me as soldiers, fighting against the undead who would later become my teachers. But while scrolling through the pictures, I stopped at those he'd taken during Zombie School. I stared at each depiction in disbelief. Seemingly heroic battle scenes showed monsters and men looking brave and defiant through the bloodshed. Only one sad, beaten creature lay curled up on the ground beside it all.

Oh my God, I thought, slamming the laptop shut. *Let no one ever see....*

Horror Camp Live!

In northern England, the old woman frowned wretchedly. She stood in a black, tattered shawl with her hands on her hips, a large hood framing her pale, grim face. Her mouth gaped open in disapproval, revealing several black teeth as she stared at us in the parking lot.

"Okay, you lot," she huffed, "pay attention. My name is Mrs. Dybuk. You are here at Camp F—ing Mass Acre. I don't like my job and I don't f—ing care what you think about it. But we're spending the f—ing night together so we better f—ing deal with it."

My eyes froze wide as she spoke. I half-smiled at her without a blink. After spending a few weeks in Blackpool following my RAM trainings, I had learned about a unique overnight endeavor called Horror Camp Live. Its website was intriguing: it stated that Horror Camp Live was a unique scare experience that mixed live actors, indoor and outdoor scare-attraction environments, dare-based challenges, and a horrifying story.

It sounded perfect.

I was joined by Dave. My thirty-nine-year-old Couchsurfing host from Blackpool stood beside me in long, corduroy pants and a winter jacket, appropriately dressed for a cool, English evening. He was also eager to make any day into an adventure. On August 2, we had decided to start the weekend by hitchhiking from Blackpool to the camp. While forty others drove into the lot at 7:00 P.M., Dave and I strolled in from the country road slightly wet and with damp bags over our shoulders from having our thumbs out in the recent rain.

Just like at Zombie Boot Camp, I had to sign a waiver that Horror Camp Live would not be held responsible should any harm befall me that evening. Dybuk also pointed out that our signature included agreeing to remain on the property until eight o'clock the next morning. No one would be permitted back should they choose to leave, and cellphone use would not be allowed.

"All right, then!" the old woman barked after the colorful introduction. "Everyone grab your s— and follow me."

Dave and I exchanged looks while the others dispersed to their cars.

"Wow!" I said, gripping my backpack straps with a grin.

Dave's pale complexion beamed. "This is great. I love it already!"

The troop followed Dybuk down a dirt path—recently transformed into mud—with rolled-up sleeping bags, pillows, and bulging backpacks.

Distant mooing and a subtle aroma from fields of tall grass told me that the site was primarily used as a dairy farm.

"I'm gonna show you where the toilets are now," Dybuk called to the crowd, "so you know where to go when you gotta s— and piss. Remember where it is because it gets dark at night. Now who's gotta take a s—?"

Giggles erupted from behind her.

"I do!" one guy eagerly exclaimed.

We inspected the bathroom's large, wooden shed, which I was thrilled to find was both clean and heated. Farther along the trail, twelve two-person tents formed a wide half-circle in an open field. A heaping pile of wood lay in a fire pit across from them, looking sad in its wet, soggy state.

"This is where you'll all be spending the night," Dybuk bellowed, "so you can pick a tent and throw your s— inside—"

She stopped as loud grunts and moans began to emit from one of the sleeping quarters.

"What the f— is going on in there?" the old woman howled.

The commotion quickly ceased. The flap door unzipped and a man stepped out. Dressed in loose leather pants, a trench coat, and cowboy hat, he scrutinized the group in annoyance while casually holding a shotgun by his side.

"What's all this?" he yelled.

Behind him, a second man emerged. His tightfitting, purple dress drew immediate laughs from the crowd. He paid no notice while straightening his wig of long, flowing blonde hair and stumbling through the grass.

"What the hell, b—?" he roared at Dybuk.

I flinched at his masculine voice.

Dybuk scolded the two for not just "f—ing around" but for doing so as brother and sister. She introduced the pair as Cleaver—Camp Mass Acre's landowner—and Incesta, his wife and sister. The three argued back and forth, swearing constantly.

"Mind your business, b—!" Incesta screamed.

"F—ing disgusting...!" Dybuk yelled back.

We followed our instructions to ignore the "trash" and dump our "s—" into one of the tents. Dave and I chose our spot in the half-circle's center. We had packed lightly for the trip: a thin blanket each, pillow, basic bathroom supplies, and clothes for the next day.

"Those three are *hilarious*," I said after hurling my bag into the tent.

Dave chuckled, unloading his own, damp supplies. "Yeah, they're brilliant. I love Dybuk."

What made them even funnier, I knew, was that Dave and I rarely swore.

The old woman demanded that we follow her back down the path. She and Incesta bickered until leading us into a large farmhouse. Inside, chairs lined the walls of what resembled a deep-blue ballroom. A large fireplace stood along the wall, appearing large enough to walk through had it not been sealed with stone. A small, coffin-shaped box stood on a table in the center of the room, and at the far end a projector screen hung above a small stage.

"Everyone take a f—ing seat," Dybuk commanded. "We're gonna watch some videos now so you can learn all about this f—ing place. Dinner will be coming in about a half-hour. We'll be having hamburgers and all kinds of s—. If you're hungry already then you have to f—ing wait."

I cracked up as she spoke. Dave stared at her as if in love. We chose seats close to the stage as our host grumpily explained how the evening would be run.

"One thing you should know is that show producers are watching and will be here all night." She pointed to a large mirror on the wall opposite the stage. "My bosses are back there with their headsets." She motioned to a small microphone by her ear that had been previously concealed by her hood. "If you have any f—ing problems, you tell me and I'll tell them. Otherwise they'll stay back there all night."

For the next twenty minutes, a home movie played out the story of a woman who had previously run Camp Mass Acre. She had died mysteriously, after which time Mrs. Dybuk had taken her job. While the story played, she and Incesta moved about the room, chatting with the campers. I laughed at pretty much everything they said.

"I love how you call everyone 'b—,'" I told Incesta when he—or, rather, *she*—approached me.

"That's right!" she said, moving her hips and neck wildly. "*Everyone's* my b—. Everyone's below *me*, b—!"

I keeled over in laughter. Dave giggled beside me. Cleaver eventually brought in trays of burgers, vegetables, and potato salad. In line, everyone shielded their faces as Dybuk threw paper plates at them.

"This place is really fun," I whispered to Dave back at our seats, "but it isn't really scary, is it?" I licked ketchup off a few of my fingers. Moments earlier, Dybuk had squirted the red sauce all over my plate after I'd asked for the bottle.

"Well, maybe that comes later." Dave shrugged. His hands remained clean, as he had opted for a plain burger after watching my ketchup attack.

Moments later, everything went black.

I felt my eyes grow wide as my food disappeared before me. A dull, gray static flickered from where the video had previously been playing. My fellow campers became a circle of silent shapes around the room. Onscreen, an image appeared. I stared, amazed, at a face looking back at us. Horrid eyes bulged out from black sockets. A large, metal brace concealed half of its bone-white head, stretching from below a pale nose down to its neck. A mass of wires attached the device to crude gears where its ears should have been, making it look like some kind of warped construction of the reanimated dead.

"Oh, f—," I heard Dybuk cry from the back of the room. "Not again!"

"Good evening, fools," came a deep, menacing voice from the screen. "My name is Lockjaw. And I am taking over this camp."

I leaned over to Dave, seeing only his outline in the darkness. "Nice!"

The creature rolled its head as it spoke, its mouth completely concealed behind the metal contraption. "If any of you hope to survive the night at Camp Mass Acre, you will put yourself at my mercy. And I want to play a game."

I smiled at the reference to the *Saw* movies. The odd monster gave us explicit instructions: we would be separated into three teams to complete a series of tasks. We would have eight minutes to carry out each one, and points would be given based on how quickly we performed them. The team with the most points at the end of the night would be the winner. If we agreed to these terms, we would survive to see the morning. And if we didn't, we would die slow, painful deaths.

I nodded in approval. That seemed fair.

Three people chose items from the small coffin in the center of the room. Teams were formed based on king, queen, and bishop chess pieces. After Dave and I were assigned to the King's team, Lockjaw described our first mission, then disappeared. A countdown clock took his place. It showed eight minutes.

"King team," Incesta called in a panic, "follow me!"

Six of us ran after her outside. With the sun now set, I understood Dybuk's earlier comment about locating the bathroom after dark. I had no clue which direction to take for finding it. Only a large, white van before us was visible. Incesta hurriedly handed out black hoods and instructed us to put them on before getting inside. The world went black as I pulled dark, thick material over my face and maneuvered through the mud. I felt Dave plop down beside me in the van, no doubt crushed in the small space. The door slammed shut. We rode in silence, bumping and sliding along the uneven road. After a short while, the van pulled to a stop and Incesta ordered us to remove our hoods and exit.

Before us, a large barn stood in a new section of the farm. I scanned the dark surroundings. I immediately envisioned a film being shot in the decrepit structure. I saw kidnapped hitchhikers being held captive in the English countryside, suspended by ropes and chains until bleeding to death and never being heard from again.

I smiled in excitement. The camp was getting better and better.

A man charged from the horrid shack. I stared at him, shocked into silence with my teammates. A surgical mask concealed half of his face. A soiled, dentist's smock covered his large frame, revealing blood and vile, yellow fluid. He stopped before us and glared. Huge, bloodshot eyes looked manic beneath greasy, matted hair.

"Everyone inside," Incesta ordered. "Follow him!"

The creature turned and stormed into the building. Dave and I rushed with the others to keep up. Past a steel door, a small room resembled a dentist's office straight out of hell. A young woman lay strapped to a surgical chair with a crude gag binding her mouth. She mumbled to us frantically, with an ancient drill jutting out from a rusting crane above her. Trays of blood-crusted tools gleamed from a counter. Buckets of what looked like muddy swamp water lay scattered around the floor. A single fluorescent bulb flickered from the ceiling, periodically plunging everything into darkness. I flinched at the smell; everything stank as disgusting as it looked.

The dentist stomped up to his bound victim, then turned back to us.

"You have six minutes left!" Incesta called. She looked tense and alarmed. "Your task is to find ten teeth in the buckets or the girl in the chair dies. You'd better move!"

Three guys immediately threw themselves down to the pails. "Go!" they shouted to one another. "Move; come on. Everybody at a bucket!"

I watched my group quickly reach into the containers of filth. Thick, slimy liquid covered their forearms and slopped over the rims.

"Ughhh...!" I exclaimed, turning to Dave.

He was already at a pail. He plunged a hand down into it. I grabbed the remaining bucket and knelt beside my fellow campers. I slowly reached into the dark, murky God-knows-what. It felt cold and gross and looked disgustingly brown. At the bottom I felt what seemed to be a thin layer of sand. Scooping up bits of debris, I opened my hand and inspected them in the intermittent light. I made out several stones, a small twig, and globs of mud—but no teeth. I dropped them onto the cement and reached back into the water, feeling around the edges and scooping out everything that remained.

"I got one!" someone in the group yelled.

"Here's one."

"Here's another!"

Water and muck splashed onto my jeans. More teeth were discovered around me. Incesta yelled for us to hurry. Everything was happening so fast. But I reveled in the rush and exhilaration of the challenge. I was immersed in a horror movie, trying to save a stranger from mutilation. I was just as much a part of the story as Incesta, Dybuk, and the homicidal dentist. And as I continued my frantic search, it felt both strange and wonderful to physically *feel* the kind of filth that I'd seen in so many haunts over the years.

Above us, Incesta shouted, counting down the minutes. The monstrous dentist appeared ready to kill both his victim *and* us the very second we failed.

I scanned what seemed to be the last contents from my bucket. A pair of tiny teeth appeared on my wet palm.

"Here's two!" I shouted.

A man jumped up from the grasping horde. "That's ten. Come on; let's go!"

Back in the main parlor, Dybuk and the remaining campers turned to us in anticipation. The clock on the wall had stopped at fifty seconds. The old woman asked for a member of our team to recount what had happened. The man who had announced our final tooth count detailed our task with pride: the blindfolded van ride, the hideous dentist, reaching into buckets of mess to find teeth. He put his hands on his hips and sighed with satisfaction while finishing the story.

In their seats, the Queen and Bishop teams exchanged apprehensive looks.

"You had all better complete your tasks," Dybuk said nervously, "or else none of us will get out of this f—ing place."

I turned to Dave and chuckled. He smiled back. It was a perfect transition: from laughs and chaos to filth and terror.

"Queen team," Dybuk said gravely. "You're next."

While six others rushed off, Dave and I returned to our seats. Within moments, the room went dark once again. Lockjaw's deranged appearance returned to the screen.

"Jeff," the creature croaked. "You will now approach the fireplace to accompany Dr. Goodkind."

A man in his late twenties, whom I presumed to be Jeff, stood up. He slowly turned to Dybuk. The old woman took his hand and led him to the stone wall that seemingly went nowhere. Jeff's friends giggled after him, waving him off to endure the unknown on his own. A dull scraping echoed around the room as a section of the wall opened in the fireplace. A large, strange figure wearing a purple suit and black vest stepped out of it.

Its head looked composed of fused fragments of metal. It stared at Dybuk's companion, and Jeff gave a nervous giggle. The creature extended a blindfold towards his new guest, allowing the man to look at it a moment before tying it around his head. Without a glance in our direction, the mysterious Goodkind then took his victim through the wall and out of sight.

Dave turned to me excitedly. "Wow, cool," he said, on the edge of his seat. "I hope they call me!"

"I know," I said. "Me, too! I like that everything here is made into a big game."

I looked towards the fireplace, wondering where the heck the life-sized puppet could have taken poor Jeff. Was he trapped in a closet like I had once been in Budapest, now three months earlier? I could only hope that he didn't need help getting out. Not a trace of him could be seen and Dybuk had already resumed her idle, insulting chitchat as if nothing had happened.

The Queen team returned with thirty seconds to spare. A young woman described their task: they had entered a doctor's office, apparently finding it just as disgusting as our dental one, only the doctor had been completely nude. The group had to find dismembered body parts in buckets of slime and filth, and one person had gotten groped during the search. Dave laughed at the thought. I stared at the team in shock, immensely relieved to have not been a part of it. But they only giggled and rolled their eyes.

As the Bishop team ran off into the night, now Jeff-less, Dybuk gave the rest of us a new task. Teams of two were ordered to make objects out of sticks and string in order to keep away evil spirits. Dave and I fumbled with the materials, musing over the game's connection to *The Blair Witch Project*. When the Bishop team returned, we learned that they had also encountered the nude, barbaric doctor. No one had gotten groped, but they had failed to complete their task in time. They were now in last place. As their leader told the story, a familiar face reappeared; the long-lost Jeff quietly crawled out of a hidden space beneath the stage. He returned to his friends, brushing off dirt from his hands and knees, then appeared to quietly reveal what he'd been through.

The next time Lockjaw brought impending doom, our team was given its next mission. We followed Incesta's lead, hopping into the van, hooded, and being dropped off outside the entrance of a large, steel building.

The bald creature that emerged was no dentist or doctor. Sweat and grime covered his tall, thin frame. A single loincloth made me wonder if this was what the others had meant when claiming the doctor was nude. Like our previous antagonist, he said not a word but grunted at us threateningly.

"Everyone inside!" Incesta called. "Six minutes. Come on!"

The grisly man turned on his heels and ran through a rusty doorway. Inside, heavy-metal music blared. Lights flickered, illuminating an old, faded doctor's chair with padding sprouting from gashes in the fabric. I watched as Incesta appeared to give instructions in the deafening noise. By my side, Dave looked at her in apparent comprehension. Before I could ask what was happening, the half-nude creature grabbed a girl in line and dragged her to the haggard chair. She hesitantly sat down, pulling her knees to her chest, and watched her captor take something from a shadowy counter and hand it to our host.

"Five minutes, thirty seconds!" Incesta called. She gave the small object to a man beside her.

"What are we doing?" I yelled in Dave's ear.

He pointed to the man holding what I could now see was a pair of nail clippers.

"We have to summon the Devil," he yelled, though I doubted that anyone else was even able to hear him, "or the girl gets it." He pointed to the girl on the chair. She watched, nervously, as her teammates passed the clippers down the line. "We each have to give this thing here," he said, motioning to the grimy creature, "one of our fingernail clippings."

"Oh my God...!" I exclaimed with a flinch.

"And then we have to pull out one of our hairs."

Dave's eyebrows shot up at the summary. *Well* that's *different,* we seemed to agree.

When the clippers came my way, I quickly searched for a nail that had any growth to spare. In a rush I took a small sliver from the edge of a thumb.

"Four minutes!" Incesta cried.

I cupped my bit of nail as Dave held his own slice from an index finger. The mad doctor approached each of us to collect the items in a grimy, plastic bowl.

Incesta consulted a stopwatch. "Now the hair!"

I watched in amazement as my teammates immediately grabbed single strands from their heads and yanked. I followed suit, adding my long, brown piece to the bowl. Despite the absurdity of it, I couldn't help but feel an even greater sense of being in a horror film. I was physically cutting and pulling out parts of my own body—if ever so slightly—to save a member of my team from a crazed killer. We certainly weren't passively going through this strange, sick story. We were trying to survive it.

The creature went back to his victim with a malicious grin. He showed the girl his bowl of human contents, stirring it with a finger. Her face contorted in amused revulsion. The madman pointed for her to return to us, and we followed Incesta back outside.

In the ballroom, I gave Dave a questioning look while inspecting my missing section of a nail.

"Well, that was unusual...," I said, back in my seat.

His eyes widened, intrigued. "Indeed!"

"Is this the kind of thing you expected?"

Dave seemed to consider it. Across from us, Dybuk looked over everyone's stick objects meant to protect us from evil. Most resembled simple stars made out of intersecting crosses. "I wasn't sure *what* to expect," Dave said. "But I'll certainly never forget it!"

I laughed as the room went dark. Onscreen, Lockjaw peered down onto his horde of captives.

"Chris," his voice boomed.

I felt my heart stop.

"You will now proceed to the fireplace and await Dr. Goodkind."

Dave looked at me and gasped. "You're so lucky!"

I slowly stood as the lights returned. All eyes in the room watched me. I immediately grinned at expressions of excitement and nervousness.

"You all right?" Dybuk asked when I reached her at the fireplace. For the first time, I saw her face grow calm and serious. I could tell that she was trying to gage my reaction: was I afraid to go off on my own?

I smiled. "I'm good."

She nodded. The stone beside us retreated. I watched in awe as the humanoid construction reemerged. His blank, glassy eyes seemed to peer right through me, and I saw that he was barely more than my height. The teams fell silent while he held a blindfold up to me, allowing me to look at it before wrapping it around my eyes and head. The room quickly became a black void. I pulled my arms to my chest in protective mode, then felt a cloth hand take my own and lead me into an enclosed silence.

The strange guide walked with me for several moments. From the echoing of our steps I could tell that a few walls now separated us from the main room. I held a hand out to my side, brushing a wall with my fingertips. Goodkind maintained a firm grip on my other. After a short time, the creature removed the blindfold and stared at me. Around us, a long, narrow hallway stood empty. Low light exposed nothing but dull, blue walls. I turned to the creature with a slight grin, knowing full well that he was trying to determine if I was scared. He spoke not a word but kept the blindfold in his hand and led me onwards.

In a small, musty room, dozens of lifeless eyes appeared. Barbie dolls, large plush dolls, and marionettes sat slumped on shelves. Others leaned four feet high against the wall, reclined in rocking chairs, or stood on their own around the floor. We stayed only a moment, then entered a large closet with hundreds of dresses, nightgowns, and pajamas hanging from racks. The humanoid animation looked at me. I scanned the clothes on either side of us, inhaling an overpowering scent of mothballs, then turned back to the thing. He was calm and silent, a creation not made for speaking. I studied him with similar interest.

This is where I live, I imagined him saying. *This is my place, another toy in the attic. And now I have a new friend.*

A long, dim hallway brought us away from the room, until Goodkind pointed to a low crawlspace. Bending down, I saw a narrow pathway along the floor extend into darkness. This, I realized, was how Jeff had made his way back to us. The creature motioned for me to go, then slowly waved goodbye. I nodded and returned the farewell. The path before me was completely dark, but I heard faint, recognizable voices from the other end. I crawled along the cement, suddenly feeling like a survivor girl from a horror film. The only difference was that the monster in *this* story had let me go—and was probably the only sane one in the camp.

The light at the end of the tunnel grew brighter until the familiar ballroom appeared once again. Dave smiled when he saw me. Dybuk shot me a scowl, and I responded with a laugh. I noticed that she asked neither Jeff nor me to recount our experience to the others. Unlike the haunt tasks, being taken away by Goodkind seemed to be left up to mystery and suspense.

After everyone's final tasks—searching for pieces of a jigsaw puzzle in a hillbilly's ramshackle trailer—points were added up to determine the winner. The Queen team beat us by almost two minutes. Each member received keychains of plush bears wearing Camp Mass Acre T-shirts. Our team came in second; we had beaten the Bishops by mere seconds.

The next time the lights were extinguished, Lockjaw appeared for the final time.

"You have played the game well...." His deformed head swayed sinisterly from side to side. I smiled at his strange grotesqueness. I hated to see him go. He had been the one to turn the camp into a living nightmare. *But all good things must come to an end.*

"And now I invite you all to attempt a restful night for the remainder of your stay at Camp Mass Acre." His black eyes cast their final gaze upon each of us. "Good luck..."

The lights returned. Dave gave me a sinister wink. "*That* doesn't sound very promising...."

"All right, everyone!" Dybuk barked. Her miserable demeanor had returned full swing. "Time to head to your tents for the night. Let's get the f— out of here!"

The mud and darkness awaited us outside. We tromped along the trail, guided by Dybuk and Incesta's small streams of flashlight. I shivered as my sneakers and jeans grew wet from the grass, passing the soggy campfire that I could only assume kept campers warm on dryer nights. With only a sweatshirt, I longed for my red jacket back at Dave's apartment in Blackpool.

Our strange hosts passed around pieces of paper with a phone number to call or text in the event of an emergency. Cleaver would come around to collect us at eight o'clock in the morning. Until then, they said, heading off into the night, we were on our own.

In our small tent, the air seemed even colder. Dave pulled on his clothes for the next day for the warmth of an additional layer.

"I wish I had sleeping bags," he said beside me.

We each lay under our own blanket, curled into balls in the darkness. I nodded, hunching my shoulders to my ears.

"I haven't gone camping in years," he said. "Not since I was a kid."

"Me neither." I shivered. "But if there were places like this back home, I would *definitely* go more often."

He chuckled. "Yeah, me too."

We lay quiet a moment, listening to the surrounding silence. Only an occasional giggle could be heard from the other tents. Dave checked his glowing watch. It was one o'clock.

"I don't think it's over," he said after a while.

I grinned, wrapping my arms tightly around myself. "Nope. Not a chance."

At some point, I eventually fell asleep. I slowly awoke to the sound of footsteps gently rustling the wet grass. They came closer, then stopped. The outline of a cowboy hat appeared above me, barely visible from the light of the moon. I recognized the shape of a long trench coat and smiled.

Now standing quietly outside, Cleaver seemed to look right at me. The shadow of his hand suddenly appeared on the canvas wall, and I watched his finger run along the fabric. I pointed at him, touching the cold, damp tent, so that he would know I saw him. His finger stopped, then drew a small circle around my hand. In an instant I felt a firm clasp grab hold of my finger. I shrieked and tried to pull it away, but it was caught in what felt like a vise grip. Suddenly, something moved beneath me. It seemed to be sliding underneath the tent. I screamed as it grabbed my arm. I shuffled back towards Dave, my finger still in Cleaver's grasp through the fabric. Although I could see nothing around me, it seemed that Cleaver could see *me* just fine. He released his grip, and in an instant I felt his other hand slide down my back. More fingers grabbed my calf. I screamed and rammed up against my sleeping roommate.

"Dave," I yelled, "wake up!"

Shrieks began to come from other tents. I obviously wasn't the only one being assaulted. I laughed in the darkness, finding the idea of an ambush at Camp Mass Acre hilarious. Dave remained still beside me. The unseen hands from under us retreated. I exhaled in relief and felt my muscles relax as Cleaver's outline disappeared.

"Dave," I said, looking towards his dark form. "Are you awake?"

He remained still. The occasional panicked scream continued from the field outside, intermixed with rustling sounds of struggle. I reached out to shake my friend awake, then stopped when a soft whining came by my feet. I knew that sound. It was a tent door being unzipped. I looked towards it and stared, frozen, at the glimmer of tiny metal arching eerily upwards on its own. I screamed, more at the thought of cold air getting inside the tent than anything else.

"No!" I yelled, then laughed. "Go away!"

The zipper completed its half-circle. The fabric flopped inwards. I saw a different sort of darkness through the opening; it was deeper and speckled with stars. Cold air rushed in like fire. I clutched my blanket to my chest and felt something grab hold of both of my feet. I gasped, trying to pull them back, but felt my body slowly being dragged towards the opening.

"Dave!" I threw a fist onto the dark lump. "Wake up—it's Cleaver!"

He didn't move. I wondered what kind of catatonic sleep he slipped into every night. I clawed at the fabric beneath me, sliding across it, and felt the drop in temperature consume my feet, then legs.

I grabbed Dave's blanket and yanked it off of him. "Wake up—he's dragging me out!"

From outside, Cleaver laughed in the darkness. Dave finally stirred. He sat up, squeezed my shoulders, and heaved me back. My feet were released. In an instant I lunged for the zipper. In the inky darkness, I saw my cloaked assailant's outline dash away.

After closing the door, I turned to Dave. "Were you awake?! Did you feel him grabbing us from under the tent?"

"Yeah," I heard his voice say. It sounded utterly calm. "I just wanted to see what he would do."

I gave him a shove. "Oh, *great*—'cause he wasn't doing anything to *you!*"

The shadow nodded. "Exactly!"

With a huff and a laugh, I curled back beneath my blanket. Screams of campers carried across the field beyond. Dave and I listened, giggling and bursting into laughter at the funniest emissions of playful panic. I thought back to Dom at ScareCON, the haunt actor who'd enjoyed scaring people as a zombie. *It's fun to make them scream*, he'd said, echoing the sentiments of my haunt trainer back at Castle Dracula. I could tell that Cleaver felt the same way, attacking people with as much enthusiasm as the actors had back at RAM. I realized that, given the choice, I actually *did* like being on this side of the game more—the role of attack*ee,* of victim. I had a sudden flashback to Clemens in Salzburg, sitting across from me in the cafe while we discussed his role as Krampus. I remembered what he'd told me about the idea of attacking someone who didn't want it.

He could always tell who did, he'd said.

I can see it in their eyes.

The actors at Horror Camp Live could certainly tell, too. And the owners obviously knew that a lot of people enjoyed being in that role. I supposed that *all* haunt owners did, since the early days of turning scare shows into reenacted slasher films. Haunters knew that people enjoyed the excitement of being immersed in a horror story, being threatened and assaulted by crazed killers on the loose. Who *wouldn't* love something like that?

Around the camp, screams eventually subsided into nervous giggles, then faded into silence.

"You know," I said to Dave, my friend and fellow victim by my side, "camping just won't be the same after this."

He chuckled. "I know. I mean, what'd be the point?"

Chapter 10

The Haunts of New Zealand

"I told yer not ta wander...!"

Joey in New Zealand

On August 18, the customs officer at Auckland International Airport looked at his computer monitor for a long time.

"Can I see your travel itinerary?" he finally asked flatly.

I hesitantly unzipped my backpack. Beside me, a fifth person in line continued through their security check without problem. Several dozen filled the queue, waiting quietly with bags and roller suitcases and kids. I hadn't seen anyone else encounter any trouble at their checkpoint. I finally handed the officer the only papers he could have possibly been referring to.

"These are your previous flights," he said, passing my tickets back across the counter. "I need your itinerary for your flight out of New Zealand."

I blinked at him. "Oh." So *that's* why he'd been staring at the screen after scanning my passport. "I haven't booked my flight yet."

His eyebrows rose. "You haven't?"

"No..." I folded my hands on the counter. Another family continued through the line as easily as I had done in every other airport. "I've been traveling for the past year, and I'm just going from place to place to see how I like it before deciding how long I'll stay."

He continued staring at me. I stared back.

"And why did you come to New Zealand?"

I felt a small smirk start to form. "For Spookers."

He squinted at me. "For *Spookers?*"

I could understand his surprise. Spookers, Auckland's haunted-attraction theme park, had caught my attention months ago. When it came to choosing where to go in the Southern Hemisphere, I knew that my budget would only allow for one place. Spookers' website had been the nail in the coffin, beating Australia hands down. "Yes," I said. "It's a haunted attraction—"

"I know what it is," he interrupted. "You came all the way to New Zealand... for *Spookers?*"

I contemplated my answer. Back in England, people had warned me against revealing the true nature of my travels at customs. Doing research for a book, they said, could fall into a gray area between getting into a country as a tourist and requiring a work visa. It was better to avoid the issue altogether. But this guy was demanding an explanation. Why would someone spend over a thousand dollars for a one-way ticket and not bother booking an outbound flight just to go to a haunted house?

I turned my smirk into an innocent smile. "Of course," I said with a shrug. "Who wouldn't?"

An hour later, my new host picked me up at the airport. I had begrudgingly purchased my outbound flight for early September before being allowed to proceed through customs. I obliged with rolling eyes. They had no reason for concern that I would decide to stay in New Zealand indefinitely.

Please, I thought. *I'm from the States, man.*

"I'm so sorry about the delay," I said to my host after giving him a hug. "I didn't know that customs would be so strict."

Joey waved it off. He was my age, dressed in loose jeans and a white T-shirt, though a thin beard made him look a bit older. He grinned. "No worries. That's happened to a lot of my 'surfers. I should have warned you." He extended a hand to take my bag. "It's okay—he'll be the only one you meet in this country who won't be totally laidback."

On the ride to his house, I gaped out the window from the passenger seat of Joey's silver Jetta. The New Zealand countryside was a seemingly endless expanse of rolling hills, trees, and farmland. Though I couldn't help but find it remarkably similar to Pennsylvania, it seemed light years away. The country was to be my final international destination before returning to the States. It felt strange to be on the other side of the planet now, and I took it all in while only occasionally reminding myself to blink.

In Whitford, a village fifteen miles from downtown Auckland, Joey showed me around his small cottage. He had moved to the country from South Africa six years earlier as an airline mechanic. Although his first language was Afrikaans, to me he sounded just as kiwi as the customs officer.

"I love it here." My host extended his arms on the back porch, admiring the view. Although neighboring houses were along either side of us, none could be seen among the trees and endless green. "It's so nice and quiet."

I nodded, stuffing my hands into my jacket pockets. Feeling the chill of New Zealand's end of winter, I happily wore my red jacket, winter hat, and gloves for the first time since Hungary. "It's beautiful."

In his kitchen, Joey added a heaping tablespoon of condensed milk to cups of instant coffee. It was my first break from an Italian-style coffeemaker since leaving Connecticut. I quickly concurred that the change in taste and its added sweetness put any cappuccino or latte to shame.

Suddenly, Joey grew serious. "I have only one rule in this house," he said from across the counter. I looked at him and froze. I had a feeling that he might be referring to his Ducati motorcycle propped up in the living room. It was shiny and pristine, and Joey had already introduced it to me as the love of his life.

But after staring at me a moment, he pointed to an open laptop on a nearby shelf. "You have to choose the music."

I turned to where he gestured. A Spotify account showed on the screen.

"This way people who stay with me can feel like they're at home," he said, "and I usually get introduced to new things."

"Ahhh..." I nodded at the idea. "I can definitely help with that!"

I chose the first song in a heartbeat.

"This is called 'Grisly Reminder,'" I said proudly, typing in the name. "It's by a group called Midnight Syndicate. They're legendary for haunters. Their music is played in attractions all over the world—and I always have it running in my yard displays on Halloween."

Joey listened as the song began. An ominous feel seemed to come over the bright, sunny dwelling as the eerie melody played.

"That's really cool," he said after a minute. "See, this is what I mean. I've never heard music like that before."

"And this show was amazing...." I pulled up a clip from *Mephistos Pakt* on YouTube, telling him about the Walpurgisnacht festival in Thale.

"I would have loved to see it," Joey said.

I paused the show after Mephisto's demonic introduction. "Yeah, it was amazing. But I'm really glad that you want to go with me to Spookers."

I watched as Joey shuddered. He straightened his back on the stool, then pulled his coffee towards him without taking a sip. "Yes," he seemed to force out. "I went there years ago." He gave a quick nod, keeping his eyes on his drink. "I'll go again."

"You liked it?"

"Well, it was scary, that's for sure...." He squirmed involuntarily. "It's run in what used to be the old psychiatric hospital. That whole place is creepy."

I smiled at his reaction. It was always a good sign when patrons were freaked out by a show's very location. It really helped to set the mood.

"Nice!" I said. "I can't wait to go."

Since Spookers was only open during the weekends, I had some time to explore the area first. Joey took me on several motorcycle rides through the country, including up to his favorite spot on Mount Wellington. The grassy volcanic peak gave a terrific view of downtown

Auckland. Interspersing water of the Hauraki Gulf looked serene with the urban sprawl surrounding it. I could understand Joey's preference for Whitford's more peaceful countryside. Back at his place, I continued following his one rule, playing songs by "Weird Al" Yankovic, Credence Clearwater Revival, and the Monkees. But when Midnight Syndicate's *Gates of Delirium* album started creeping him out after nightfall, he decreed that the one rule would be changed.

Spookers

A few days later, I watched my host clench his teeth in the driveway. He exhaled deeply from the Jetta's driver's seat.

"Okay," he said, more to himself than to me. "We're going...."

I regarded him curiously from the passenger seat. He started the car, kept it in park, and looked through the windshield pensively. It was getting dark now. The weekend had finally come. In a flash, Joey pulled out his iPhone and typed something into it. I leaned over and watched him post on Facebook: *Off to Spookers... Why??*

I laughed, slumping back into my seat. "Are you scared *already?* What's the matter with you? We're not even *there* yet!"

He frowned and gave a sarcastic scowl, then put the car into gear.

After the forty-minute drive, I understood Joey's comments about the spookiness of the area: a long, winding road took us past dark, multistoried buildings, long-abandoned and eerily illuminated by our headlights. It looked like a prime location for a future *Paranormal Activity* film—or an overnight massacre camp.

"See," Joey said, his shoulders slowly rising towards his ears, "this place is just creepy...."

"No way!" I scanned it all excitedly. "This is perfect!"

A single brick building revealed the only light within the grounds. Inside, a man in a black Spookers T-shirt sold us tickets for $55—the equivalent of $42.50 U.S.

"These will get you into the Haunted House, Disturbia 3-D, and the Freaky Forest," he said. "You can also have a complimentary Spookers torch. You'll need that to get into the Freaky Forest."

I smiled at the image of a green, roaring zombie printed on the pocket-sized flashlight. I handed it to Joey, then quickly turned at the sound of a gut-wrenching scream off in the distance. I grinned at my host, presuming that the noise had come from one of the haunts out back.

"Ugh!" Joey said, wincing at the sound. "Why am I here...?"

I turned to the worker and thanked him for the passes. "This place is great already!"

Across a courtyard out back, a woman stood outside a large, wooden building resembling a small warehouse. Red tissue gleamed where skin had seemingly been ripped off the entire left side of her face. She let two young couples in the entrance, then turned towards Joey and me. Joey wrinkled his face as we approached her.

"God," he said, turning away. "I can't look...!"

"Why not?" I studied the woman's makeup. I suddenly wondered if she used the same materials that the kids did back at RAM. "She's awesome."

After the vision of horror let us inside, we inched our way down a dark hallway. I listened for the slightest sound, hearing nothing beyond our slow-moving steps. The only light was a dull glow from a roped-off room down the path. As we approached, I saw TV monitors, recording equipment, and keyboards filling a control room covered in dust. Specks and streaks of red shone ominously throughout. I envisioned a serial killer who had gone on a rampage sometime back in the seventies. An office chair in the center whirled around, and in a flash I recognized a red-haired doll facing us. I gaped at its distorted, plastic face with gashes along its forehead and cheeks. I remembered seeing the thing as a kid and changing the channel whenever a preview for its movie came on TV. I had pictured the toy with a twisted, evil smile running through my house with a knife. Now in its dusty chair, the doll was much larger than it had been on the screen, dressed in denim overalls and a striped sweater. In a flash it hopped up. Clumps of wild, red hair flew in all directions as it rushed across the room, holding a butcher knife as if to attack. It was undeniably played by a dwarf actor.

Joey jumped back and shielded his face. "Chucky!" he screamed.

I stood motionless, marveling at the mutated toy. It grunted maniacally and jerked its weapon over the rope, trying to stab us.

"Oh, man," I said in admiration, "that thing sure scared me as a kid!"

From behind, Joey grabbed the sleeve of my jacket. "Yeah, me too." He endured my staring at the living doll for only a moment before pulling me away.

Back in the hall, my host's hand felt like a claw slightly piercing my arm. It tightened at the sound of a low, rhythmic creaking from a second room. We shuffled towards it and looked in to find a large crib slowly rocking of its own accord. It was long rotted and stained with age, surrounded by moldy stuffed animals slumping over crooked shelves. In an instant, the concealed mover of the bed appeared. A teenage girl lay awkwardly inside it. Blood covered her lips and mouth. She gazed at her new visitors while Joey and I stared from the doorway. Before either of us could say a word, she drew her knees up to her chest, brought her legs over the side of the crib, and stepped out. Her back arched as she bent over backwards, looking as though she might snap in two. She effortlessly rested her palms flat on the floor, then began crawling towards the doorway. Her long, greasy hair dragged along the floor, and her inverted face turned mad with a smile.

Joey jumped back from her warped approach. "Goodness me!"

I laughed. It had been years since I'd gone through a haunt with someone who was genuinely afraid of them. I looked at the incredible, crawling invalid. She had the appearance of some kind of human crab. I wondered if *I* could have pulled off something like that while haunt acting. I had a feeling that I would have landed flat on my face.

"Wow, she's cool...," I said. I continued looking at her until Joey took a half-step away, eying her nervously.

"That was insane," he said after we'd moved on. "This place has changed a bit since last time."

I walked beside him in the hall, his grip like a vise on my sleeve. "What was it like before?"

"I don't remember." He shook his head as if to remove the thought. "I've managed to block it out. There's nothing like this in South Africa, you know!"

Farther along, pig carcasses hung by rusty chains suspended from the ceiling. Bones protruded from partial legs, and scales overflowed with hooves and pig flesh. As we took it all in, a grisly butcher slowly emerged from the filth. He eyed Joey and me maliciously while gripping a bloody knife before a red-stained jumpsuit. A large gash covered half of his forehead, with blackened skin peeling around the wound.

Joey immediately released me from his hold and hid his face behind quivering arms. "Gross!"

The butcher grinned and stepped towards his shivering form.

Joey shuffled away and threw a nod in my direction. "You *like* this stuff?!"

"Well, this is really gory." I smiled at his retreat. "Very slasher-movie inspired. But well done. Besides, Joey, I thought you *liked* being introduced to new things!"

He ignored me with a groan and hid behind a metal slab oozing with pig guts.

The butcher's eyes grew wide. "Joey...!" The creature teasingly waved his knife. "Come here, Joey!" he moaned.

"Oh, *great*..." Joey backed away, wincing at the sound of his own name. "Why isn't he coming after *you*?!"

The butcher's wild eyes turned in my direction. I laughed at his rotting teeth.

"Are you kidding? With you being so terrified, he doesn't even *see* me!"

The creature completed his circle around the slab, making Joey bolt down the hall. I gave the actor a thumbs up as I followed. He responded by sticking out his long, charred tongue, then winking.

"That guy was freaky!" Joey said when I caught up to him.

"I know...." I smiled with approval. "Wasn't he great?"

He answered with a heated shake of the head.

We wandered on. Sickly surgical rooms led to fallen-down elevator shafts. Grime and gore encompassed Spookers' old Kingseat Hospital. Burn victims crept after us with horrid, melted faces. Joey shuddered at it all, but I noticed that his fear seemed to escalate whenever we were alone. The anticipation of whatever was coming proved to have an even greater effect than anything we actually faced.

He finally sighed in relief when we stepped out into the courtyard once again.

"My goodness...!" he said. "I hate when they jump out. And why do they have to get so *close?*"

I laughed. "Well, you wouldn't see them as well if they didn't! That wouldn't be as fun."

He flinched in astonishment. "I'd like that much *better!*"

"But it's not like any of this is *really* scary," I said, trying to bring him back to reality. "It's all fake!"

He threw out his arms in exasperation. *"So?!"*

The Disturbia 3-D house proved much tamer. Paintings of neon zombies staggered along the walls. Polka dots hovered and danced. Colorful, sunken tombstones jutted out behind open graves. We admired each one through plastic, 3-D glasses, reaching towards the illustrations to confirm that they didn't actually move.

"I like that it's so quiet in here," Joey said after a while.

I smirked behind him. In a long hallway, paint of every color streaked the walls as though it were the home of an artist gone berserk. It *was* unusually quiet. We had seen about a dozen people waiting in line outside, but not one scream or giggle could be heard from anywhere. But I knew that Joey was referring to the actors.

"Don't be so sure...," I said.

"Why?" He jerked his head to the side. "Is something in here?"

I nodded, silently laughing. Before I could comment, a high-pitched cackle erupted behind us. Joey jumped and whipped around. I turned to face two hideous rows of yellow, razor-sharp teeth. The pasty-white face behind them seemed almost insignificant. The thing wailed relentlessly, throwing its head back over a cheerful, spotted clown suit. My skin crawled as the noise echoed off the walls. It sounded strangely metallic. When it finally stopped, large, white eyes faced me, shining through inhuman slits. I heard Joey scurry down the hall behind me. I slowly followed, keeping my eyes on our new pursuer, who stomped after us in red, floppy clown shoes.

"I had a feeling that might happen...!" I told Joey back outside with a chuckle.

He gave a violent shudder. I got the feeling that he was trying to shake off the experience entirely. "God, they're everywhere!"

I laughed and nodded. As much as I'd enjoyed the horror games in England, it was nice to be back in the types of haunts I'd grown up with: mazes structured around nightmares and the element of surprise. I could only hope that Joey was enjoying it on *some* level. How could anyone not? There was excitement in the simulated danger, wasn't there? Dave had felt that way that back at Horror Camp Live. I remembered something that Thomas had told me in Dublin: *The people I know who like those types of shows actually want to feel scared.*

"There's still one more to go, though," I said with a glimmer of hope.

Joey turned as I pointed across the green. A muscular man in a black sweatshirt and jeans manned the entrance to a trailhead. Beyond it, not a single light was visible within the dense woods. It looked as though a few steps into the terrain would mean entering a void comparable only to deep space.

When we approached, the worker confirmed my theory.

"The path isn't lit," he said. He asked to see our torch, then made us flip it on to ensure that it worked. He shined a larger, metal flashlight onto our miniscule, plastic one, then gave each of us a dour eye. "So you'll be dependent on that."

"Are there any monsters in there?" Joey asked flatly.

The man only stared. I chuckled, shaking my head. The worker slowly turned towards the forest, pointing his light onto the narrow trail. He gaped at it as if in wonder.

"I don't know *what's* out there...," he said mysteriously. He turned back to us, his eyes mad with fear. "But *I'm* not going out there...!"

Joey grabbed my arm as I burst into laughter. "You *owe* me for this."

On the trail, our sneakers crunched in the darkness. The trees quickly eliminated any light from above. Only our feeble, yellow stream showed the way. Joey moved it from side to side, revealing tiny particles swirling in the night air. Colorless leaves and branches made up the world around us. I constantly scanned the narrow tunnel, feeling my eyes grow wide.

"Man," I said, "it's *so* dark!"

"It *is* so dark," Joey mocked beside me.

"This is very manly of you, by the way...."

He scoffed in reply.

Beside us, five skulls suddenly took form from the brush, gaping above thick, wooden stakes. Joey held the light over them, intrigued. An instant later, he jumped back and I felt his foot crush one of my own.

"Ouch!" I yelped.

Beside the skulls, the dim image of a face appeared. It stared directly at us. I began to make out the form of a young man behind the leaves. Large, red gouges ran from his forehead to his cheeks and chin. His eyes seemed to glow bright white. He leapt up in a flash, exposing a thick trail of blood down his bare chest. A long, deafening wail erupted from his mouth and I recoiled from the same unnatural cry that the clown had made in the 3-D house. It went on and on, pervading the previously dead silence. Joey released my arm and threw both hands over his ears. Our small light left the howler, revealing only dark branches above. I felt Joey grab my sleeve once again and yank me forward until the screaming behind us ceased.

"How the heck do they *do* that?" I asked, hustling to keep up. "I wish *I* could do that."

"It's freaky! I can't believe that guy is just sitting out there in the dark."

"Are you kidding? He loves it! Who *wouldn't* want to do that?"

I shut my mouth as soon as the words came out. I remembered the night I'd sat in the insane asylum back at Castle Dracula. I hadn't exactly *loved* it. My reaction had more closely resembled Joey's panic right now, but he didn't need to know that.

"Isn't it cool that they don't put any lights out here?" I asked. "I like that we can't see anything until we find it ourselves. It has a really cool effect."

I got no reply.

"Want me to take the light?"

Joey's grip tightened. "No!"

"This isn't so bad, you know. I've been in camps where the monsters literally grab you and drag you away."

"If anyone did that to me," Joey said flatly, "I'd punch them."

We continued on. The air was brisk, not cold, or at least it didn't seem cold as I focused on the eerie silence. Joey's attention seemed sharpened by it. An intensity came over him as he strained to hear even the slightest sound. It was as though he thought that it could mean the difference between life and death. It was all very different from the well-lit rooms of the Haunted House. The danger here didn't just hide. It remained as unseen as everything else, including the two of us who were mere outlines in the middle of nowhere.

Subtle illumination finally appeared ahead. Rustic lanterns dangled above a small section of the trail. A white tent had been set up beside a small campfire. A cooking kettle hung from a wooden tripod next to it. Stretched deerskins and thermal underwear dried from frayed ropes. We slowed down to look about, grateful for the visibility, as a woman emerged from the bush. Long, disheveled braids fell over her plaid shirt and overalls. She gave an enthusiastic smile, revealing several gaps between crooked teeth.

"Well, I'll be!" she exclaimed. "I here gotten visitors."

I immediately cracked up at her accent. For a New Zealander, she sounded perfectly Virginian. Beside me, Joey eyed her suspiciously. But the woman seemed not to notice as she approached me.

"Do y'all like goat pie?" she asked with wide eyes.

The hillbilly grabbed my arm as I laughed. She led me away from Joey to a wooden shack tilting along the trail. Pots and pans hung from a patched ceiling. A wooden washtub leaked soapy water onto a broken table. She walked me through, grinning wildly as if thrilled to have company after years of solitude.

"Just go on now and y'all find ma brother up yonder...."

I giggled back at Joey, who slowly followed. I could only assume that he was grateful to not be the center of attention for once.

"Just don't go wanderin' off the path, now!" the woman called, waving me off. She gave Joey a crooked smile as he slinked past her.

"She's hilarious!" I said once he caught up to me.

He gave a half-nod. Still looking behind, he kept an eye on the woman of the woods until the darkness took over once again.

After several yards, additional lanterns revealed bare bodies hanging upside down among the trees. Large sections of skin had been stripped from their backs, arms, and legs—to be eaten, I had a feeling. Joey groaned in repulsion, then took the light off them in defiance. We continued through the darkness. More hidden howlers threw out explosions of wails. A small graveyard exposed short, peaked tombstones barely visible in the grass. Joey continued his strained silence, keeping his attention on the darkness as if it were the greatest enemy of all. Eventually a sharp rustling came from the bushes ahead, and we stopped to see our hillbilly friend reappear.

"Where y'all been?" She grabbed me out of Joey's grip. "Y'ain't done found ma brother?" She pulled me close with a stern look. "I told yer not ta wander...!"

I exploded in laughter after she let me go. Within moments, the familiar courtyard came into view. Lines of people stood outside the entrances to the indoor shows. Others waited before the forest, their tiny lights glowing in the night.

"See?" I asked Joey when we were safe again. "That wasn't so bad."

"Ugh!" He exhaled deeply. "Thank *goodness* it's over."

"But you liked it though, right? Wasn't it fun?"

He only looked around at the crowds, trying to regulate his breathing. "I'm just glad it's over...."

I playfully punched him on the arm. When he finally looked at me, he gave a weak smile.

"Hey look!" I said, motioning away from the crowds.

Across from us, a creature dressed in a white doctor's coat emerged from the building where we'd gotten our tickets. Its black, hollow eyes scanned the people waiting in line. Long, disheveled hair made it look female, though I couldn't tell for sure, with a bluish-gray face that seemed to have been decomposing for months. It clasped a dismembered leg to its chest and slowly approached a small group outside the Haunted House. The teens smiled and stepped close to each other. The strange doctor brought its bleeding appendage to its mouth, then bit into it with a demented smile. It encouraged each of them to take a bite of his snack, making them giggle wildly.

I laughed and gave Joey a nudge.

"See?" I pointed. "Everything here is just funny." *How could that customs officer have ever questioned my draw to this place?* I wondered. *He's obviously never even been here.*

Joey only stared at the corpse-eating fiend.

"These guys aren't *really* scary," I said. "It was just *you* getting freaked out by it all. Look at how much fun everyone is having...."

My host didn't blink. He continued watching the decomposing doctor nibble on dead toes. After a moment, it spied a girl across the courtyard. It sneered at her, then crouched as if to attack. In an instant it took off, running straight towards the girl and chasing her back into the building. Her screaming echoed down the hall as the two disappeared.

Joey turned to me, looking mockingly morose. "No," he said. "It wasn't *just* me."

Fear Factory

On New Zealand's South Island, I stood before a gateway into hell.

Deep-red lettering glowed against dark stone. A female corpse stood miraculously upright beside a black pillory, casting a piercing, deadened stare. I smiled at the image and an ominous sign above: *Fear Factory. New Zealand's Scariest Haunted House.*

After surviving Spookers, I had learned about a second haunt in the country. Fear Factory was a single-venue attraction located in Queenstown. The website revealed very little about the show. Not a single actor was shown—no demented butchers or evil clowns—only multiple shots of patrons screaming while the object of their terror remained concealed off camera. Supposedly, the show was so terrifying that thousands chose to be removed before completing it. After reading the website's claim, Joey insisted that I would be doing *that* one on my own.

My host also referred me to Transfercar: a company that allows people to rent a car free of charge if they pick it up at one designated airport and return it to another. On September 4, I flew into Christchurch airport and stepped into a blue Sirion Daihatsu for the 300-mile drive southwest to Queenstown. I blared the radio while there was still reception, watching the rising moon cast a blue hue upon the surrounding mountains. A wave of bliss washed through me at being behind the wheel for the first time in a year—even while driving on the opposite side of the road. Five and a half hours later, I saw hordes of exceptionally fit teens and tweens walking the Queenstown sidewalks. Dark windows of closed shops showcased colorful kayaks, climbing ropes, and helmets. I had heard that the town was renowned for extreme sports and could only wonder if Fear Factory had been created with that unique theme in mind.

After passing the bleeding dead, I found the haunt's lobby resembling a Victorian hotel. Black-and-white photographs crookedly hung on pale-green wallpaper. A line of people filled the room, waiting outside a plain, black door. A man in a Fear Factory T-shirt guarded the entrance. I noticed that, unlike the crowds outside, no one here resembled the perfect specimen of health; they ranged from their twenties to their sixties and were no more muscular and toned than I was.

Before I could approach the ticket counter, a second door flew open. Screams erupted beside the queue. Four people burst into the quiet waiting room. One middle-aged woman threw her hands over her face, then stopped to shake her head and laugh. Another looked at the staring faces around her, clutching her chest while catching her breath. Two men with them rolled with laughter, then let out sighs of relief.

"Oh my God," the second woman said while calming her heartrate. "That was insane!"

"I am never doing that again," the other said, laughing.

"You guys were so scared!" one of the men teased.

"So were you."

"Not as much as *you*, though!"

I exchanged smiles with the woman at the counter. She stood in a similar shirt as her fellow worker, with hands folded casually before her. After paying thirty-five dollars' admission, I noticed a cartoon chicken on the wall behind her. It blushed meekly, with a sign beside it reading: *Will you join our Chicken List?*

"That's how many people have backed out after going inside," the woman at the counter said, spying my interest. "And people who decided that they didn't want to go in after buying their ticket." She smiled, appearing proud of the statement. I looked at the tally in amazement; the number read almost five thousand.

"How much do you know about the show?" she asked.

Beside us, the hyperventilating couples began sorting through merchandise—mugs and T-shirts—while the others in line watched.

"Not much," I said.

"Inside it will be completely dark. No lights are allowed, not even a light from your cellphone or camera." She cast me a kind but warning look, as though I might be considering pulling out my phone at the very thought. "You'll see a glowing, red dot in front of you at all times. Just follow that. It'll take about twenty minutes."

"Ohhh..." I stared at her. I had been to those types of shows before. I knew exactly what they entailed. There were no sets or scenes or characters inside. There were no moss-covered crypts or mental hospitals where the doctors were the ones insane. There were only empty, dark rooms. But by the woman's proud and pleasant smile, I could only presume that she was the owner, so I decided to hide my disappointment.

"Okay," I said, nodding.

I joined the queue behind two girls exchanging nervous looks. I got the distinct impression that they had just overheard the conversation. But before I could ask for their opinion, more screams erupted. Five people rushed out the exit door beside us. They flew into the gift shop just as frantically as the previous group had, circling the room with eyes pressed tightly shut. One woman shook her hands as if trying to remove an image from her head. They regrouped a moment later, clutching each other and laughing. From across the room, the woman at the ticket counter smiled at me.

"Are you two ready?" the man guarding the door soon asked.

The girls ahead of me instinctively drew their arms to their chests. They giggled and nodded.

"If at any time you want to be removed, yell, 'Chicken!' and you'll be immediately escorted out."

The pair slowly stepped forward as the ominous door opened. They pressed tightly together, forming a single unit of panic. I heard a final, excited cry escape them before the door removed them from view. Silence immediately resumed.

"You came here alone?" the guard asked, turning back towards me.

I nodded. From behind, I heard others join the queue.

The man folded his arms. "Then you go in alone."

I froze. Low gasps came from my unseen, would-be groupmates.

"I do?"

The worker nodded with a smile. "Yep."

Well, that's *different,* I thought. I had never encountered that rule before. But suddenly, the show seemed a lot more exciting. "Okay."

I confirmed that I understood my option for "chickening out" and stepped through the mysterious door of doom. With a final glance back, I saw several, young pro-athletes-in-training behind me. Two frowned in empathy and terror. I chuckled and waved. The door slowly shut and I watched the light of the room narrow to a slit. It soon disappeared completely and everything went pitch black.

I stood still a moment. I felt my eyes begin to widen. I couldn't see a thing. It wasn't just dark; it was like an abyss. I turned around in what felt like nothingness. I couldn't believe the effect of it when a well-lit room was just the other side of the wall. Somewhere before me, I made out a lone, red light from what I could only presume was a far wall. It looked about the size of a bottle cap and for all I knew was miles away. I brought my hands to what I estimated to be the height of my chest, then began walking slowly towards it.

Eventually the spot disappeared. From the corner of my eye, I saw another emerge somewhere to my right. It looked just as far off. I turned and walked carefully towards it, hoping that I wouldn't run into a wall. This, I remembered, was exactly what other, similar haunts had entailed: walking through an empty maze, blind. There was nothing interesting about that—at least, not for me. And there was certainly no creativity in it.

After spying a third light, I picked up on a distinct giggling from somewhere in the distance. I smiled. It had a positively eerie effect. I inched ahead, trying to imagine where the hidden actor could be standing. A moment later, I felt the distinct impression of a finger stroke the back of my hand, then withdraw.

I flinched and laughed. I quickly turned as if I had any chance of seeing who or what had done it. But all was dark.

Well played, I thought.

I continued following the little light until it, too, disappeared. Another took its place, now off to my left. I turned, still feeling nothing with my outstretched hands but knowing now that unseen actors were around and could see *me* just fine. Upon spying another light, I felt two fingers touch my right calf. I burst into laughter and tried seeing their source in the blackness below. I could certainly imagine some people becoming hysterical over something like this: the unseen having their way with them when they had no idea from where or when it would happen. I thought back to Joey being scared out of his wits from the very darkness of the Spookers trail. Here, people weren't even given the smallest torch to guide them. Joey would have been next on the Chicken List for sure.

Continuing onwards once again, I stopped at the sight of two red lights. One was directly ahead while a second glowed off to my left. I looked at one, then the other, confused as to which I'd just been following. Neither looked familiar. Where was I going again...? After a few moments, a red flash raced across what I could only imagine to be the floor. It dashed to the left. I took the hint from the unseen actor and followed it.

Additional silence followed. It continued for what felt like eons. The darkness began to feel tangible. I felt as though I were floating in another dimension, light years away from anyone or anything, moving my feet without the sensation of moving at all. Not even my sneakers made a sound. But the isolation was extinguished as a loud growling came just inches from my face. I laughed at it and continued ahead.

Now this *is cool,* I thought.

The noise moved from my left to my right. It sounded just inches away from my ears. I imagined a gigantic werewolf standing beside me, foaming at the mouth and ready to tear me to shreds. Strangely enough, I couldn't feel even a trace of its breath. Eventually the noise ceased. I continued walking, smiling in the darkness, amazed at how silently the actors could move.

After what felt like a second eternity, I stopped at a blazing light. My eyes pressed shut as the room seemed to explode before me. In an instant I forced them back open. An object came into view, and I flinched at the sight of another human being. A young man lunged towards me. His arms were wrapped tightly around himself, bound by the sleeves of a padded straitjacket. He screamed in uncontrollable rage, revealing crooked, discolored teeth. I made out large stitch wounds running along his face beneath a wild mop of hair. All around him, the metal bars of a prison cell shimmered in the light. I gaped at the scene, completely in shock. The man's hollering continued mere feet away from where I stood. The noise and blinding light seemed to fill the entire world after an eternity of darkened silence. In a moment the inmate disappeared and the void returned.

"Cool...," I said, more to the actor than myself. My hands slowly resumed their position: floating in the darkness as I headed towards another spot of red.

Additional long moments passed. I felt a finger trace the length of my back. A soft voice mumbled erratically in the distance. Another followed, inches from my face. I laughed, picturing deformed figures living in the bowels of the earth with transparent skin and black eyes watching my every move. A face eventually appeared. Subtle light below it revealed white pupils against dark, cruel eyes. It hissed loudly, and I saw deep veins running along dead flesh. In a second the light went out and the horrid figure disappeared.

Similar episodes followed. Dim voices whispered incoherently. Heavy breathing rushed into my ear. Eerie laughter broke long bouts of silence. I was brushed, touched, grabbed. I laughed every time, picturing curious deformities playing with a strange life form that had lost its way in their midst. It was unlike any show I had ever gone through: walking through the unknown in eternal darkness, immersed in a game of death stalking life. But I could understand how some people would run screaming through it, like the couples I'd seen panicking out in the lobby. I could see how some could find the disorienting abyss too intense to handle and would gladly up the count on the Chicken List.

I eventually pushed against a flat surface, then stepped out into the light. The familiar gift shop appeared once again. I felt an immediate sense of comfort at being able to see everything in front of me: new faces in the queue line, shirts and souvenirs, even the ancient walls of the Victorian hotel. I couldn't help but feel as though I'd been away from it all for days.

One man waiting by the entrance gaped at me. "Oh my God—you went in there *alone?!* Are you *okay?!*"

I laughed at his sincerity. "Yeah—it was awesome!"

Behind the queue, the woman at the ticket counter beamed with pride.

"Did you like the show?" she asked when I approached her.

I nodded. "I did. It was very different—and a lot of fun!"

She pulled up a laptop between us. On the screen, I saw images that had evidently been taken while I was inside. I recognized the same wallpapered hallway from the photos on Fear Factory's website. But unlike the screams of terror that had caused Joey's refusal to join me, I was laughing in all of them.

"I actually wasn't sure if I would like the show at first," I said, lowering my voice to a whisper. "I'm used to other kinds of attractions. You know, with elaborate scenes."

The woman nodded. She moved the laptop to the side and leaned against the counter. "But you'll notice," she said, keeping her voice equally low, "that those kinds of shows are based on the imagination of the *creators*. We wanted to put on a show where the scares come from the imagination of the *patrons*. It makes it much more personal."

I nodded in thought. "That's true."

"In complete darkness, the unconscious takes over. And when people can't see what's around them, they envision things that *really* scare them. And that will always be worse than anything they actually see."

I considered it. I thought back to the Spookers trail with Joey and his death grip on my arm in the darkness. I remembered going through the Haunted House and seeing him much more terrified *between* the scenes than whenever a killer clown or bloody butcher appeared.

But I also knew that Joey wasn't the *only* one who had let his imagination run wild. As a kid, I had been just as terrified of the infamous

Chucky doll whenever seeing its mangled face on TV. I remembered believing that I would be permanently traumatized if I ever watched those movies. It was only years later when I finally did that I learned the things in my head were far worse than anything in the films.

From across the counter, the woman nodded to another group approaching the simple, black door. I turned to watch four thirtysomethings giggle after agreeing that they would yell, "Chicken," if they wanted to be removed. By their expressions, I got the feeling that they would keep the word on the tips of their tongues at every turn.

The woman rested her elbow on the counter, then put a hand to her chin. "People often feel powerless when they can't see what's coming. That's when fears really come out." She squinted at me pensively. "It affects us more than we realize."

Chapter 11

American Halloween from Hawaii to Florida

"Will I be able to build a haunt here? Otherwise what's the point of even owning a house?"

The Return of Halloween in Waikiki

Although I flew to Honolulu on September 16, the International Date Line made my arrival a day earlier. I was now an international haunt investigating time traveler.

In the airport, I reveled in the familiar accents of my fellow Americans. I recognized vacationers from the South, California coast, Midwest, and Northeast, all excitedly making plans for going to luaus and spending a week on the beach. I locked my eyes on the American flag hanging over the security check and felt a greater sense of peace than any monster-based attraction had filled me with all year. The customs officer smiled while handing back my passport—without, to my relief, even the slightest hesitation.

"Welcome home," he said.

It took all my strength not to hug him.

It was my first time on the Hawaiian Islands, and I knew of no better way of experiencing the fiftieth state than at the haunted attraction drawing me there. Dr. Carnage's House of Horrors would be opening during the first weekend in October. After a year of attending dark shows around the world, I basked in the thought of going to an American haunt at long last. I also had three weeks to explore the island in the meantime, but my wandering mind stopped at the sight of another long-sought image. Bags of mini Hershey bars and Reese's Peanut Butter Cups seemed to glow from the airport gift shops. Strands of colorful, plastic leaves adorned them. Rubber skeletons dangled beside small, pointed witch hats and tombstone-shaped candles. They were the same objects I'd seen in stores every autumn from as far back as I could remember: the symbols of the Halloween season's grand return. I looked at the scene and felt an immediate wave of joy and nostalgia—but it also seemed strange, somehow. For the past year, I'd gone to so many shows about the living dead, about witches and monsters that weren't associated with the American holiday at all. I browsed through what I used to associate with trick or treating and costume parties, smelling the familiar aroma of chocolate and plastic, but saw the icons reflecting just a small fragment of an entire world that enjoyed those things—my own culture being just one of many.

My host, Brent, listened to stories of my travels in his living room. He slouched over one end of a long, curved sofa, hands folded behind his head and bare feet crossed over a glass coffee table. He was my age, tall and exceptionally thin, and wore the same things I would come to see people wearing all over the island: a bathing suit and flip flops, which he referred to as "slippers." He had moved to Waikiki years earlier from Ohio and now rented a four-bedroom house with three roommates.

"So...," he said after I described the void at Fear Factory, "you just, like, left it all?"

I turned to face him. My attention had veered to a wall completely packed with board games, rollerblades, and skateboards. I smiled at both his question and his voice. Like everyone at the airport, his accent was music to my ears. I felt as though I had just found a longlost brother.

"You, like, left your job and apartment to go traveling?"

I crossed my feet over my duffel bag across from him. "Yup. Just left it."

"And got rid of all your stuff?"

"Almost everything." I glanced at a rack along an opposite wall. It held more than ten surfboards of various sizes. "I have a few boxes at a friend's house and I kept my bike. But everything else, I just gave away. It was very liberating."

Brent looked off into space as if considering it. "Huh. I've always wanted to do something like that."

I felt my face light up. "Really?" I'd heard many people say that during my travels. But I had a feeling that Brent was serious.

I thought back to what my day-to-day life had entailed since leaving the U.S., now eleven months earlier. The last thing that I wanted was for a future wanderer to get the wrong impression of what living as Hobo Zero actually involved.

"Let's see...," I said. "I've slept on more couches than beds the past year, my diet has pretty much consisted of eating whatever the grocery store was selling for a dollar, and the only time I've had to myself was when I camped out in a car for a week in New Zealand."

Brent nodded. "Have you blown through all your savings?"

I shrugged. "Almost. But don't let thoughts like that stop you. You can always make more money."

His pensive look returned. "That's true."

"I've also picked up any new clothes I've needed at thrift shops." I motioned to my faded, California-surfer T-shirt and cutoff shorts, both of which I'd gotten in England. I shot him a look of mock misery. "God knows I've gained enough weight this past year to need them!"

He chuckled. "Sounds like quite the lifestyle."

I nodded with a grin, reflecting on everything I'd been through that year. "I *highly* recommend it."

Dr. Carnage's House of Horrors

The blood-soaked doctor before us was beautiful. Red stains covered his gloved hands and apron. A malicious smile spread over his face, evidently inspired by the gleaming machete he held before him. His dark eyes stared at us from a billboard. I had a feeling that Brent and I were in for quite a show.

I was surprised to find Dr. Carnage's House of Horrors set up in the middle of a parking garage outside Windward Mall.

"This is typical Hawaii," Brent said as he parked his Chevy van. "Fit it wherever you can."

Well over a hundred people stood in line. As we joined it, I gloried at the screams and delirious laughter coming from behind a wall of wooden backdrops. I was also relieved to not be dripping in sweat for once; the island had been experiencing record humidity since my arrival. Although it was only in the mid-eighties, it had felt like more than a hundred degrees every day. But Brent and I hadn't let that stop us from hiking around the island or going to the beach. It had been nice to wear shorts and a tank top every day for the first time since Mexico, but I also understood why some vacationers never leave the comfort of their hotel pools.

While waiting in line, I asked my host about the last time he'd been to a haunted attraction.

He thought about it. "I think I was fifteen. So quite a while ago. And I remember that it looked a lot like that." He pointed to a teenage boy interlocked with his young lady friend. I smiled at the sight. I had a feeling that no amount of horror behind those barriers could tear them apart. "I asked a girl to go with me so I could put my arm around her if she freaked out." Brent laughed, thinking back on it. "It worked."

I chuckled. "I see that a lot."

"Hey..." Brent extended his arms in defense. "You do what works."

After paying twelve dollars' admission, we wandered through an enclosed maze with four teenagers. Grimy, deranged creatures crept out of the shadows, half-alive with faces completely rotten or partially removed. Ghastly looking hillbillies shouted crude insults, getting right into our faces with broken teeth and hard breath. Filth-covered women clambered through a junk pile of dead bodies. The teens screamed and clutched at each other around every turn, appearing both horrified and thrilled at the spectacle. I noticed that Brent regarded it all in the same fashion that I did: with curious interest at the creative depictions of doom.

We eventually came to a girl strapped to a hospital bed. Her body had been torn wide open and a gaping wound was exposed in her midsection. Her arms and legs dripped with blood, lying limply on the soiled mattress. Amazingly, she looked at our group, still very much alive.

"Please," she screamed, "help me!" She reached out for us, trying to lift herself up. Aside from her ruined limbs, she only seemed able to move her neck and head of matted, sweaty hair. Around her, the entire room was covered in human butchery.

"Ugh!" gasped a girl from our group. She stared at the patient in shock while holding on to her boyfriend.

"Hurry, please!" the victim begged. "He's coming back."

"Uh oh...," Brent said. "That's not good."

Within moments, a man barged in. I stared at a horrid contraption of tubes and wires strapped to his back. It looked as though the device was meant to hold together a twisted mass of parts. The man looked only partially human, stomping across the room in a bloodstained surgical gown. This was unmistakably the star of the show: Dr. Carnage himself. After growling down at the girl, the thing reached into the gaping wound in her stomach. Her entrails were immediately ripped out—long, gray intestinal tissue falling to the floor as the victim screamed in pain. My hands flew to my mouth as I stared, transfixed, at the gruesomeness.

The girl's cries began to fade as her head slumped back from weakness. Her entire body fell limp. Neither Brent nor I moved. The couples beside us cringed and recoiled, moaning in disgust. A huge pile of innards lay at the mad doctor's feet, looking like some kind of horrid snake. The doctor whipped around and snarled at us, still up to his elbows in the carcass. The teens screamed and ran out of the room, pushing against each other in a panic. Brent and I finally snapped out of our stupor and shuffled after them.

"Wow," my host said, shaking his head.

"Yeah..." I blinked, still processing the scene. The show certainly reflected how far haunted attractions have come from the original spook houses in the seventies. "This one's brutal."

Brent calmly pushed aside a sheet of thick plastic hanging in the hallway. "The sign outside said, *Face Your Fear.*"

"Ahhh, see?" I asked from behind him. "This stuff is healthy. Good for us."

Our skittish companions waited in the next room. They faced a young man, whom I was relieved to see was completely intact, lying strapped to a gurney. Trays of surgical tools glistened all around him: long amputation knives, metal extractors, and rusty forceps, each evidently well used, judging by the gobs of blood and fluid they dripped onto the floor. Smears of similar filth covered the wall behind him. Our four companions started moaning at once, looking nervous but excited to see what would happen.

"Help me!" the bound man pleaded. "I don't want to die like this."

"Oh man." Brent shook his head. "He's *dead.*"

I laughed at his deadpan humor. I loved seeing his enjoyment of it all. He was no more appalled by the horror than I was. Even our nervous companions seemed to be having fun, facing their fear through screams and shudders. I could only wonder if Joey would have enjoyed Spookers more had we gone through with a group like them. I had a feeling that their fear was *part* of their enjoyment.

A new doctor, void of any metal or tubes, entered, but his gown and mask were marked by as much mutilation as his sadistic counterpart. He shuffled to a table of tools and, after finding nothing that caught his eye, pulled a large, gleaming backsaw from beneath it. My hands immediately retracted to my chest at the sight. Without losing a moment, the doctor turned his back to us and stood above his trembling victim. The prisoner screamed hysterically. The horrid blade was thrust into his midsection. The doctor proceeded to saw. Behind the human butcher, I saw bloody feet twitch and shake while the victim's upper body writhed to and fro. I stared, unblinking, unable to look away. Judging by the doctor's movements, the weapon seemed to descend deeper and deeper into the flesh. Brent and I inched across the room to try and see the human destruction. With the grinding metal now deep in the bedframe, we saw that the young man had become two large parts, with thick blood covering the mangled flesh. He howled in agony.

Though I felt my stomach turn at the sight, I couldn't help but admire how well the actors were pulling it all off. They didn't base their performance on quick scares or intimidation; they seemed happy just completely grossing us out. Brent's face contorted as he gaped at the slaughter. It was all so extraordinary that we couldn't help but stare. I remembered Johan telling me back at Zombie Boot Camp that simulated violence was an outlet for aggression. Perhaps I felt no *conscious* desire to be violent, but watching a manlike monster pretend to tear someone to pieces was spellbinding. Human misery and murder—so long as they were *fake*—were intriguing, and we, as a group, could glimpse them from the safety of a show.

Back in the parking lot, the line had doubled.

"Wow," Brent said. We had long lost sight of the teens from our group. They had practically run through the rest of the show after the surgical nightmare had threatened us with his backsaw. "That was... intense."

I nodded with eyes wide. "Yeah..." I listened to the sounds of additional screams emanating from the maze of horror. Gore-crazed young couples waiting outside it clutched at each other. They looked at one another in anticipation, exchanging widening, nervous smiles as cries of suffering echoed across the concrete.

I sighed at the sight of it all. "God I love this country."

The Couchsurfing Haunters of Anchorage

On October 6, single-digit temperatures hit me as I stepped out of Anchorage International Airport. In my beloved red jacket once again, I practically danced off the plane. I felt like a penguin being released onto the ice after barely escaping the flames of Hawaii.

At 7:00 A.M., I hopped off a city bus and faced a small, quiet neighborhood. The Chugach Mountains looked majestic arching high above the suburban streets. I checked the address on my paper and toted my bag down a few frosty roads, until the evil smile of a jack-o-lantern caught my eye.

My new hosts, Paul and Shawna, had contacted me a week earlier. After reading my open Couchsurfing request for Anchorage, they messaged me immediately. *You have to stay with us,* Paul wrote. *We eat, live, breathe, and dream Halloween. I'm the store manager of a Halloween party store and we throw a huge Halloween party every year.*

I couldn't believe it: *Couchsurfing haunters!* I had never encountered that before. For the first time I would stay with Couchsurfers of my own culture, my own *breed.* Although I was new to the Last Frontier, I felt as if I was meeting family.

But my hosts had warned me that my arrival time was far too early for them to come to the airport.

We usually sleep until noon, Paul had written. *But we'll leave the door open and you can let yourself in. The house will be easy to spot.*

He was right. Beside the pumpkin hanging from a white birch tree, a four-foot skeleton stood locked in a set of stocks like a Vlad Tepes captive. Gargoyles perched on the roof, with red eyes peering down towards the driveway and claws gripping the tiles as if ready to attack. Arched tombstones throughout the lawn read *RIP,* and miniature gravediggers plunged shovels into heaps of dirt before them. I smiled from ear to ear at it all, then stepped onto a black welcome mat reading: *Haunted: Come Right In.*

While trying the handle, I found that the couple had, in fact, left the place unlocked. I stepped quietly inside, spying a silhouette in the window to my left. The shadowed image pressed his hands against the glass, with red smears below his fingertips and palms. I found the light switch beside it, then scanned the room.

Decapitated zombie heads sat above a mantel. A gray-faced witch flew from the ceiling. Jars labeled *Wolfsbane, Zombie Virus, Snake Venom,* and other potions lined shelves, intermixed with skulls and faces floating in unidentifiable, yellowish fluid. On the fridge, a small whiteboard listed weekly chores. Number thirteen read *MURDER A COUCHSURFER* in bold red. I shook in silent laughter while reading it. Now these were my people.

It wasn't long before movement came from the hall. Past the kitchen, I saw a young couple slowly stagger my way. Both wore long, flannel robes and tired expressions as if they had just woken up from hibernation. I took a few steps towards them and spied framed, Victorian-style portraits hanging along the hallway, each changing into the image of a decayed corpse at a certain angle.

"Good morning!" I said excitedly.

"Good morning," they replied sleepily with a wave. Shawna squinted in the light, scrunching her long, brown hair. Paul combed a hand through his thick, dark-blond beard.

"I'm going for the Charles Manson look," he said before I could comment on it.

The two were barely awake as they began showing me the house. Every prop had been purchased from Paul's party shop. They had plans for further decorations in each room and expected about sixty people at their Halloween party. Even their bathroom was themed. The Grim Reaper gazed down from a large poster on the ceiling. Plastic spiders covered the soaps on the sink. Bloody handprints marked the bathmat and shower curtain.

As the three of us drank coffee in the kitchen—my first cup from an *actual* coffee machine in almost a year—the couple asked about what I'd seen abroad. I happily described haunts such as Spookers and Underground Fear and the more interactive adventures such as Zombie Boot Camp and Horror Camp Live. But Paul and Shawna laughed when I mentioned the confusion that some of my hosts had shown about my interests. I couldn't help but join them. While red lightbulbs in the ceiling cast the entire room into shadow, resembling some kind of porthole into the depths of hell, we mused at how anyone could find bloodied, flesh-torn creatures to be anything but mesmerizing.

Later that morning, dressed in jeans and a flannel shirt but no coat, Paul took me to his shop.

On Arctic Boulevard, he opened the door of a small, stand-alone store that was part of the Party City chain.

"I keep it about 90 percent Halloween all year," he said. "The rest is stuff for birthday parties and other holidays."

I smiled at him before entering, keeping my hands inside my jacket pockets. How my host could withstand the cold without a coat was beyond me. "Nice ratio."

Inside, my eyes grew wide. Aisle upon aisle bore everything needed for making the ultimate Halloween party or display. Grim Reapers and skulls embellished Styrofoam tombstones. Standing skeletons ranged from one foot high to six. A wall of zombie masks showed rotting, mutilated skin and eyeballs dangling from the sockets. Foam pumpkins smiled cheerfully, with others appearing confused or menacing. Brains and other organs were wrapped in plastic as if they'd come straight from the deli. I recognized a few jars of floating faces from Paul's living room. We walked every aisle, and I picked up plush cats and plastic skulls to touch the familiar images. Above us, webbed corpses hung from the ceiling like victims from a fifties science-fiction movie. Behind the counter, a whiteboard listed several street addresses under the title, *Best Halloween Displays in Town.*

"People love seeing their addresses on the board," Paul said when I pointed it out. "And it inspires newbies to make their own displays so they can be put on the list. Alaska's population is small, but people still love to go all out."

In addition to choosing which items to put out for sale, my host enjoyed making displays for the store. Life-size vampires crawled and hissed in a graveyard. A crazed-looking doctor performed surgery on a withered corpse. Imprisoned skeletons hung chained to a faux stone wall.

"I get to make all the sets here," he said, "and most of them stay up all year. Sometimes it really freaks out the kids." He smiled peacefully, gazing off into the distance. "My day is not complete unless a child has cried."

I keeled over in laughter. "Can I just say: you guys are *awesome!*"

Around town, Paul's store items had been put to good use. A suburban, two-story home sat behind a lawn covered in tombstones. More than a dozen zombies crawled up from the grass. A thirty-foot spider hung from cloth webbing between the trees. Red handprints and splattered gore covered an entire side of the house, with a skeleton dressed in a doctor's gown laughing crazily beside it.

I looked at it all with heartfelt approval. It reminded me of so many displays I'd seen in New England for Halloween, right back to the days when I was a kid. I remembered running to houses with cemeteries in their yards that seemed to stretch on for miles. I remembered ghosts hanging from the trees that had looked even more enchanting than anything from the movies. Similar specters flew before me now. I realized that, after encountering so many monstrous, cultural icons abroad, *these*

were the ones from *my* country. Other places had Krampus or the Busós, Oni, Namahage, or Mephisto. But these zombies and ghosts and mad doctors were part of my heritage. They came around every October with the fun-sized candy bars and pumpkins for transforming into jack-o-lanterns. Just like so many displays that had shaped my experience of Halloween and monsters, this Alaskan one had been made for the entire neighborhood to enjoy. I had a sudden memory of something that Clemens had told me back in Salzburg. *Halloween is just commercial,* he'd said. *There's no meaning behind it.* What stood before me now was no sheer commercialism. It was the American Halloween culture that I knew and loved—built around a shared sense of community.

Beside me, Paul beamed at the display with pride. I got the feeling that he remembered selling every single prop to the people who had made it.

"It's too bad you won't be sticking around," he said, folding his arms and frowning at me. "These people are coming to our Halloween party!"

Religion and Halloween with Larry

Shortly after my arrival in Alaska, I received an e-mail from another Anchorage resident. His name was Larry. According to his message, he had seen my open Couchsurfing request and was intrigued by the unique theme of my profile.

I'm really interested in the project you're working on, he wrote. *If you're free, I'd love to meet you for coffee and hear more about it.*

After almost a year of haunt traveling, I was used to messages like this. Some Couchsurfers were eager to recommend ghost tours and themed restaurants in their area. It wasn't unusual for others to offer their own couch should my current host suddenly become unavailable. But Larry's reason for wanting to meet caught me completely off guard.

"I'm fifty-three years old and grew up in Alaska," he said, sitting across from me in a booth at Sarah's Sandwiches cafe. Like Paul, he had a thick beard, as gray as his short hair, and wore a rugged, leather jacket. "Up until recently, I've been a member of a Christian church that had very strict views on things. I was raised to believe that Halloween is evil, and anyone who celebrates it is evil."

I looked at him, holding my paper cup of coffee. From his expression, I could tell that he was discussing something that had been troubling him for quite a while.

"But for one reason or another," he said, "I'm no longer part of that faith. And I've spent the last few months questioning everything they've led me to believe."

He looked at me in silence, choosing to leave it at that. I nodded in understanding. I couldn't help but feel touched that he trusted me enough to be so honest. It was another feature that the Couchsurfing community was known for: open-minded individuals who could exchange ideas without criticism or judgment.

"Ever since I was young," Larry went on, "I was told that doing or believing the wrong thing was enough to get you into hell. It's kept me living in fear my entire life. And I don't know what I think about all that anymore. Then I saw your profile, and I see that you've been all over the place looking at things that my religion would have said were evil. But you have all these references from your hosts that say you're nice, and that doesn't sound like an evil person to me."

I smiled at him and nodded. "I know what you're saying. I had a few friends growing up with parents who held similar views about Halloween. I'm not religious, so I don't associate it with anything like that. But I *can* say that the traditions have nothing to do with the devil or anything evil. And most people I know who like Halloween and all these other types of shows I've been going to like them for the entertainment of it all."

Larry looked at me curiously. He seemed to have an almost searching expression. "But most people don't seem to do the types of things *you're* doing. You seem to be almost fanatical about it. People from my church would say that someone like that was a bad person. But you don't seem bad, or even negative. You seem very happy. And you're not dressed in black and don't have tattoos everywhere or weird piercings. That's not what I expected."

I laughed, both at this mentality and the fact that even if I *did* have tattoos, he would never see them under all my layers. Larry smiled, appearing to relax.

"Even the people I know who *do* look like that aren't evil," I said. "I think 'evil' refers to the intent to do harm to someone. But I've found that most people who share my interests—and there are a *lot* of them— are happy and good-natured. Even my parents, who *were* religious, never considered Halloween to be bad. It was always seen as a time when we could have fun with our friends and neighbors. And for the past year, I've seen the same mentality in people going to these types of shows all over the world."

"I've lived almost my entire life in fear," Larry said. He shook his head with a sigh. "Not anymore. I can't believe that just a year ago I would have instantly judged you based on what my church told me."

I looked at him for a moment. I suddenly remembered a thought that I'd had back in Florence, when I was walking through the exhibit based on Dante's *Inferno* at Santa Croce. It was ten months earlier but somehow felt like a lifetime ago. I remembered realizing that as much as I admired scenes of demons and ghouls inflicting horrors on sinners, I only felt that way because I viewed the story as fiction. Larry was a perfect example of how interpreting works such as Dante's as fact could affect a person so traumatically. But I also knew better than to scorn religion entirely. The Day of the Dead celebrations had also stemmed from Christianity. And like everything else, there were positive *and* negative aspects to it.

"Well, the good news is," I said, "that you don't look at me that way *now*."

Larry nodded pensively, then grinned.

I gave him an ironic smile. "Thank *God!*"

Zombie Manor, Arlington, Texas

The old corpse grinned on the porch. She appeared rather content in her rocking chair, her decayed flesh pulled back over rotting teeth and black gums forming a grim smile. Her pale summer dress looked as though it had once been yellow, and the withered bouquets of flowers beside her concealed any lingering aroma that may have offended her visitors. The old bag was my welcome to Arlington.

The next stop on my journey was Texas. When my friend Duane had learned that I'd be returning to American soil after haunt-trotting abroad, he invited me to check out his own. His small, professional attraction was called Zombie Manor. He had been running it for eight years and its ghouls, he claimed, always welcomed new guests.

I found Arlington a stark contrast to Anchorage. Highways arched across the sky like eerie, concrete rainbows. Endless sprawl had been made out of big-box stores and chain restaurants, and every house on Duane's block had a Dodge Ram and even larger SUV in the driveway. But when I entered Zombie Manor in the middle of a small business complex, all of that seemed miles away. I was now in an abandoned plantation. Thorny vines stretched across brick columns speckled with decay. Branches dripped Spanish moss upon a splintering porch discolored from age. And unlike so many shows I'd seen constructed as indoor mazes, the entire venue had been built as an actual plantation within a massive storage unit.

"Everything we make is based on Zombie Manor's background story," Duane explained in a room of gloom where crooked, ancient portraits gathered dust on curling wallpaper. Duane stood slightly taller than me, his short, black hair matching his T-shirt and his cowboy boots shining below his jeans. I was happily back to wearing T-shirts and long pants in the warm, Texas climate. I watched him motion around the set of a small parlor where a female corpse smiled its welcome.

"The story goes that a man named Branson Delacroix built Landrun Manor beside an old cemetery." The floorboards creaked as Duane stepped across the room. I hid a smile over his Texas drawl, which I'd been forcing myself to do from the moment he picked me up at the airport.

"He had many servants," Duane went on, "including a Haitian Creole named Bedule. She was very devoted to him and was a practitioner of Voodoo. One day, Branson tried something that was, shall we say, inappropriate with Bedule's daughter."

He paused, giving me a knowing look. I took my eyes off a lamp made out of a human head and met his gaze. "I see...."

"As you might imagine, Bedule didn't like that very much. So she placed a curse on Branson and everyone who worked in the manor. The entire plantation soon fell sick from plague. But after they died, they returned as zombies. The entire crew remained on the property and to this day terrorizes anyone who enters."

"That's a great story," I said. "You wrote that with the other show owners?"

"Actually my friend Greg wrote it. He works security here. He and I got together with the owners and built Zombie Manor around the story. So after coming up the porch, patrons come through here to the dining room...."

I followed him through the doorway. In another fully constructed room, a dozen rats covered an ancient dining-room table. They pierced tiny, plastic fangs into plates of long-rotten meat and heaps of flesh. Dismembered bits of fingers and toes bled onto silver platters.

I smiled and groaned at the inventive representation of plague. "Very nice." All around the room, a thin layer of what I could only presume was a mixture of mold and bodily fluid dripped along the walls.

"Our actor stands over here," Duane said, motioning to a corner behind the door. "She's all decomposed and staggers up to people after they come in. They're usually so distracted by the scene that they don't even see her until she sneaks around."

"Yeah, I'll bet," I said, gawking at it all.

"Then they go through the courtyard, then into the parlor...."

Duane's lights-on tour brought me through an entire plantation in ruin. Mildewed rooms were coated in flesh and fluid. Webbed corners stank of rot. Twisted vines and shrubbery made up a fully constructed greenhouse. Hanging, mutilated pig carcasses displayed more animal innards than I ever wanted to see. Duane's love and pride shone through as he described each set. It was the same way in which Paul had shown me his home decorations and shop displays back in Anchorage. I loved Duane's enthusiasm. And the creativity and detail made up everything that I loved about haunts—and certainly brought the Delacroix story to life.

Passing through a screen door barely hanging by its hinges, we stepped into what looked like the Everglades.

"This is our newest addition," Duane said. "The swamp shack."

Before us, stunted, malformed trees loomed over a wooden boardwalk. Some stood ten feet high with Spanish moss falling into a small pond below. The lagoon of dark water lay still, green and vile, as if the liquid itself had been poisoned by the Delacroix curse. Roots and ferns surrounded it as well as a small, wooden shack on the other side of the water.

"This place is unbelievable," I said, taking it all in. The entire area smelled of muck. I could barely believe that we were actually still inside a storage unit. "How long did it take you to build this?"

Duane considered it. "We finished the swamp in about... two weeks."

"Two weeks?!" I reached up and touched a thick branch arching over the walkway. I was almost surprised to feel the light, foam texture rather than genuine tree bark.

"We take a lot of pride in making sure everything looks authentic," Duane said, watching me gape at the tree.

"It certainly does." I looked to the distance beyond the fake marsh. Steel walls were only barely visible and somehow seemed even less real than the trees. "We *are* still inside, though, right?"

Duane chuckled. "Yes, we are."

The following night, my new host brought me back to Zombie Manor before it opened to the public. I met the cast: more than thirty actors, as well as backstage technicians, security officers, parking attendants, and ticket handlers. Everyone greeted one another with big hugs, then shared hot dogs and sodas that the owners kept in full stock onsite. The actors helped each other with makeup in the bathrooms and backstage hallway, laughing and talking about their day. As living skin began to peel and decay, the assembly started to resemble a big, zombie family reunion.

In a control room, a flat-screen TV showed twelve slots of feed from hidden cameras within the set. Posters and pictures of the cast covered the walls. Framed certificates read, Zombie Manor Award of Excellence. A large schematic showed the entire show's layout, reminding me of a hotel evacuation poster.

A half-hour before show time, one of the owners, Dean, called everyone to a preshow meeting. The zombie horde sat in a small parking lot, with the entire plantation amazingly residing on the other side of a concrete wall. I looked over the decaying troupe in awe; the tattered, living corpses revealed absolutely no trepidation about acting. Their red and white eyes stayed locked on their monstrous leader while they listened to any changes about who needed to work each scene. Blood trickled down Dean's gray and white beard. He would be playing the role of the plantation owner back from the dead.

After the crew filed back inside, I joined Duane for a final spot check. All around us, Landrun Manor had become even more ghastly. Fog hung

over the swamp. Plantation rooms buzzed with eerie sounds. Foul odors accentuated mold and rot. We switched on electric candles in séance scenes and on Voodoo altars. Projectors were run to make silhouettes of the living dead stagger across windows. Duane topped off fog machines so that they would have enough juice to last the night. Stepping into the den, we found that one device had gone haywire; so much fog filled the room that we could barely see a thing.

Duane coughed as he made his way through it. "We turn down the fogger if it gets to the point that people can't see," he said, waving an arm in front of him. He crouched down beside a table and adjusted a knob on the metal device. It looked like a small film projector. "Otherwise, what's the point?"

I chuckled, straining to see him through the dense vapor. I remembered thinking the same thing back at Fear Factory. But I only muffled a cough. The dense fog gave off an almost overpowering aroma of chemicals.

Beside me, Duane's form slowly disappeared into the haze. "And too much would make the actors sick."

"I would think so," I said.

All around us, shuffling came from behind the walls as actors moved through the scenes. Within moments, a horrid odor suddenly grew out of nowhere.

"What is *that...?!*" I exclaimed, pushing my hand against my nose.

"Ugh..." I heard Duane sigh along the floor. "That's Patrick. He loves wearing the Rotting Flesh scent."

Before I could question it, a man dressed in a grimy jumpsuit stepped out of the cloud. His long, greasy hair partially covered a filthy face. I hadn't seen him sitting at the meeting, but it looked as though a barrel of human waste had recently been dumped all over him.

"Like it?" he asked, giving me a crazed smile. "It always gets a reaction."

"Patrick!" Duane stood up through the fog, which had finally started to clear. "We get complaints!"

With the show ready for opening, I joined my friend in the control room. A small screen on the monitor revealed roughly sixty people waiting in line. Duane flipped a switch on a control board to signal for the worker manning the door to let in the first group. A set of large, oak doors opened, and I watched a young couple inch their way onto the porch. I smiled as they pressed tightly together, remembering Joey's death grip on my arm back at Spookers.

The pair flinched in repulsion as they entered the dining room. They stared at the rat infestation, then jumped and screamed when a hiding, female zombie crept out from behind the door. She lurched towards them, stumbling as though her joints had long since been broken but still allowed the cursed creature to move. The pair immediately bolted out of the room. I chuckled to Duane as the actor skipped back to her hiding place.

"It looks like the crew has a lot of fun with this," I said.

Duane reclined in his office chair and nodded. "Oh yeah. They love it. They look forward to it all year."

Through another hidden camera, I saw the same couple nervously glance around decapitated hedge sculptures in the courtyard. A ghoul lurked until his prey had moved past a fountain of green, vaporous water. He slowly emerged from the bushes. They jumped back in fright. A rusty,

DRAWN TO THE DARK

square cage was locked around his head. He staggered towards them with outstretched arms and long, padded sleeves hanging eerily to the ground from a straitjacket he'd managed to undo. The young couple's screams were muted on the video feed but no less funny as they took off running out of frame. When they encountered the grisly Patrick, I saw the young man finally let go of his girlfriend and sprint straight into a wall. Duane and I bent over in laughter. My host then wrote something in a small notebook beside him.

"This is a list of scares we'll show at our cast party in November," he said. "The actors love to see this stuff. And it shows them what gets the best results."

"Wow," I said, looking at the list. There were at least ten entries already from previous shows. "That's a great idea!"

"You bet. And, of course, they all go through a lot of training."

Over the next few hours, I watched hundreds go through the manor. Its undead crept out from the fog, lunged out of closets, and shuffled after the living, who panicked at the sight of them. The actors sometimes danced with joy after their visitors had fled, ecstatic over causing their better scares. Through the playful torments, I could see that they loved playing their roles as much as Duane had loved making the very sets around them. This was what the Halloween season meant to them: putting on a show to make visitors tremble, scream, jump, and laugh all at once. I was more than happy to sit back and watch. Despite what I'd learned about the fun of engagement at Castle Dracula and Zombie School, there was definitely something to be said about a nice, peaceful, outside perspective.

At eleven o'clock, the cast finally plopped down onto their chairs backstage. Their hair looked even more disheveled after three hours of screaming, pouncing, and chasing their victims. They smiled but stayed silent, their evil-looking eyes only half-open, as Dean praised everyone for a great show. He seemed to be the only actor still capable of standing. The blood running down his face looked old and faded and his pallor was more from fatigue than makeup.

"And remember," he said, beaming down at the seated troupe, "come hungry tomorrow night because we'll be ordering pizza!"

Patrick's sigh carried from across the room. He sat in a corner, alone due to his stench. It had received yet more complaints from both patrons *and* actors. He slumped down in his chair, flopping his filth-covered arms to his sides.

"Ugh," he said, exhaling. "I can't even think about tomorrow."

Midnight Syndicate's "Legacy of Shadows"

In Sandusky, Ohio, Cedar Point Amusement Park had transformed for October. I stood out front, my forty-dollar ticket in hand, facing twelve enormous jack-o-lanterns lining the entrance and the steel railings of a rollercoaster arching across the sky. With the sun beginning to set, the crowds eagerly swarmed in for the evening's HalloWeekend event. I knew what awaited inside: six haunted attractions, each as big and elaborate as Zombie Manor back in Arlington. There were also "scare zones," where chainsaw-wielding phantoms chased visitors through passageways of blinding fog. But the posters all around me advertising them didn't capture my attention. Instead, I was drawn to the forty-foot projector screen below the pumpkins grinning their evil. *Midnight Syndicate presents "Legacy of Shadows,"* it read. *Live!*

I had learned about the concert weeks earlier. My funds may have been running low, but that didn't matter. I immediately booked my flight and rental car for the trip. It was the group's very first live performance. I could hardly believe my luck. After going through so many shows that prided themselves on knowing what terror *looked* like, I knew that Midnight Syndicate was the only music group that knew what terror *sounded* like.

Along the drive to the park, I admired the Ohio scenery all around me. The beaches in Hawaii and mountains in Alaska had each been gorgeous, but the leaves exploding in orange, red, and yellow from every tree managed to top them all. Over the radio, my familiar Voice from

Photograph by Steven Franczek, Invertalon Photography

Hell ominously described local haunts where people could go to get the wits scared out of them. I smiled at the commercials while savoring a Dunkin' Donuts pumpkin-flavored coffee. Together, it all created the epitome of a perfect autumn day with sights, sounds, smells, and even tastes of Halloween in America's heartland.

The size of the crowds made Cedar Point park practically burst at the seams. I swam through the masses. The festivals back in Hungary and Japan suddenly felt like small, intimate gatherings by comparison. People waited in lines for the attractions for over an hour. I bypassed them for now, grinning at the display of skeleton cowboys roasting marshmallows around a campfire. I loved the park's incorporation of humor *and* horror for Halloween. I ran from roaring chainsaws in the fog only to face a statue of Charlie Brown dressed like a pumpkin. Around every corner, Midnight Syndicate music played. Their eerie, ominous melodies put me in the mindset of walking through some twisted, endless nightmare, regardless of how many rollercoasters soared over my head.

In the Good Times Theatre, I sat in the center row. A world of enchantingly crafted horror lay before me. Vines of ivy crawled along a crumbling, Gothic mausoleum. Low fog hovered among ancient tombstones. Blue light cast everything into twilight, with an enormous full moon hanging above. Once every seat had filled, I recognized the two musicians as they took to the stage.

Edward Douglas appeared in an eighteenth-century-style black undertaker's cloak and hat. Gavin Goszka walked beside him in a gray, Edwardian suit. I clapped with the crowd, then held my breath as the pair took their places behind two keyboards—each, I realized, cleverly concealed behind large, stone altars. The pair turned to each other, keeping quiet and mysterious, then began to play. In an instant I recognized the tune. It was "Alchemist's Chamber." I immediately became lost in the music as the mystifying notes penetrated the theater. I was no longer in Cedar Point now, or anywhere else in the "normal world." I was immersed in a place of eerie things. I pictured strange creatures emerging from the ancient graveyard before me. I could see them being summoned by the music. They were the same creatures that I had envisioned in the darkness at Fear Factory, back when all I had to guide me were tiny glimpses of light and my own imagination. The musicians played slowly and elegantly, then picked up in momentum as the song grew powerful.

My eyes lit up again with the next tune. The familiar sounds of "Grisly Reminder" cast a sinister feel over the theater. I had a sudden flashback to playing the song for Joey at his house in New Zealand. I remembered him insisting that I no longer play that song or any other like it after sundown. I smiled at the memory, perfectly picturing his fear in the quiet countryside. I could only wonder if he would be as nervous listening to it now with hundreds of others around him before an ancient graveyard.

Onstage, the players added to the enchanting feel of the notes. They looked piercingly out into the crowd. Edward lifted a hand, then slowly clenched a fist as if trying to capture the very essence of the music. The intensity of his emotion was captivating. I had seen that look before. It was the same passion that Duane had exhibited while giving me the tour of Zombie Manor. It was the same that Paul and Shawna had shown in Alaska, along with Clemens in Austria, my monster trainers at RAM, and so many others who put their heart and soul into their performance and art.

A slow, thick fog began to encompass the mossed boneyard. It glowed eerily orange, then purple, then red. The music changed and intensified. It sounded as if hell itself had been unleashed. I imagined the very spirits of All Hallows' Eve being conjured all around us, the risen dead that the Celts had believed could enter the world at this time. I had a feeling that those scenarios were what Edward and Gavin wanted in the minds of their listeners. They wanted us to lose ourselves in the daunting music and step into strange worlds that only we could create. No external stimulus was even needed. No actor or set or scene could put us there. The magic and wonder and thrills came from only ourselves. I suddenly realized that after years of looking forward to the return of monstrous creatures at Halloween and in the movies, every one of them produced a specific feeling, an emotion, that I looked forward to more than anything. And there was never any shortage of that. It could be found in the most unlikely of places: a tent in a campground, a trail in the woods, a shop hanging masks in their window. The feeling never really left so long as we brought it with us. It could follow us around the world and was where the spirit of Halloween truly lived.

Hellview Cemetery, St. Petersburg

On October 30, my bus pulled into the St. Petersburg Greyhound Station. During the ten-hour ride after a short stop in Savannah, a smile never left my face. At long last, after more than a year, I was approaching my final destination.

Through the window, I saw my friend Mark waiting for me. It seemed like a lifetime ago that we'd last seen each other at the Halloween Extreme Conference in Orlando. We'd kept in touch ever since, and when I mentioned that I wanted the grand finale of my trip to be a Halloween celebration encompassing an entire neighborhood, my friend had replied to my message within seconds. He invited me to join him at his home haunted attraction called Hellview Cemetery. Like so many home haunters, Mark was passionate about putting together a show for his entire town to enjoy right at his house. It also gave him the opportunity to turn his place into something that reflected his own character: an elaborate theater of monsters ranging from lovable lunatics to menacing ghouls—while still remaining suitable for all ages.

Mark threw open his arms as I stepped off the bus.

"Chris!" he cried. "You made it." He stood over me at more than six feet, smiling from ear to ear in baggy jeans and a button-down shirt. I had always seen him as a kind of jolly, haunter Santa, just without the beard. He hugged me, then shook his head in disbelief. "*Man*, you've been all over!"

I exhaled at the thought. "Yes...!" The excitement of my travels was temporarily put on hold; instead, I brushed off the tiring bus rides and planes and hours spent lost in new areas. I felt the warm, Florida sun on my face and let my backpack fall to my duffel bag on the sidewalk. I couldn't help but feel as though I'd just shed ten bags off my shoulders. My arrival meant knowing that I would no longer have to plan future travel routes or housing stays or festival dates. "Can I just say, you have *no idea* how nice it is to be here—and just before Halloween!"

Mark beamed at the word. "That's right! Come on...." He reached down and lifted both bags over his shoulder as though they were made of feathers. "I'll take you home—to *Hellview!*"

In his Ford Taurus, adorned with large Hellview Cemetery magnets on the doors, Mark eagerly recounted his show's happenings from the past two weeks.

"Everything's gone great!" he said along the drive. "We're raising money for two charities this year: the Florida Bat Conservancy and Kind Mouse. That's a nonprofit organization that helps feed the hungry."

"Wow," I said beside him. "That's great!" I realized that I could pick up on Mark's slightly Midwestern accent much easier than I could two years ago. Although he'd lived in Florida most of his life, Mark was originally from Ohio.

Photograph by Black Eyed Susan Photography

We pulled into a small driveway and my friend turned to me excitedly. "Here we are!"

I leaned forward and gazed up through the windshield. "Wow...!"

The house, I saw, had been turned into a small castle with its own Gothic mausoleum. What I could only presume to be Mark's garage stood concealed behind an arched, gold-studded oak door. Skulls bordered either side, with a circular stained-glass window above. Ancient-looking pillars resembled stone altars throughout the quarter-acre lawn. Massive, faux stone walls covered the house, with long strands of moss slithering out of slit windows.

"This is incredible!" I said, taking it all in.

Mark stepped out of the car, then threw open his arms as if to encompass it all. "Welcome to Hellview!"

Inside, the house was exactly what I would have expected for the day before Halloween: a disaster area. Witch cloaks, undertaker robes, and ghillie suits concealed a sofa. Zombie masks, top hats, and an assortment of wigs hid a recliner. Tubes spilled white and gray makeup onto folding tables beside cans of colored hairspray. The kitchen looked like a murder scene; half-filled bottles of "blood" stained a dining-room table. A knot of entangled extension cords as big as a basketball lay on the floor between buckets of fog juice. I smiled at open boxes of Count Chocula, Boo Berry, Frankenberry, and Fruit Brute.

While Mark gave me the tour, I saw a framed picture of a happy, monster family on the wall. A pale and ghastly Mark smiled in a black top hat and cape. A teenage girl was beside him, grinning menacingly with blood streaking down from dark eyes like horrid tears over undead skin. On Mark's other side, a second set of female-looking eyes glared out from behind a Jason Voorhees mask.

"My daughters are both in the show," Mark said, gesturing to the picture. "They're really looking forward to meeting you. That's Beth's in the Jason mask; she's nineteen. Callie's sixteen, with the pigtails. We've all been following your travels."

I cocked my head in emotion. "Awww, that's so nice to hear!" I could only imagine what the journey must have looked like from the other side of a computer screen. I presumed that it would be rather peaceful—staying in one place and looking at pictures rather than hopping from couch to bus to plane.

"My daughters have worked at Hellview from the very beginning, in 2006. They were both raised on horror and science fiction."

I laughed, nodding with approval. "As it should be!"

Back outside, Mark led me to the large, oak door serving as Hellview's entrance. It opened with a loud, eerie creak, which I could only imagine sounded even more sinister after dark.

"I write a new script every year," my friend said, extending a hand for me to enter, "and my crew and I build Hellview around that. When we have a good story, we can put on a better show. This year we're basing it on the Blackwater Clan hillbillies and Swamp Water Maggie."

"Wow...," I said. "I love the names." I stepped through the entrance, feasting my eyes on everything around me. "Just look at all this...."

Inside, a stone altar stood at the back of a dismal chamber. A pentagram had been spray-painted onto it, with partially broken skulls demonically grinning between its five, glowing points. A silver chalice suggested dark rituals, with black roses encircling a soggy, dismembered head on a puddle of blood.

I pointed to the woeful dead. "For sacrifice or consumption?"

"Both," Mark said with a smile.

I giggled.

We continued down a passageway of faux, aging brick along the side of the house. I felt as though we were walking through the remains of an old town that hadn't seen residents for centuries. A village in decay appeared past it: chipped blocks of cement formed multiple, connecting rooms, each made out of large sheets of painted, crafted Styrofoam. Black sheets and sheer coverings cast them into darkness even in the daylight. The walls stood more than ten feet high, making the size of the yard impossible to determine. In one area, a trail disappeared into towering cornstalks. In another, dead foliage fell from wooden fencing to create the look of a dense forest.

"This is incredible," I said, admiring it all. "You made all this?"

"Oh yeah." Mark gave me a crafty smile. "The dumpsters of St. Pete are very generous. It's incredible to find people throwing away perfectly good building materials. Wood, tarps, foam... Most of this stuff came from an abandoned motel they were about to tear down on the beach."

"Wow...!" I looked around the set with new eyes; it was a very different approach to haunt building from what I'd seen at Zombie Manor. But it all appeared so professional that I never would have known the difference. "Nice score!"

Mark smiled excitedly. "Right? So the undead come out from over there, just before visitors enter the corn maze." He motioned to a dark tarp concealing a chunk of missing wall. Tall husks rose above our heads as we entered the corn, and I saw rubber rats and spiders peeking out from thick, entangled webs between them.

"We have a few scarecrows that hide in here," Mark said, "one of which being my younger daughter."

I laughed, envisioning the framed, black-teared teenager creeping after people in the darkness.

Outside a small shack, we approached an old hillbilly sitting in a rocking chair. The gray and shriveled mannequin glared at us while decapitated heads swung above her. A tattered, broken screen hung by a hinge with a large cow skull mounted on the wall beside it. Behind the small home, a row of skulls lined a tall fence separating Mark's yard from his neighbors.

"Then people meet our hillbillies Meemaw and Peepaw Blackwater. We have twenty actors in the show, and those two will join this little lady here," he said, gesturing to the seated prop.

"They're perfectly named," I commented.

Mark smiled cordially. "Thanks! They're quite the characters. And it's good to throw in a few laughs and diversions. It creates a nice, false sense of security between the scares. There's a whole psychology to it."

I nodded. I remembered hearing something similar back at ScareCON. "That's true."

We continued on, exploring the bowels of Hellview. Bloody dolls and stuffed animals filled a children's room. A fully stocked bar showcased blood wines and jars of eyeballs. Crooked portraits hung in an aging den, each ruined by crude, spray-painted images. Along a tilting section of wall, a poster showed Frankenstein's monster beside a disclosure I'd seen in many scare shows over the years: *This attraction features the music of Midnight Syndicate.*

As we walked a path lined with brush and barren trees, Mark eyed me devilishly. "And this is where Swamp Water Maggie resides." He gestured to a small plot of evil: bone mobiles hung beside a rotting shelf of candles, skulls, and stones. A short fence separated the area from the trail, creating the perfect spot for the witch to terrorize her victims. "She was the town healer at one time but now brings death and disease from the land of the dead."

I nodded, having the distinct impression that Duane from Zombie Manor would have appreciated it as much as I did. "Very nice."

A long, narrow crypt led us to Hellview's final scene: a cemetery with skulls and crossbones marking ancient-looking tombstones. Celtic crosses leaned beside stone benches, and random remains of the dead lay inside mossed, rock alcoves.

"This place is unbelievable," I said. "I love how you've used every square inch of the yard."

"Absolutely." Mark turned around, scanning his world of elaborately crafted death. "That was the main thing I looked for when buying a house. I thought: will I be able to build a haunt here? Otherwise what's the point of even *owning* a house?"

I cracked up at the sentiment. I had a feeling that Paul and Shawna in Anchorage would have become Mark's best friends for sure.

Mark laughed with me, putting his hands in his pockets. "There's not a lot of room for parking, but my neighbors know that a few weekends per year the street gets crazy. The rest of the time, I stay pretty quiet."

"Those are some nice neighbors," I said, admiring them at once.

Mark nodded, sighing in relief. Not everyone, I knew, approved of their neighborhood turning into chaos every October. "That's for sure. And, of course, it helps that they love Halloween."

The morning of the thirty-first, I woke up feeling more at peace than I could last remember. It was the Big Day: the day when the entire country, from Hawaii to Florida, seemed to have a sense of magic in the air. After a full month of skeletons and ghouls emerging in the stores and people's yards and haunt shows, it was the day when similar faces could be seen walking down the street or driving through traffic, delivering the mail or handing a tray of coffee through a drive-through window. It was the day when people of all ages felt something call them out to celebrate—to dress up as the living dead, who knew no social norms and had no desire to. Even those who didn't feel a sense of otherworldliness the rest of the year, for whatever reason, could come together in unison. It was my long-awaited Halloween.

It was also the day that my travels had come to their end. After going through dark shows of virtually every type for over a year, I could now celebrate with Hellview Cemetery as the grand finale. As haunters do, my new host family slept until noon. I sat in the living room with a bowl of Count Chocula, savoring the chocolaty goodness while admiring the endless artistry around me. The bottles of blood took me back to my friendly zombie teachers at RAM. I could picture the kids from Zombie School decaying their faces in the dressing room, then charging after victims as the raging undead. The mound of black and brown wigs on the recliner made me envision cowering before Krampus in the cold of Austria, then hugging the lovable Busós months later in Hungary. There had been so many celebrations around the world, with dances and bonfires and concerts in the mountains. I had seen deep meaning in the celebrations in addition to the revelry. Now, I felt more grateful than ever to be back in my own country and enjoying my own traditions. I was looking forward to helping Mark and his crew get ready for the show, then handing out candy to the trick-or-treaters at Hellview's donation table. I could only imagine how the small St. Pete neighborhood would bustle with haunt-seekers after sundown. I had a feeling that, as each looked upon the majestic display that was Mark's yard, I would relate to their excitement completely.

Hours later, the transformation began and Hellview came alive with the undead.

Twenty actors arrived one by one. Hillbillies bled from gunshot holes in their T-shirts and jeans. A living scarecrow bid its welcome through the stitched mouth of a saggy, leather-skinned mask. A Haitian princess painted white designs around her sunken eye sockets and cheekbones. Beth, Mark's older daughter, wore a mask of burnt flesh. She knelt on what little space she could find on the living-room floor, leaning over a laptop in a tattered red-and-green sweater.

"I'm Fan Girl," she said to me proudly. From the floor beside her, I watched Beth upload her character image onto Facebook and Twitter accounts. "My character absorbs the abilities of anyone she focuses on. Tonight, I have the power of Freddy Krueger. I can enter people's dreams and tear them to pieces." She enthusiastically thrust a razor-clawed hand through the air, then laughed demonically.

Callie, Mark's younger daughter, stood in a dingy bathrobe splattered in blood. The ten or so actors maneuvering all around her didn't faze her one bit as she put her long, brown hair into pigtails. They instantly made her look about ten years younger than she actually was.

"My character's name is Emily," she said. "Sometimes I attack people in the cornfield, but tonight I'll work in the den." She gave me a crazed smile, resembling the horrid image of herself on the wall. "To spice things up."

I laughed at her wickedness. Tru, the show's makeup artist, joined us. In her early twenties, Tru sat on the edge of the recliner of wigs while corpsifying a zombie for the cemetery. The actor knelt before her in a ragged, gray suit covered in holes and dirt. It complemented Tru's costume perfectly: a nightgown equally stained with filth. I admired the two, then looked down at my own clothes with a frown. My jeans and T-shirt suddenly seemed pretty boring by comparison. I had been so excited about the idea of giving out candy to the kids that I'd completely forgotten about dressing up.

But as each actor excitedly recounted their exploits from the past two weeks, I gave them my undivided attention. They imitated visitors running and screaming through their scenes, sometimes before the actors even had a chance to fully emerge from their hiding places. The crew laughed at each other's stories and passed around Kit Kats, Twizzlers, and Peanut Butter Cups. The mixed aroma made me feel eight years old again. Just like back at Zombie Manor, I could see the actors enjoying their time together as much as they did turning into the monstrous creatures of Hellview.

Before long, Mark popped his head into the chaos. He had changed into his black cape and hat, no longer making me envision him as a haunter Santa but now more of a diabolical ringleader. His role would be greeting visitors at the door, then letting them in as Hellview's caretaker. I carefully stepped through the cast after he called me over.

"Hey, Chris," he said, "do you mind playing Swamp Water Maggie tonight? Our regular just called in sick."

I froze before he even finished the question. My stomach immediately tightened in objection. *Oh God,* I thought. *Not again…*

"She called in sick?" I asked, hoping I'd completely misheard.

"Yeah. So we're down one scene."

I stared at him. I felt the familiar wave of panic arise. I had almost forgotten the sensation. It was now three months since I'd battled the living and the dead at Zombie Boot Camp and Zombie School. I'd spent my subsequent days floating in a kind of euphoria, believing that my acting days were behind me. I'd never mentioned any of my fears about acting to Mark, though he knew that I'd been part of the shows at RAM and Castle Dracula.

But now, either choosing to ignore my look of terror or else hoping that the idea would grow on me, my friend smiled in anticipation and need of help.

"Okay," I finally forced out.

Mark jumped in excitement. "Awesome, thanks!" He slapped me on the shoulder. "You'll do great! You've done this stuff before."

Minutes later, I found myself sitting before Tru. A long, black dress had replaced my previously boring clothes. My clenched hands formed balls inside my long, velvet sleeves. As the undead artist dabbed a makeup pad on my cheeks, I thought back to the swamp scene I'd toured with Mark. I vividly remembered it being very exposed—at the end of a long walkway where every visitor would be able to see me in plain sight. I had loved the scene only yesterday. Now, I wanted to run screaming from it. I couldn't help but find it ironic that in all my years transforming into a ghoul on Halloween, it had never brought any feelings of dread. I'd always enjoyed the pleasant, more passive experiences of putting together yard displays and handing out candy to trick-or-treaters. I had never felt the desire to *act out* the role of a ghoul—especially not to an audience who had come to see a good show. But all around me, my fellow actors grew more and more hyper, as anxious for the night to begin as I was for it to be over.

Eventually, Tru handed me a small mirror.

"What do you think?" She gave me a nervous smile, reading my silent expression perfectly.

I was almost afraid to look. But in the small, oval image, I barely recognized myself. Deep-sunken eyes stared at me from bloodied-looking skin. Dark lines and cracks made me look decades older. I smiled immediately. It seemed that the Chris I knew wouldn't be part of Hellview, after all; Swamp Water Maggie would.

"I love it," I said, my breath coming much easier now. "Thanks!"

Tru smiled and exhaled. "You're one of us now."

Above us, Mark's voice caught our attention. "Okay, everybody, listen up." He looked around with glowing eyes, now bright white from his contact lenses. "Everyone take your places. Remember that Kind Mouse will be going through the whole set to film it before we open, so we'll be doing that first."

I craned my neck up at him, feeling my shoulders instinctively scrunch.

"You'll see the cameraman coming, so just do your scene like you normally would. We'll let you know once everything's been recorded. Just please keep quiet until it's all wrapped up."

I looked at him in horror. "They're *filming* it?"

"Chris!" Mark bounced when he saw me. "You look great! Yeah, they'll be showing the video at an award ceremony next week when we give them the donation check."

I barely heard him. I only stared, unable to blink. Performing in front of a crowd was bad enough, but on *camera*? That was even *worse*! That meant being recorded on something that could be *replayed*. I fought the urge to lunge after the scarecrow and hide beneath his mask. Instead, I turned to Tru.

"Did *you* know they were filming it?"

She smiled sheepishly. "Yeah. They film it every year."

I suppressed a sigh; Mark had *definitely* forgotten to mention that.

Outside, my panic subsided. Hellview had completely transformed. With the setting sun, a pale, blue light shone from the cathedral window, casting an eerie glow above the entrance. The séance altar radiated red and purple. In the yard under the tree shadows, the brick and cement looked completely authentic without revealing even a hint of faux materials. Wolves howled in the cornfield through hidden speakers.

Banjo music played in the hallways. I walked behind Mark, barely able to believe that we were in the same set. Hillbillies fresh out of the grave took their places. Tru reclined in a rocking chair in the children's room. Callie sat before a glowing organ in the den. But when the swamp scene appeared around the corner, my nerves returned. The flickering candles cast perfectly creepy shadows throughout it, as though intentionally reflecting the sense of doom that I couldn't force myself to shake.

"You can hang out back here," Mark said. He motioned behind the small fence separating the scene from the trail. I looked at it and nodded. At least I had something to hide behind. "Jonesy will be a few feet away as a Bushman." He pointed down the path where we'd just walked. A six-foot pile of brush lifted a leaf-covered arm and waved.

"Hi," it said.

I chuckled. I hadn't even noticed the ghillie suit.

"And Fallon will be across from him on the other side of the window." Mark pointed to a black curtain in the fence across from the brush. The concealed Jonesy did the same with a mossy finger. "People will be able to see you when they turn the corner, so you can distract them before these two scare them."

I looked at the spot. I tried to imagine anything I could possibly do to distract *anybody*. Run away and hide? That would get their attention.

Mark put a hand on my shoulder. "You'll do great! Remember, this is all for fun; that's what it's about. So just have fun with it. Right?"

I nodded slowly. It was good logic. And it helped not one bit. "Okay."

He stepped into the crypt, leaving me with my terrified thoughts, then stopped beside a small window between the scenes.

"Oh, want some music?"

I turned to him with a sudden glimmer of hope. "Music?"

He reached through the opening in the wall. A portable MP3 player lay concealed behind my shelf of evil. He flipped the switch. In an instant, the world changed. Slow, sinister tunes permeated my swamp. I knew that music. I had heard it a week earlier in an ancient, glowing graveyard. I could still picture every detail of the concert as my creepy little dwelling began to transform.

I envisioned a wave of spirits rising all around me. I saw them emerge from the very darkness, entering into the world through hidden veils. But they hadn't come on their own; Swamp Water Maggie had called them. I felt the mystical creature whom I'd only glimpsed in the mirror suddenly return. She was powerful and devious. She had created life from the brush. She had raised spirits to scream from dark portals in her midst. And as Mark disappeared down the crypt corridor, I became that bringer of death and took my place within my enchanted realm that was Hellview.

Within moments, the surrounding scenes grew quiet. My brush friend stood equally still, roughly ten yards down the trail. I could only assume that the unseen Fallon was behind her curtained window. I waited behind the low fence until a tiny, red light rounded the corner. I almost flinched when I saw it. It looked exactly like the glowing pinpoints that had guided me through New Zealand's Fear Factory. I thought back to the disorienting void of the almost scene-less show. *But that's not Hellview*, I reflected. *Here, the undead wait and watch you. And you must face your fear.*

The tiny light moved closer. I slowly extended a black-sleeved arm towards it. With a curl of my finger, I beckoned the ember to continue through the darkness.

It drew closer. I began to make out blue jeans and a gray sweatshirt behind the camera. Its holder walked towards me, inching along the trail until reaching the wall of shrubbery.

The mound of brush leapt out in a flash. "Come with me!" it growled.

The cameraman jumped back. I saw his body convulse while he turned to capture the swampy creature on film. I felt a sly smile form on my face as I watched.

The camera panned back my way. I continued gazing at its little light, until, after a few more steps, the faceless filmer jumped. A loud scream pierced the silence from his left. He grinned excitedly and faced the wall to find only darkness before him.

He finally turned back towards me. I watched the round, reflecting lens come closer. It moved in to mere inches from my face.

I stared boldly into it.

"Welcome to my swamp...," I hissed. Leaning in slightly, I felt my small grin grow wider and more devilish. In my mind I pictured other characters I'd seen give that look: Krampus, Namahage, Mephisto. Each of them smiled with me now, oceans away from their own dwellings.

The cameraman continued on, filming my unending glare while he walked. He turned the corner, entering the crypt, until his camera disappeared behind the faux stone. With a silent step, I slid to the window through which Mark had flipped on my music. I reached my arm through the opening as the filmer reappeared. The cotton from an unsuspecting shoulder felt soft on my fingertips. The lens turned my way. I hissed at the dark, gleaming glass and heard a loud crack come from the Styrofoam beneath us. A sudden shift moved the window, and in an instant the entire frame crashed down to my feet.

I jumped back in horror. A large, gaping hole now stood between me and my would-be victim. The cameraman darted back from the other side

DRAWN TO THE DARK

of the wall. Without a thought, I ducked behind what remained of my shattered porthole into evil and made myself disappear out of frame.

Oh my God, I thought, crouched on the ground, *Mark is going to* kill *me!* But as quickly as the thought came, it disappeared. Another took its place: *after a year of globetrotting to shows around the world, I've seen all kinds of strange things—but never anything like* that! I immediately covered my mouth and shook with silent laughter.

After what felt like an age, I could only assume that the cameraman had moved on. Perhaps he was wandering through the cemetery by now, filming more professional actors who *knew* what the heck they were doing. Hopefully he wouldn't mention to Mark—or anyone else— about how Swamp Water Maggie had fallen on camera like some kind of drunken Voodoo queen. I stood up, then recoiled at the sight of a red light glowing in front of me. It looked suddenly demonic. From behind it, its shadowed owner giggled uncontrollably, then flinched. As he quickly moved on, I could only presume that my gaping expression had made him regain himself.

I ran over to Jonesy.

"Oh my *God*—did you see that? It was horrible!"

The tall brush slapped a foliaged hand on what I presumed to be his leg. "That was *hilarious!*"

"No, it wasn't." I buried my face in my hands. Eerie music or not, Swamp Water Maggie had retreated to the netherworld. "And of course it had to happen *on film!*"

"Nahhh..." Jonesy waved a leaf. "They'll just edit the footage. You're fine." He chuckled, making a slight rustling sound as he shook.

"What happened?"

From the darkness across from us, a black hood appeared. It concealed all but a young-sounding woman's nose and lips.

"It was great," Jonesy said. "Chris fell through the window on camera." I felt rough plastic touch my arm as he playfully pushed me.

Fallon gasped. The hood turned towards me. "You did? Are you okay?"

I groaned. "I'm fine, thanks. But I ruined the set!"

"Oh no...," she said casually. "Alex will come and fix it. We break stuff all the time."

Mark expressed a similar reaction. During a walk-through to confirm that everyone was ready for opening, he looked at the window in confusion through vacant, white eyes.

"What happened?"

I felt my head disappear between my shoulders. "Ummmm... it broke."

Mark shrugged. "Oh well. I'll send Alex to fix it." He turned to me with a smile. "Having fun?"

I exhaled happily behind my fence. "Yes! Now I am."

The mysterious Alex appeared within moments. In charge of electronics and repairs, he pulled an electric screwdriver from his workbelt, replaced the foam in less than a minute, then tipped his cowboy hat and disappeared.

The setback was forgotten as the show began. Processions flocked through. Six-foot black cats walked arm in arm with their vampire boyfriends. Three-foot princesses held pumpkin pails beside five-foot Batmen and butterflies. Swamp Water Maggie beckoned them all with her enticing eyes and bewitching ways. There was no need to terrorize or scare anyone in her bog. Instead, I cackled as they jumped from my cursed hedge. I giggled evilly when they screamed before my gateway into the abyss. I lured in every mortal who found themselves in my mystical swamp—the *fools!*—then slyly invited them to enjoy additional nightmares in the depths of the crypt.

Hundreds went through, couples, families, and whole neighborhoods all having fun with the frights and charade. Smiling children sometimes contrasted their trembling parents. I saw wide, gazing eyes as they approached me, my eerie lights and sinister tunes helping to steal their minds in the swamp. I recognized those looks; they were the same expressions of enchantment that I'd had myself as a child, lost in a world of monsters lurching out of the darkness. I'd seen it in every country I'd visited, with people drawn to other, devious characters that delighted in haunting them. My visitors—my *victims*—were some of them now. It was Halloween that had drawn them out. It was enjoying our centuries-old traditions together on a night of wonderful things when magic truly *does* exist and the living really do walk with the dead.

Afterword

The Difference of the Dark

I began November 1 the way I had been dreaming about for months. I e-mailed each of my Couchsurfing hosts—all now good friends whom I'd kept in touch with since staying with them—and thanked them for making my travels possible. After twelve months, eleven countries, and 56,000 miles, the travels were over. I would, at long last, begin writing about the adventures. To my surprise, Brent quickly replied from Hawaii. He had given his notice at work and was planning his own eighteen-month backpacking trip around the world.

I beamed when I read it. I could only hope that he would include at least a few dark shows along the way.

The trip had cost me a grand total of $11,000. I spent more than my initial Kickstarter goal but felt grateful to have never received those funds. Without a specific agenda agreed upon with any backers, I had been able to change my itinerary at will. It had allowed me to stay in some areas much longer than anticipated and alter my route on a whim.

I thought about all the people I'd met and the things I'd experienced that year. Although I had been fueled by a desire to see dark and devious characters, I realized that the highlights were whenever I was able to share the enjoyment of them with someone else. In Couchsurfing, there simply are no strangers. Many of my hosts had jumped at the opportunity to go to the shows with me. Some had grown up with the traditions, while others got to enjoy them for the very first time. Together we'd laughed and explored, sometimes battling fierce creatures, other times getting battered *by* them. Looking back on it all, I began to wonder if what may be of even more interest than the way sinister characters are portrayed across cultures is our own, personal draw to them. For me, there has always been a thrill about it all, about entering seemingly magical worlds with creatures that foreshadow the grave. Maybe it all stems from Halloween and the feelings I got when my whole neighborhood transformed after sundown. Maybe it came from idolizing my older brother as he fearlessly watched cackling skeletons well into the night. Or maybe it's simply the allure of the unknown and a desire to see just how fun and frightening we can make it out to be.

But wherever I went, I found others sharing my draw to the dark. Both at home and abroad, in the people running their cultural games and the ones who attended, I saw it evoke primal, human emotion. I witnessed people losing themselves in a sense of wonder. It transcended language and culture and in many places kept history and tradition alive. Each dance and *lauf*, performance and tour created celebrations based on tiny glimpses of the unknown that, in the end, we, ourselves, fill in. But no one escapes *every* demon. We all have our fears to face. Some may take the form of a killer doll running through our bedroom or a room of watchful eyes as we perform before a crowd. But with the company of friends, we can challenge those fears. We can battle through them and come out stronger on the other side. We feel more fully alive when we do, embracing the darkness together in, dare we say, the most *monstrous* proportions.

Kind Mouse never did show the footage they filmed at Hellview Cemetery. But as a thank-you for the $2,600 donation, they gave a copy to Mark. He got a good laugh when he watched. I sat beside my haunter host family on their sofa, cringing at my performance on the screen.

"Great job, Chris," Mark said. He laughed from his chair no longer reserved for wigs and costumes. "With this video, Swamp Water Maggie will forever haunt the swamps of Hellview!"

I hid my face in my hands and groaned. "Oh my god," I said, "now *that's* scary."

Sources

Bannatyne, Lesley Pratt. *Halloween: An American Holiday, an American History*. Gretna, LA: Pelican, 1998.

Delsol, Christine. "La Catrina: Mexico's Grande Dame of Death." SFGate.com (2011).

Goethe, Johann Wolfgang von. *Faust*. gutenberg.org.

Stoker, Bram. *Dracula*. Barnes & Noble, 2006.

Kyoto
sbarnhill.mvps.org
thekyotoproject.org

Bran Castle
brasovtravelguide.ro
designlike.com
romaniatourism.com

The History of Vlad Tepes
ucs.mun.ca

Bram Stoker
news.bbc.co.uk

The History of Halloween
paganspath.com

The Evolution of Haunted Attractions
americahaunts.com
bhamwiki.com
cincinnati.com

Index